To the north-east the Germans were only about 80 miles from Petrograd on both sides of the Gulf of Finland. To the west the German and Austrian line ran in front of Pskov and Minsk; to the south-east in front of Kiev and Kharkov. In the south the White Cossacks, under Krasnov, occupied the Don, and under Denikin the Kuban. In the south-west the Roumanians and Turks were on the shores of the Black Sea and in the Caucasus, while the British were advancing to the Caspian. In the west the Czechs, now linked up with Admiral Koltchak, had taken Sumara, Simbirsk, Kazan and Viatka, and in the north British, French and Americans were preparing to attack from Murmansk and Archangel. The Bolsheviks were completely encircled by their enemies and it only remained to see which of them would reach Moscow first to administer the *coup de grâce*.

# BY DENNIS WHEATLEY

## NOVELS

The Launching of Roger Brook
The Shadow of Tyburn Tree
The Rising Storm
The Man Who Killed the King
The Dark Secret of Josephine
The Rape of Venice
The Sultan's Daughter
The Wanton Princess
Evil in a Mask
The Ravishing of Lady Mary
  Ware
The Irish Witch*
Desperate Measures*

The Scarlet Impostor
Faked Passports
The Black Baroness
V for Vengeance
Come into my Parlour
Traitors' Gate
They Used Dark Forces

The Prisoner in the Mask
Vendetta in Spain
The Second Seal
Three Inquisitive People
The Forbidden Territory
The Devil Rides Out
The Golden Spaniard
Strange Conflict
Codeword, Golden Fleece

Gateway to Hell
Dangerous Inheritance

The Quest of Julian Day
The Sword of Fate
Bill for the Use of a Body

Black August
Contraband
The Island Where Time Stands
  Still
The White Witch of the South Seas

To the Devil—A Daughter
The Satanist

The Eunuch of Stamboul
The Secret War
The Fabulous Valley
Sixty Days to Live
Such Power is Dangerous
Uncharted Seas
The Man Who Missed the War
The Haunting of Toby Jugg
Star of Ill-Omen
They Found Atlantis
The Ka of Gifford Hilary
Curtain of Fear
Mayhem in Greece
Unholy Crusade
The Strange Story of Linda Lee*

## SHORT STORIES

Mediterranean Nights                Gunmen, Gallants and Ghosts

## HISTORICAL
Old Rowley: A Private Life of Charles II
*Illustrated by Frank C. Papé*
Red Eagle
*The Story of the Russian Revolution*

## AUTOBIOGRAPHICAL
Stranger than Fiction*
*War Papers for the Joint Planning Staff of the War Cabinet*
Saturdays with Bricks*

## SERIOUS STUDY OF THE OCCULT
The Devil and all His Works
*With 215 illustrations in colour and black and white*

*All these books, with the exception of those
marked\*, are available in the Lymington Edition*

*Dennis Wheatley*

# RED EAGLE

A Story of the Russian Revolution
and of
Klementy Efremovitch Voroshilov

ARROW BOOKS

Arrow Books Limited
3 Fitzroy Square, London W1

An imprint of the Hutchinson Publishing Group

London Melbourne Sydney Auckland
Wellington Johannesburg and agencies
throughout the world

First published by Hutchinson & Co (Publishers) Ltd 1936
Arrow edition 1964
New illustrated edition 1967
Second edition 1968
This edition 1976
Illustrated edition © Dennis Wheatley 1967

Made and printed in Great Britain
by The Anchor Press Ltd
Tiptree, Essex
ISBN 0 09 912370 3

*To my wife*
**JOAN**
*with all my love*
*on the sixth anniversary of*
*our marriage*

# Contents

## Maps

# Introduction

The greatest event of this century to date is the Russian Revolution. More people lost their lives owing to it than in World Wars I and II together, yet that was only the beginning of its repercussions. The transformation of the old, inefficiently governed Czarist Empire into a vast, highly organised (so-called) Workers' State, directed by able and determined men, has divided the nations of the world into two camps—those who accept Totalitarian rule and those who still strive to maintain a degree of Liberty for the Individual. And now, in this nuclear age, the final outcome of that Revolution may be to wipe civilisation from the face of the earth in an atomic holocaust.

When this book was first published twenty years had already elapsed since Imperial Russia had become the Union of Soviet Socialist Republics. Already an immense literature had appeared on various aspects of this great upheaval, so the basic facts about it were common knowledge. To them I was able to add a small contribution from numerous untapped sources.

A British Communist, who must still remain nameless, provided me in secret with forty-six records translated from the Russian, giving intimate details of the early lives of the Bolshevik leaders—and particularly about Marshal Voroshilov, whom I took as the central character in my account of the Revolution. These documents included one upon the Soviet Union's future strategy in the event of another war with Germany, which happily enabled me to predict correctly the course that events were likely to take when, five years later, I became a member of the Joint Planning Staff of the War Cabinet.

To His Imperial Highness Prince Dimitri I owed an introduction to Mr. Anatol Backileff. He was the head of the Siberian Co-operative, under cover of which during Czarist days the revolutionaries distributed their propaganda. Imprisoned

at Irkutsk for his activities, he spent a long period as a 'trusty'
there ; and it was in that prison that the revolutionary leaders
arrested in European Russia were confined, often for several
months, before being despatched to exile in remote villages in
the Arctic. In consequence, he came to know many of them,
including Stalin, intimately. On the success of the Revolution
Backileff was made the first Commissar for Siberia, then the
first Soviet Ambassador to Japan. As a genuine Liberal, he became revolted by the murderous excesses of his colleagues so,
one night, quietly left the Embassy and, with his family, took
ship for England where, it is a pleasure to record, he settled
happily and his son became an officer in our Army. Mr.
Backileff's personal memories naturally proved invaluable to
me.

Finally, I was given much very useful information by the
late Major-General Sir Vernon Kell, then the head of our
Secret Service.

These sources enabled me to give an account of the genesis
and course of the Russian Revolution which is as valid today
as it was over a quarter of a century ago, when it was first
written.

# 1

# The Birth of a Nation

The Czar of All the Russias. Those words have something of the same romantic ring as 'Grand Cham of Tartary' or 'Great Mogul,' yet they were far more than an empty and almost legendary title, for there are, in fact, many Russias; and if we would understand the mighty people whom we vaguely term 'Russians', we must have some idea of the lands which make up the vast territories of the Union of Soviet Socialist Republics at the present day.

Vast is the only word applicable when trying to visualise this one immense area of plain and forest, desert and mountain which stretches unbroken from the Baltic Sea to the Pacific Ocean and from the borders of tropical Persia to the ice-floes of the North Pole. It occupies over 8,500,000 square miles.

The United States is less than half its size, and the area of England, Scotland and Wales together being approximately only 90,000 square miles, Russia is over 90 times the size of our 600-mile-long island.

The present population of the Soviet Union is 226,000,000[1] against our 54,000,000 odd, so, excluding our overseas territories, there are, near enough, four Russians to each Briton.

By taking the two sets of figures together we may get a rough idea of how the Soviet lands are peopled. Set our island down in Russia and give it for its area the same density of population that Russia has. From a mighty metropolis of 8,000,000 London would shrink to a city of 355,000. Manchester from 660,000 to 34,000 and our innumerable hamlets, with their 100 odd villagers, would each be marked by a single cottage with a family of five.

We consider here that if our house is 12 miles from a railway station we live in the very back of beyond, but, on the same scale, in Russia we should have 270 miles to go instead.

1. These figures are the 1964 estimates

Enough of figures. Let us try and get some idea of the people who live in these great wastes and, in the course of time, have come to populate the Soviet cities.

There is a mistaken idea that a great proportion of them are Asiatics, but actually only a small percentage are Non-Aryan. Great, or true, Russians predominate. Little Russians, White Russians, Swedes, Letts, Serbs, Poles, Bulgars, Lithuanians and Czechs, all different races but all Slavs, form the great bulk of the population. Finns and Esthonians in the north, Georgians and Circassians in the south, innumerable Turko-Tartar tribes in the east, contribute a smaller quota, and the whole is leavened with a fair sprinkling of Jews.

Later the Poles, Finns, Bulgars, Lithuanians, Serbs, Esthonians and Czechs were to secure independence, but their stock has been mingled with that of the Russians for generations, and large numbers of them still live within the borders of the U.S.S.R.

Except for a period of two hundred years, when she was dominated by the Golden Horde which swept down upon her from Mongolia, Russia has always been essentially a European power. Fifteen out of every sixteen of her people live in Europe, nine-tenths of her great cities lie there; from time immemorial she has drawn her wealth and life-blood from the great grain-fields of the Ukraine.

The land is one vast plain with few mountains, except in Asia.

In classic antiquity the Russians were called Scythians. The Greeks and Romans knew them as hardy fighters, and on burial urns left pictures of them in costumes which differ little from those which are used in South Russia at the present day.

Their early history is much confused with myth, but there is ample evidence to show that those amazing adventurers, the Vikings, who sailed the unknown seas even to the distant continent of America, were equally hardy travellers by land in the ninth century, for they founded the two great cities of Novgorod and Kiev, and were responsible for forming the nucleus of what was afterwards to become the mighty Russian Empire.

Three brothers who came out of Sweden are credited with the feat, and after one of them named Rurik, it is said, the land became known as Russia.

Rurik's successor, Oleg, penetrated to the Black Sea and

laid siege to Constantinople; the first we hear of an enmity which dominated Russian policy for many centuries.

Oleg gave his daughter Olga to Rurik's son. She became a Greek Church Christian in 957, and their grandson, Vladimir, was the first Russian Christian king. He added Galicia and Lithuania to his territories. The next sovereign, Yaroslav, gave Russia her first code of laws, and it is interesting to note that these, although debased later by Asiatic influences, were entirely European in conception.

There then came a time which is known as the 'Period of the Appanages'. The country was divided into principalities which owed no allegiance to any sovereign overlord. Those of Kiev, Smolensk and Novgorod were the principal among them.

That Europe was not, in those days, lacking in communications and, as we are sometimes inclined to suppose, in a state where one people were totally ignorant of the existence of another, is proved by the fact that Vladimir Monomakh, Prince of Kiev, married an English girl. His princess was one Gytha, the daughter of our last Saxon king, Harold, who died in battle resisting the invasion by William the Conqueror.

Curiously enough, no other marriage between the two royal houses took place for nearly eight hundred years; the next being when Queen Victoria's son, the Duke of Edinburgh, married the daughter of the Czar Alexander II in 1874.

This Vladimir's son, George Dolgoruki, founded Moscow, but the town did not assume any real importance until some centuries later.

The year 1224 brought a new era to Russia. From that date right up to 1462, and periodically afterwards, her cities were laid waste and her feudal barons dominated by the Mongols.

Her great open plains lent themselves to easy invasion. There were few mountain chains in which the Europeans could make a desperate stand and her cities were poorly fortified. The yellow-skinned hordes under Jenghis Khan poured down from south-eastern Siberia on their wiry ponies and drove the white peasants like cattle before them.

Comparatively little is known of Jenghis Khan, but he was certainly a most remarkable man. Having amalgamated several loosely related Tartar tribes under his leadership he swooped upon the ancient Chinese Empire and captured Pekin in 1212, took Samarkand and subdued the huge Khoresmian Empire, which stretched from Asia Minor to Middle India, by 1218, and was well on the way to the Baltic by 1224.

In its great extent the Mongol Empire makes the conquests of Alexander the Great look insignificant. It included, or almost touched, Warsaw, Mandalay, Pekin, Moscow, Lahore and Budapest.

The Tartars were a rude, hardy people living in tents and existing mostly on mare's milk products and meat, yet it must not be imagined that their Great Khans remained nothing but the leaders of huge ill-disciplined robber bands. Their early wars with China taught them much and, infusing the old Chinese strategy with their extraordinary vigour of execution, they became superb generals. Their campaign of 1241, conducted simultaneously against Hungary, Germany and Poland, was conceived upon a scale hundreds of years ahead of anything the European commanders had ever visualised. No one else in fact, either before or afterwards, right up to the Napoleonic era, operated armies upon such tremendous lengths of front as the instance of one central directing brain.

Such feats cannot be carried out unless the fighting troops are backed by a high degree of organisation, and here Jenghis Khan showed his fine judgment in selecting the brilliantly gifted Chinese statesman, Yeliu Chutsai, as his right-hand man. Yeliu outlived his master by many years, and the consolidation of the Mongol Empire was almost entirely due to his genius.

We Europeans have been taught to regard the Tartars as barbarians, and it is true that they laid waste much property, destroyed many townships, and kept subject peoples under by an iron discipline, but there is little doubt that the highly cultured Yeliu Chutsai regarded us also as barbarians, and with some reason, since he was imbued with the traditions of the oldest unbroken civilisation in the world. He organised a vast espionage system throughout the enemy countries, an adjunct to warfare with which they had never had to deal before, and Western Europe was only saved from conquest because his spies informed him that the difficult country of mountain chains and great forests was not suitable to Tartar operations. It was at his instance that many monuments of antiquity and works of art were saved from spoliation by the soldiery, and he was responsible for complete religious toleration being ordered throughout the whole of the enormous territories overrun by the conquerors.

In view of his wisdom and power it is not surprising that the Mongols rapidly became more and more dominated by the Chinese influence, so that when the Empire split up the last of their great Emperors, Kublai Khan, moved his capital to Pekin, very wisely contenting himself with founding a dynasty in what must have been by far the most beautiful and agreeable part of his dominions.

Afterwards, Russia, with which we are alone concerned, formed part of the great Khanate of Kipchak. Mongols, picturesquely known as Khans of the Golden Horde, continued to rule there for nearly two hundred years. During this time the Russian Princes, or Grand Dukes as they were coming to be called, paid tribute and were compelled to raise armies for the use of their Asiatic masters. Yet the *life* of the country went on much as before the conquest and the practice of Greek Church Christianity was in no way interfered with.

Although at first sight it may appear that the Mongols differed little from Attila's Huns in an earlier century, and that after battening for a number of generations on the countries they conquered they disappeared from history having contributed little or nothing to civilisation, this is by no means the case.

They played the exceedingly important part of breaking down the barrier which had hitherto existed between East and West. At the splendid, if ephemeral, court of the Khan of Khans in Karakorum, Arabs mingled with Chinese, Europeans with Hindus, and Malays with Finns. For the best part of a century men of almost every nationality met in that Central Asian metropolis exchanging news, merchandise and beliefs under a benign autocracy that encouraged learning. With the removal of Kublai Khan's capital to Pekin the Siberian city fell into decay, but many of the bonds which had been established were never afterwards entirely broken.

Russia was one of the principal beneficiaries since, as an integral part of the Mongol Empire, her nobility had to travel to Karakorum in person to swear fealty, and for two and a half centuries they intermarried freely with the Mongol aristocracy. It is largely from these contacts that the households of the Grand Dukes derived the barbaric splendour for which they continued to be famous long after the Mongol Empire had passed away.

The Greek influence must not be discounted, however, since

contact had been made with Byzantium at the much earlier period of the Norse rulers and was never discontinued. It was from the Graeco-Romans of Byzantium that the Russians adopted the humiliating practice of knocking their heads on the ground when in the presence of the Czar, until this was abolished by Peter the Great.

Nevertheless such influences left the bulk of the population quite untouched, as is evidenced by the fact that there is little Tartar or Greek in the Russian language. The mass of the people remained as they had always been; essentially European in blood and custom.

The ancient city of Novgorod in the far north, not to be confused with Nizhniy-Novgorod of later fame in the south, had always succeeded in maintaining its independence and, as one of the Hanseatic League, had become an immensely wealthy Republic City-State with a population of 400,000. It is now, however, at the end of the Mongol domination, that Moscow first begins to rival it in importance.

Ivan III, Grand Duke of Muscovy, surnamed the Great, won the confidence of the ruling Khan and by his favour secured sovereignty over a number of neighbouring principalities. In 1480 he revolted and drove the Tartars out; thus becoming the first independent Russian sovereign of note.

He later broke the power of Novgorod, which from that time fell into decline, and also smashed up the Kingdom of Lithuania, then a state nearly twice as large as his own, extending from the Baltic to the Black Sea.

Ivan the Great was a skilful statesman as well as a good general, and married Zoe, a daughter of the Imperial House of the Palæologi, the last sovereigns of Byzantium. Constantinople had fallen to the Turks in 1453, and with it collapsed the last crumbling ruin of the once mighty Roman Empire. From this alliance Ivan took the Double Eagle for the Russian crest and from the disinherited family of his wife the title of Czar or Cæsar for his successors.

Like England after the Norman Conquest, Muscovy was never to be totally subdued again, although parts of it were ravaged from time to time by the barbarians, a Polish King occupied its throne for a brief period and it was invaded by Napoleon. From the successful insurrection of Ivan the Great in 1480 dates the true birth of the Russian nation.

# 2

# The Making of an Empire

Some wit once remarked that the only thing wrong with Froude's *History of the English People* was that it contained nothing about the People.

That may be true, but, in defence of Froude, it should be remembered that the life and habits of a whole people can be radically changed by an autocratic ruler. Anyone who doubts this should consider the revolutions in outlook and custom which took place in Turkey, Italy and Germany as a result of the dictatorships of Kemal Ataturk, Mussolini and Hitler.

At the present day such changes can be brought about with great rapidity owing to a high level of education which facilitates the absorption of new ideas, rapid communication, and Government control of press and broadcasting. Up to the twentieth century, however, it took months, and before the nineteenth, years, for new ambitions, prejudices and fashions to percolate as far as the common people. Yet they were, even if slowly, affected by the policies of their rulers, and particularly during the longer and more important reigns. Moreover, without their participation the imperialistic wars could not have been fought, and certainly not won if all the rank and file had been unwilling conscripts.

In any attempt to assess the Soviet people of today, therefore, it is essential to give a brief résumé of Russia's development under her most outstanding Czars and Czarinas.

After Ivan the Great the next monarch of note was Ivan the Terrible, a madman who practised incredible barbarities on his subjects yet seems to have had periods of sanity during his long reign. His nickname came from the awe that he inspired and a more correct translation of it is 'John the Dreaded'.

In character he appears to have been not unlike Louis XI of France. He sequestered himself from fear of assassination, was deeply religious and spent much of his time in theological disputation, but he built many fortresses and considerably strengthened his kingdom.

Personally he was a great coward and left Moscow to be sacked by slave-raiding Tartars from the Khanate of the Crimea in 1571, but his general, Prince Kurbski, won many battles, and Yermak, the Hetman of the Don Cossacks, seized Western Siberia for him as far as Tobolsk. For the purposes of this book it is interesting to note that Siberia began to be used as a penal colony for political prisoners almost immediately afterwards.

One matter in which Ivan showed sound sense was his prolonged endeavours to open up his country to the traders, craftsmen and scholars of Western Europe. In this he was seriously baulked by his arch-enemy the King of Poland, who would not allow them to cross the Russian frontier, but assistance reached Ivan from an unexpected quarter.

In 1553 Richard Chancellor sailed from England in search of a north-east passage to China. He failed to find it, but having arrived in the White Sea made his way to Moscow. Ivan said that he would receive him, and a Court official told Chancellor that he must kneel and knock his forehead on the ground in the presence of the Czar. Chancellor replied: 'I do not do that even when given audience by my own sovereign, Queen Elizabeth, so I certainly will not humble myself so before any foreign Prince.'

When this was reported to Ivan he said: 'She must indeed be a great Queen who is served by such proud and courageous people.' He waived the ceremony, received Chancellor with every honour and sent him back to England with the first Muscovite Embassy. While still cut off by land from communication with other European powers Ivan was soon able to secure by sea from Britain the things he coveted. A thriving trade was established, a considerable colony of Scots and English settled in Moscow, and Ivan entered into negotiations for an alliance with Queen Elizabeth.

Ivan had seven wives and selected for the eighth an English girl, but hearing accounts of his cruelty she funked it at the last moment and, probably wisely, refused to sail. He killed his eldest son by striking him with an iron staff and died in a fit.

He left two sons, Feodor and Dmitri. The elder, vitually an imbecile, married the sister of the clever, unscrupulous and powerful noble Boris Godunov; the younger died in mys-

terious circumstances. Godunov was all but Czar during Feodor's reign and became so in fact upon his death by compelling
the nobles and Provincial *Zemstvos* to elect him to the throne.
These *Zemstvos* were representative bodies which had sprung
up in the times of the Mongols and on occasions of crisis sent
members to a central *Duma*; but this was not summoned between 1698 and 1905 and the powers of the *Zemstvos* became
purely confined to matters of local government.

Godunov was a tireless worker but never popular. He fortified Smolensk as a barrier against Russia's hereditary enemy,
the ancient and powerful Kingdom of Poland, and founded
Archangel in the far north. His main importance in the development of Russia is that he broke the power of the hereditary nobles; his death was sudden and there is good reason
to believe that he was poisoned.

There followed a period of troubles. At one time a pretender, the false Demetrius, who declared that he was the son of
Ivan, was on the throne, at another the boy Czar Michael, the
nominee of the *Boyars,* as the great landowners were termed.
They forced him to associate them jointly with himself in the
Government, but their success was only temporary, and the
next groping attempt towards some sort of Constitution was
not to be made for another hundred years.

Poland and Sweden both proved difficult neighbours. The
Poles overran the country and made their King, Ladislaus, its
sovereign for a couple of years; Gustavus Adolphus of Sweden
forced through a treaty in 1617 by which he acquired lands
shutting Russia right out of the Baltic. Yet, in spite of this, the
country developed rapidly. Dutch, Swedes, Danes, Germans,
English and particularly Scots settled in the Russian cities in
ever-increasing numbers and brought to the land of their
adoption the knowledge and customs of the Western world.

By the middle of the seventeenth century the barbaric splendour of the Mongols and the elegance of decadent Byzantium
had been tempered by the artistry of the Italian Renaissance
gradually creeping north. There were still few large buildings
of stone except in the principal cities, but the Court of the
Czars rivalled any of that date for magnificence; the priceless
furs of the courtiers and the lingering influence of the East
adding a glamour to the cloth of gold, velvet and gems common to all state functions of the period.

The Czar Alexis reigned towards the close of this unsettled

time; he was a humane man compared to the majority of his predecessors, but the ferocity of the average punishments inherited from the Tartar Khans can be judged by Alexis's *revised* code of laws in which it is set down that a man found guilty of smoking a pipe of tobacco should have his nose cut off.

In this reign we see the first concerted action of the people, unled by any discontented noble, against the throne. A revolt against crushing taxation took place in 1648; several *Boyars* were killed and much blood shed before it was put down.

Alexis generously helped to finance Charles II during the period of his exile, and on the Restoration received an Embassy bearing cordial thanks from Great Britain.

The Cossacks of the Don, as has been seen, came under Russian sovereignty in Ivan the Terrible's day; the other main body of this mixed Turko-Russian race, the Cossacks of the Dnieper, were subject to Poland. In the latter part of the sixteenth century Stephen Batory organised six regiments each 1,000 strong to act as a frontier force against the Tartars, but these Dnieper Cossacks were treated with ill-judged harshness by their Polish masters, and in 1652 ceded from John Casimir of Poland to Alexis. This gave Russia a loose sovereignty over another great slab of territory to the south and ultimately resulted in her regaining her ancient city of Kiev.

Peter the Great next claims our attention and slight as this historical outline must be it is necessary to devote a few more paragraphs to him than any other sovereign because he changed the life of the whole nation.

Had he lived two centuries later he would almost certainly have been a Bolshevik, and there is much in his determination to achieve sweeping reforms, for the ultimate benefit of Russia, however ruthless the methods necessary, which resembles the attitude of the early Commissars.

He despised pomp and luxury, had simple tastes, wore old clothes, loved talking to homely people and scandalising conventional, pompous persons, was extremely quick-witted, possessed an insatiable craving for practical knowledge and had immense bodily vigour. He took as his second wife a captive peasant who could not even sign her name.

The only thing he retained of the Asiatic heritage was the ferocious cruelty with which he punished the reactionaries who opposed his plans; in all other things he showed a fanatical desire to Westernise Russia—and he succeeded.

The bold Scottish adventurer, Patrick Gordon, was already established at the Russian Court on Peter's accession. The new Czar made this great captain his right-hand man and took innumerable other foreigners into his service. Not content with what they could teach him he set out to travel in 1697 and see other countries for himself. Intense interest in engineering and shipping caused him to put in a spell as a worker in the Dutch shipbuilding yards at Saardam and another at Deptford near London.

His rough mode of life is illustrated by the bitter complaints of Captain Benbow who rented Says Court, Deptford, to him. When the Czar had gone Benbow put in a claim against the Government because all his furniture was smashed, the locks broken off the doors and 'All the grass worke is out of order, and broke into holes by their leaping and shewing tricks upon it.'

William III thought very highly of Peter after talking to him and he evidently thought well of Britain since he often said in after years that it was a happier life to be an Admiral in England than a Czar in Russia.

After visiting Vienna he returned in haste to Russia at the news of a rebellion of the *Streltsi*; a large body of household troops not unlike the Roman Prætorian Guards, but composed at this time of old-fashioned Muscovite soldiers who detested Peter's foreign advisers and the reforms he was instituting. When he arrived in Moscow Gordon had already suppressed the rebellion for him, but he slaughtered the imprisoned mutineers with the most savage brutality.

In 1709, Peter's Ambassador, Matvéive, was arrested for debt in England. The Czar's amazement and indignation on receiving this news was so great that it led to the law of Diplomatic immunity being passed which later became common in all countries.

Owing to the splendid courage and leadership of Gustavus Adolphus in the earlier part of the century, Sweden was at this era a power of the first rank in Europe. Charles XII, a restless and ambitious prince, soon came into collision with Peter. The Swede was brave but incredibly foolhardy; he devastated Poland which, for once in its history, was fighting on the Russian side, but met his match in the Czar. The gallant

Swedish army was decimated and Peter enabled to annex
Esthonia and Livonia, thus realising his dream of being able
to establish a seaport on the Baltic. Later he also acquired
Finnish territory in the north, took Baku, thus clearing the
way to the Caspian in the south, and extended his Siberian
dominions as far as Lake Baikal in the east.

With incredible labour and at an immense cost he built the
great stone city of St. Petersburg, which became the new capital. It was constructed with slave labour, on piles, in the middle of the desolate marshes at the head of the Gulf of Finland,
and so many tens of thousands of lives were lost before it was
completed that the Russians said of it that it was built on a
foundation of human bones. Peter, having achieved his dearest
ambition of a capital on the sea, equipped it with libraries,
museums and picture galleries. He also founded the Russian
Navy.

In 1717 he undertook a second foreign tour, visiting Copenhagen, Lubeck, Amsterdam and Paris. It is not, however, as a
conqueror or traveller that Peter commands our attention as
much as for the extraordinary revolution which he brought
about in the everyday lives of his people. He did for Russia
what Kemal Ataturk has done for Turkey in our own time.

Russia, like Turkey, had been influenced by Asia to the extent of keeping her women in seclusion and allowing her religious orders immense power. Both dictators emancipated
the women and broke the thraldom of the priestly caste.
Kemal forcibly confiscated the fezzes of the Turks, Peter cut
off the beards of the Russians. Both abolished many senseless
fasts and by a hundred ordinances compelled their people to
accept the customs of more advanced nations.

His tragedy was his son Alexis who proved a die-hard reactionary, wanted to become a monk, openly declared that he
was only waiting for his father's death to undo all his work and
bring the capital back to Moscow, betrayed Russia to her enemies and conspired against his father's life. Peter had him tried
by the highest functionaries in the land and, when Alexis was
found guilty, had him executed to save the new Russia.

Peter the Great found his country a mediæval kingdom and
left it a modern Empire.

We now enter the period of palace revolutions, largely due
to the bitter strife between two irreconcilable parties, the clericals and reactionaries, led by the Princes Dolgoruki, who

wished to revoke Peter's innovations, and the capable foreigners who had helped so much to bring them about.

The Germans at first got the upper hand and Ostermann, the son of a poor Lutheran clergyman, set Catherine, Peter's illiterate widow, on the throne. She was the first of Russia's women rulers, and, like the others, caused continued jealousies and conspiracies at court by giving power into the hands of male favourites. Menshikov, who started life as a baker's boy but had shown great ability under Peter, governed Russia through her; among the many presents she gave him were 50,000 peasants.

Soon after his succession the young Czar Peter II exiled Menshikov to Siberia, whose limitless snows many favourites were now soon to travel, and the Dolgorukis led the reactionaries into power; but only for a short time as Peter died of smallpox.

The great nobles decided that in future the power of the monarch should be limited and virtually retained in their hands, as was the case in Poland. They offered the Crown to the Princess Anne conditionally upon her granting a Constitution. The draft of this stipulated that she should consult the High Council on all Government affairs, and not declare peace or war, levy new taxes, confer any important offices, marry, or choose a successor without its consent. Neither was she to condemn any of the nobility to death or confiscate their property unless their crime had been proved. In addition no property was to be alienated from the Crown, she was to have a fixed sum for her expenses and no control over troops except the guard at her palace. A Supreme Council of twelve with a Treasurer to control State funds was to be appointed, a Senate of thirty-six to report upon all business to the Council, a House of two hundred lesser nobility to protect their interests and an Assembly of gentlemen and merchants to see that the people were not oppressed.

These measures would have almost entirely nullified the powers of the throne, and if the Constitution had gone through, the history of Russia would have been very different. As it was the lesser nobility preferred one master to twelve and the more able ministers like Ostermann secretly opposed it because it would have robbed them of their great personal power. The palace guards revolted in favour of the Crown retaining its ancient and absolute prerogatives, so Anne was crowned Czarina without having granted any concessions at all, and ruled through her hated favourite Brien, a German Courlander of low extraction.

More palace revolutions followed the death of Anne until at seven o'clock one fine morning Elizabeth, the only surviving daughter of Peter the Great, seized the Winter Palace. The moving spirit in the plot was a French surgeon, one Lestocq; this being the first sign of the French influence which was to play so large a part at the Russian Court for many years afterwards. The tutelage of the German adventurers was ended; and when soon afterwards we find Russia for the first time involved in the wars of Western Europe, she is allied with Austria and France against Prussia.

The Seven Years War, which opened in 1757, was waged against that extremely able soldier Frederick the Great, who initiated a policy which many other enemies of Russia were afterwards to adopt; often with disastrous results to her gallant army and loyal people. He offered big bribes to Russian statesmen and generals, who treacherously accepted them as the price of delaying the campaign, or deliberately refraining from exploiting Russian victories to their fullest extent. Yet this did not save Frederick in the end as the Russians carried their eagles to Berlin in 1760, the year before Elizabeth's death.

A serious abuse, dating from this period, was the establishment of a Government office to deal with the reports of an unofficial political spy system. Informers gave secret evidence of criticisms made in casual talk against the Sovereign and high officers of State, upon which the indiscreet were seized and sent upon the terrible journey to Siberia. This practice was never long discontinued, but grew with time to be a brooding terror which threatened the life and happiness of every Russian citizen. It was perhaps, more than any other, the root cause of the Russian Revolution.

As a nominee of the reactionaries Elizabeth favoured the clericals, built many churches and performed pious pilgrimages, but these acts were probably dictated more by policy than inclination, since she had numerous lovers, encouraged the arts, and took pride in her beautiful person.

Her nephew, Peter III, was permitted to reign only a few months. Having a passionate admiration for Frederick the Great, the new Czar's first act was to make peace with Prussia and restore to her all the fruits of the recent Russian victories.

This quixotic gesture caused great resentment in the Army. His next move was an attempt to possess himself of all the great monastic properties. He was not a strong man like Henry VIII, and very soon found himself embroiled up to the ears with the Church.

Even then he might have saved himself for a time had he not for some years previously abominably ill-treated his exceedingly beautiful and vivacious young wife, Catherine. She was a German by extraction, but having become a Russian and a member of the Greek Church on her marriage she thenceforth devoted herself to the country and faith of her adoption with unfailing loyalty.

About her charming person centred the most famous palace conspiracy in Russian history. Most readers will know the story and several million people must have seen the version of it in one of the films for which Marlene Dietrich or Elizabeth Bergner played the part of the Czarina.

Catherine gathered about her, largely by the lure of her personal favour, a number of powerful lords: the Orlovs, Dashkov and Potemkin being particularly prominent among them. During the night of July 19th, 1762, she visited the barracks and won over the soldiers personally. To the honour of the conspirators it should be said that no blood was shed; the only sufferer being the unfortunate Peter, who is believed to have been strangled four days later. The *coup d'état* succeeded without a hitch and the lovely Catherine found herself Empress of all the Russias, which she ruled for the following thirty-four years with outstanding ability.

Her wars and treaties extended the Russian dominions in nearly every direction. After the three partitions of Poland, the last of which took place in 1779, that country ceased to have any independent existence; there being no lion to dispute the prey, the eagle's share of the ancient kingdom went to Catherine. To the west she secured the Duchy of Courland, the country of the Letts, which added greatly to her Baltic seaboard. To the east more and more Russians were establishing themselves in further Siberia, while Turkey was forced to cede many provinces, including the Crimea, which gave her an outlet of the first importance in the Black Sea.

Far bolder and much cleverer than Peter she carried out his scheme for transferring the religious lands to the Crown. Over two hundred great monasteries had been founded in the past four centuries; they possessed immense wealth and owned more than a million peasants.

A terrible *pogrom* in which great numbers of Jewish children were slain took place in the Government of Kiev during her reign, but she executed the Cossack leader who was responsible. A pretender also gave her trouble and his revolt became a kind of *jacquerie,* resulting in the burning of many manors by the peasants and slaughter of the landed gentry. She put down this revolution with a firm hand, but was humane by nature and punished with the utmost rigour members of the nobility who she found to have ill-treated their serfs.

In 1787 she undertook a Royal Progress to her new possessions in the Crimea. Potemkin, wishing to impress her with their fruitfulness showed her only specially prepared areas, but he was not the first or last to fake a show in order to please a gullible Sovereign or foreign trade-union leader. He was only anticipating, however, as Odessa and Sevastopol were founded upon the sites of tumble-down Turkish villages, and the Crimea blossomed into the beautiful Russian Riviera.

Potemkin was Catherine's greatest minister and the able Suvorov her most famous general; in addition she had many favourites who achieved a certain importance for a time as her lovers of the moment.

Catherine amused herself at times by writing fairy-tales, comedies, and even did a Russian adaptation of the *Merry Wives of Windsor.* She was a small person and is reported to have been, as it were, a pocket Venus ; but flatterers may have exaggerated her charms. In any case she was certainly a great lover, and a great woman; deservedly she ranks in the history of her dearly loved adopted country as Catherine the Great.

Paul I, the only child of Catherine, is known to us as 'the Mad Czar'. Two forms in which his insanity showed itself were colossal arrogance and playing the tyrannical martinet over his household troops. Once he ordered an entire regiment which displeased him on parade to march off to Siberia then and there. So absolute was the Czar's power that they obeyed and did not dream of turning back until his order of recall reached them.

Alarmed by the French Revolution he joined Turkey, England, Austria and Naples in attacking France in 1799. Most of the fighting was in Italy; one Russian army was routed there and another in Switzerland. The veteran Suvorov, who had covered himself with glory in other campaigns, arrived on the scene too late to do anything but unite the remnants of the defeated armies, after a fine march across the passes, and bring them home. He was disgraced for his pains.

Napoleon Bonaparte now enters the picture. Wishing to gain Paul's friendship, the shrewd Corsican sent back all the Russian prisoners in nice new uniforms, with his compliments. Paul fell for the generous gesture, broke with the Allies, and planned with Napoleon an invasion of India.

The original scheme never matured, as the Pahlen conspiracy took place in March, 1801, and Paul was assassinated.

His successor, Alexander I, immediately made peace with England, and in 1804 the British Cabinet agreed to subsidise him to the tune of £12 a head for every soldier he put into the field against Napoleon. The French Emperor beat the Russians at Austerlitz in 1805, but again generously repatriated the prisoners.

The ancient Christian Kingdom of Georgia, Stalin's country, which lies on the borders of Turkey, was absorbed into the Russian Empire in 1801, but Alexander was having considerable trouble in that neighbourhood at this time, so his situation was by no means easy, although a few years later he succeeded in conquering Bessarabia. In 1807 his troops were again defeated by the French at Eylau and Friedland, after which he met Napoleon personally on the River Niemen and signed the Treaty of Tilsit.

One of the Treaty's stipulations was that Russia should place an embargo on all British imports; this caused considerable distress among Alexander's subjects when enforced by him, as, for generations, they had depended on shipments of British goods for certain necessities. The alliance did not last.

For over six centuries Finland had been subject to Sweden, but was ceded to Russia in 1809. Alexander, however, granted this sturdy people a constitution by which they retained their own Diet and a separate army.

In 1812 Napoleon invaded Russia with an army of 600,000 men. After some preliminary fighting, 370,000 Russians, under Kutuzov, made a stand against him at Borodino, about fifty miles outside Moscow. This terrible battle is magnificently described in Tolstoy's great novel, *War and Peace*. The carnage on both sides was ghastly; the French were victorious, but the Russians were not routed. Napoleon occupied the ancient Muscovite capital.

The citizens of Moscow then showed an incredible degree of courageous stubbornness, refused to disclose the where-abouts of their hidden stores even when shot in batches and, six days later, set fire to their city. Nine-tenths of it were burnt to the ground.

Napoleon occupied the ruins for five weeks, but his troops were already on short rations, winter was approaching, and to secure supplies became the one paramount necessity. On October 24th the disastrous retreat began. Only about one in seven of Napoleon's men succeeded in staggering back to Germany; the Russian campaign contributed more than any other single factor to break him, but in it Marshal Ney covered himself with deathless glory.

He commanded the centre at Borodino and was named Prince of Moscow on the evening of the battle. In the retreat he was ordered to cover the retirement of the Grande Armée. Through short, sunless days of icy wind and long, freezing nights he fought one of the most gallant rearguard actions in the history of the world. Day after day, with indomitable cou-rage, he kept Platonov's fur-clad Cossacks at bay while guns and wagons were manhandled through the ruts of snow and slush. Unshaven, filthy, sleeping but two hours in twenty-four, eating and fighting with his men, Ney carried the army that Napoleon had deserted across the Berezina, and then, by sheer will power, over the Niemen into safety; being himself the last man to fire the last musket on the bridge of Kovno before reaching the safety of Polish soil. It is virtually certain that had it not been for his incredible bravery and endurance, the whole of the Grande Armée would have died in the Russian snows. As it was, 80,000 men were saved to form the nucleus for the following year's campaign. Ney's name will live in his-tory on account of that epic as an example to the soldiers of all nations for all time.

In 1813 Napoleon was again defeated at Leipzig by the Allies; in 1814 the Russians occupied Paris. The Congress of Vienna awarded Russia the Duchy of Warsaw, a further chunk of Poland which had till then remained outside her borders. Alexander was crowned King of the Poles and gave them a constitution.

In spite of these many wars, Alexander's reign was one of

progress. Owing to the Liberal views of the minister Speranski, the conditions of the serfs was ameliorated; but during the occupation of Paris in 1814 the Russian officers had come in contact with the French who had comparatively recently guillotined their King and Queen and dispossessed their clergy and nobility. Many of them naturally returned chock-full of revolutionary doctrines and secret societies were growing in the land. These societies were almost entirely composed of army officers and liberal-minded nobility who wished to see Russia brought up to modern standards. The 'Union of Salvation' was formed, with the object of securing freedom and justice for all by forcing the Czar to grant a Constitution. The knowledge of these movements made Alexander suspicious and unhappy during the last years of his reign. Towards the end he adopted the counsel of the reactionaries, brought military despotism to the country areas by settling regiments of soldiers among the peasants, and ordered a far stricter censorship of the press.

Nicolas I succeeded him in 1825 and the proclamation of the new Czar was the signal for an immediate insurrection. Ten years had been quite sufficient for the revolutionary seed to germinate and considerable numbers of people of the upper classes now belonged to underground organisations; the movement being known as that of the 'Dekabrists.' A new era had arrived in which monarchs no longer had to fear strangulation in a palace plot, but an explosive bomb hurled by a representative of the oppressed workers.

The Dekabrist revolt was put down, five of the ring-leaders being hanged and the remainder sent to Siberia. Nicolas entered on a Persian war, annexing two more provinces to Russia, and then began a campaign against the Turks.

The year 1830 saw the first Polish insurrection. A number of Russians were massacred and the Poles raised an army of 90,000 men. They fought with heroic bravery, but were defeated. Poland became a Russian province, its Constitution was cancelled and the University of Vilna suppressed. Nicolas then assisted Franz Joseph of Austria to deal with his rebellious Hungarian subjects. This other brave people who for many centuries had maintained a glorious independence was also mercilessly crushed, but Russia derived nothing from it.

In 1854 the Crimean War flared up. Russia had long cast

covetous eyes on Constantinople, but Britain and France went
to the assistance of Turkey. It was a bitter struggle in which
nobody gained anything of note and only remarkable for the
Russian's heroic defence of Sevastopol. While the siege was
still in progress Nicolas died.

His eldest son, Alexander II, succeeded him and the Treaty
of Paris, in 1856, closed the Crimean War.

The year 1861 proved of particular importance as the Czar
passed a law emancipating the serfs; a measure which had
already been under contemplation by Nicolas.

A second Polish insurrection took place in 1863 in spite of
attempts at conciliation. Finding these useless the Russians
seized in their beds a number of Poles who were known to be
irreconcilables and drafted them into the Army. The result
was an immediate outbreak, although the Poles had little but
their fervid patriotism to throw into the combat. Their secret
nationalist movement, the Ryad, carried out numerous assassinations, but they lacked arms to fight against the well-equipped soldiers of the Russian Viceroy, the Grand Duke Con-
stantine. The revolt was stamped out and as a penalty the use
of the Russian language was forced upon the Poles.

Alexander II conducted wars against the Circassians, Persians and Turks. He was largely responsible for the establishment or enlargement of the Christian States in the Balkans at
the expense of Turkey.

The conclusion of his reign was disturbed by many plots
against his life. In 1879 alone three attempts to assassinate
him very nearly proved successful.

During his time Russia subdued the Caucasus and annexed
Turkestan, thus bringing her frontiers to within 500 miles of
India. She also acquired by treaty from the Chinese all the
territory on the left bank of the River Amur and in 1860 Vladivostok was founded on the Pacific.

It has now been seen how Russia increased during the
course of exactly four hundred years, by conquest after conquest, from the little Grand Duchy of Muscovy to a vast and
many-peopled Empire. We are free to turn to another story.

In 1881 a pale, sickly boy of eleven was already showing unusual brilliance at his studies in Simbirsk on the Volga; a
ragged brat aged two was tumbling about the filthy, cobbled
alleyway outside a poor shoemaker's hovel in Tiflis, and a

baby son was born to a vagabond peasant miner in the Don Basin.

In that year the Czar of All the Russias was killed by a Nihilist hand-grenade, but the children referred to were destined to change the course of history. They were, respectively: Lenin, Stalin and Voroshilov.

# 3

# Masters and Serfs

At the outbreak of the Great War Voroshilov was still only thirty-three years of age—*yet his father was born a slave.*

Let us be plain about the matter. When we say slave we mean it. The French serf, before the Revolution, could not really be described as a slave although he had to give so many hours' work a week free to his master. The Russian, in addition, could be flogged, imprisoned, sent to penal servitude or exiled to Siberia without trial and solely at the will of his owner. He was, further, an object of barter; his family were of no account and without reference to his wishes he could be sold to another landowner in a distant province just as though he were a sack of corn or an animal.

What a fantastic situation! How utterly unthinkable it is to any Anglo-Saxon of today that his father should have been an owner of slaves or a slave himself.

The very word 'slaves' conjures up a mental picture of ancient times. We think of the Roman nobility employing them in their houses; the cruel whip of the overseer as it lashed the naked backs of the rowers in the Phœnician galleys, or of ten thousand nebulous figures straining upon the ropes to draw into position some great block of stone under the blistering Egyptian sun.

In Western Europe slaves ceased to exist as saleable property nearly a thousand years ago because, with the gradual spread of Christianity, it was recognised that no baptised Christian could observe his religion and traffic in a human body that housed another soul.

It is vaguely accepted that slavery still continues in barbarous countries where the white man's writ does not yet run, but for generations we have suppressed it wherever possible and even the Negroes who laboured in the cotton fields of the United States were liberated in the remote days when men still wore three-cornered hats and swords.

How can it be then that the father of a man amply qualified to sit at the council table on equal terms with any European statesman, who also commanded the largest peace-time army in the world, could conceivably be the son of a slave?

That he is only one of millions of living Russians whose parents were slaves or who were actually born in slavery, goes without saying. We know that the Scythians were a free and independent people, honoured by the Romans as an uncultured but courageous race. How is it that their descendants should have come to such a shocking pass?

If we would understand this extraordinary enigma we must examine the structure of Russian society and the conditions which led to a great mass of her people still being in a state of serfdom less than a hundred years ago.

The Russian monarchs were autocrats. They had absolute power over the lives and property of all their subjects irrespective of rank or degree. Witness the peasants given away in herds to Court favourites and the favourites themselves exiled or executed without trial when they were no longer able to please.

Yet up to the time of Ivan the Terrible the peasants were not in the absolute state of bondage into which they afterwards fell. Until the early sixteenth century their state was similar to that of most European land workers in mediæval times, but they were not bound to the soil.

Among the great nobles there was always a party which wished to limit the autocracy and we have seen how, in the time of Michael, they succeeded to some degree, *ukases* then being issued in the name of the Czar and *Boyars,* but this success was only temporary. We have seen, too, how at a later date they failed to force a Constitution on the Empress Anne. In early times they held their lands by inheritance and wielded extensive power, but these powers were greatly curtailed by Ivan the Terrible, and the last vestige of their independence was crushed by Peter the Great.

A Great Council existed called the *Sobor* which was presided over by the Czar himself. About twenty of the great Barons and about twenty high dignitaries of the Church were usually summoned to it when it met, but none could claim the right to be present and invitations to it *depended entirely on the will of the Czar.*

The nobility consisted of four distinct grades.

B

The *Udielnia Kniazia*. These were the greatest hereditary princes to whom were attached appanages outside the original Duchy of Muscovy. Ivan the Terrible filched many of their ancient privileges from them by cunning and decreased their number by forcing some to remain unmarried and sending others to Siberia.

The *Boyars,* a Tartar word meaning 'exalted.' Their revenues came from lands assigned to them by the Emperor which they held only at his pleasure. They also received a further payment for serving in his wars.

The *Vioevodes*. Members of the lesser nobility who had done fine work in the wars and proved themselves successful generals.

The *Kniazia,* who had no patrimony but the bare title and were descended from the younger sons of the great nobles.

All the children of a *Kniaz* took his title and it is this which makes princes so numerous in Russia right up to the Revolution. As early as Elizabethan times an Englishman living in Russia wrote of them: 'Of this sort there are so many that the plentie maketh them cheap: so that you shall see dukes glad to serve a meane man for five or six roubles or marks a yeare, and yet they will stand highly upon their *bestchest* or reputation of their honours.'

This 'standing upon their honours' was carried to excessive lengths, and right up to the latter part of the sixteenth century they slavishly followed an absurd custom by which no man could fill an office which was inferior to any which his ancestors had held, or would accept a post under any man who counted fewer ancestors than himself.

Such a farcical adherence to precedence based solely on heredity naturally debarred many of the ablest men from any but inferior positions. On the advice of the wise Prince Galatzine the Czar Feodor made an attempt to destroy the system; he sent for the famous 'Book of Pedigrees,' under the pretext of wanting to look something up, and burnt it.

His act paved the way for the drastic reorganisation of the aristocracy by his successor, Peter the Great. Peter's scheme was diametrically opposed to the ancient custom; his view was that rank should correspond with the importance of official duties. In consequence he established the Chin, a graduation of ranks, and arranged all nobles in three classes, civil, military, and religious, with appropriate titles.

The word *Chinovnik* later became one of the most hated in the Russian language, since many minor members of this official class were not only petty tyrants but lazy in the extreme and had to be heavily bribed before they would attend to any matter concerning their department of the vast bureaucracy which ran the whole country.

Paul, however, removed from the nobles the obligation to perform public duties and many of them lived, when on their estates, like independent princes except that they were subject to the least order of the monarch. Their journeys to the capital resembled Royal Progresses and they were often accompanied by several hundred personal servants. They rarely travelled outside Russia and therefore held the strange belief that it was more highly blessed by nature than any other country. The state of education among them was extremely low and most of them were much too ignorant to be entrusted with a foreign Embassy. In consequence, up to the opening of the eighteenth century, the Czars generally employed foreigners: English, Scottish, or German adventurers principally, as their Ambassadors.

Until Peter the Great's time the women of the aristocracy led lives of oriental seclusion and were entirely in subjection to their husbands. They were even more ignorant and superstitious than the men, ate great quantities of sweetmeats regardless of their figures, and lazed away innumerable hours while their lords were hunting, in listening to fairy stories recounted by their female serfs, or the prognostications of fortune-tellers.

On the formation of Russian society at the later courts they appeared with their faces painted to an extreme degree, a practice probably acquired originally from the decadent Greeks of Byzantium and further fostered by the Chinese influence during the period of Mongol domination.

An old Court chronicler tells us: 'They paint so palpably that if they laid it on with a brush, and had a handful of meal cast in their faces when they had done, they could not disfigure themselves as much as the paint does. But the custom is so general, that the most handsome must comply, lest they should discredit the artificial beauty of the others: whereof we saw an example in the wife of Barrissowits Cirkaski who was the most handsome lady of all Muscovy, and was loath to spoil with painting what the rest of her sex took so much pains to preserve thereby: but the other women informed against her, and would not be quiet till their husbands had forced that Prince to give way, that his wife must daub her face after the ordinary manner. So that painting is so common in Muscovy, that when any are to be married, the bridegroom that is to be sends among other presents some paint to his bride.'

The weddings of the nobility were celebrated with great pomp, prolonged feastings, and the buffoonery common in the rejoicings of people having a low standard of intelligence. Before the eighteenth century the husbands were rarely allowed to see their future wives until the wedding day and many tricks were played upon them. To make herself appear taller the bride stood on a stool or the recumbent body of a beautiful female slave. The Russians are great eaters and drinkers, so they feasted far into the night and as a point of honour the male guests generally drank until they collapsed unconscious and were carried to bed by their body-servants.

Although many attempts were made to bring them over to Rome the Czars have never acknowledged any form of Christianity except that of the Orthodox Greek Church, acquired upon their ancestors' first conversion from paganism.

Until 1589 the Russian clergy remained under the Patriarch of Constantinople after which a separate Russian Patriarchate was established at Moscow. On Palm Sundays the Czar held the bridle of the ass upon which the Patriarch rode, a menial task that many Rulers did not relish, but so great was the hold of religion upon them at that time that they feared to discontinue it.

The suppression of this custom and the Patriarchate resulted indirectly from our own Reformation. Centuries later when Peter the Great visited England he observed with interest the supremacy of the Crown over the highest religious dignitaries. In his great reform of the privileged orders he nominated no Patriarch, but merged the office into that of Metropolitan of Moscow, who thereafter held a somewhat similar position to our Archbishop of Canterbury.

Catherine the Great, as we have seen, despoiled the monasteries of their lands and regulated their incomes.

In Russia, right up to the Revolution, there were two types of Orthodox Clergy; the *white* clad—parish priests, and the *black* clad—monks. Both were exceedingly numerous, but there was only one monastic order, that of St. Basil, in all

Russia. The ignorance, venality and filth of the Russian clergy have shocked travellers in the country from the earliest times up to the epoch when they were slaughtered or driven out by the armed proletariat.

Here, until the last century, there was practically no middle class at all. Even the lower ranks of *Chinovniks* were drawn from the poorer families of the aristocracy. The Slav has always been an indifferent business man and trade was entirely in the hands of foreigners, mostly British; such physicians as practised there, apart from the village wise men— mere witch doctors—were foreigners, too. It was before the age of factories in their modern sense, and there were practically no industries at all; the arsenals and army equipment plants were Government owned and their labour supplied from State serfs. The nobility imported their furniture, clothes, and luxuries from abroad. During the long winter months when the villages were snow-bound each specialised in some home-craft such as the making of wooden spoons, leather goods, agricultural implements, boots, etc., which they traded with their neighbours at the spring fairs; that of Nizhniy-Novgorod, in South Russia being particularly famous.

Even on the land there was no yeoman class of small independent farmers. The actual labouring peasant, and only the peasant, made up the one other class outside the Nobility and the Church—namely the People. Right up to 1914 over 82 per cent. of the total population still lived outside the towns.

In the time of Ivan the Terrible these *Muzhiks* were not in an absolute state of bondage and they still consisted of two distinct kinds of land-workers.

The *Krestiani*, peasants attached to the soil and long nominally free, with the right of quitting their masters on St. George's Day each year if they wished to make a change.

The *Kholopi,* who were real slaves; men captured in war, or the descendants of debtors who had been sold into slavery.

This system was in practice from very early times in Russia. Where the land-owner was a humane and benevolent man, and in later times there were many such, he regarded his peasants as grown-up children; the Czar himself was the 'Little Father' of them all. Good masters looked on their serfs as a grave responsibility, dispensed a rough justice among them, protected them from bands of robbers, and made serious inroads on their coffers to support them in times of famine. It is easy to see, however, that such an arrangement gives the land-owner complete control over his peasants. Without invoking any court of law he could virtually sentence a worker who had been troublesome to death by starvation. He had only to refuse the man the facilities granted to the others. The peasant might be nominally free, but the estates were so big that if a few neighbouring landlords agreed not to take on peasants who had been dismissed by the others the man might be faced with a journey of many hundred miles on foot before he could hope to secure fresh employment. Most of them had wives and families and it was like making a decision to go to another country with no secure opening there and no capital to live on until they had established themselves. Naturally, with very rare exceptions, they acquired the habit of kow-towing to the master even if he were a scandalously bad one.

The other class of land-workers were slaves already, but it became customary to give them plots of land by which they could support themselves and their families as more convenient than issuing them with daily rations.

In the course of time each of the two land-worker classes contributed something of its own characteristics to the other, and from the early sixteenth century they began to merge into one caste, the serfs, with such liberties as the old free *Krestiani* had enjoyed becoming more and more restricted.

It was the Czar Boris Godunov who first bound the peasants to the soil and forbade them to seek service under another master. From then on serfdom became more and more actual slavery.

Feodor's minister, the liberal Prince Galitzine, who instigated the burning of the 'Book of Pedigrees', was the first to propose the serfs' liberation. This was at the end of the seventeenth century and he wished to see Russia on the same footing as the Western nations. His view was that the first step to this must be the emancipation of the peasantry and the handing over to them of the lands they cultivated; but nothing came of his revolutionary proposal.

Peter the Great ordained that domestic serfs might enter the army and that those who had saved a certain sum might enrol themselves as inhabitants of towns for purposes of trade; in both cases without their necessarily obtaining the consent of their owners. In other ways, however, he much increased the powers of the masters as he abolished tax collectors and made the landowners responsible for the collection of all dues. Their hold upon the serfs was further strengthened by his successors who went to the length of allowing them to send recalcitrant workers to Siberia without any reference to a higher authority.

The Emperor Paul extended serfdom eastward, but in some parts he limited the free work which the serf-owners might demand to three days a week and forbade them to sell their peasants apart from land. In this condition the serfs continued until their emancipation in 1861.

The method adopted was that the Crown purchased the land from the landlords and then gave it to the Commune on the basis of about thirteen and a half acres for every male peasant. The Commune then had to repay the Crown over a period of forty-nine years with interest at 6 per cent.; so the deal was to be concluded only by 1910 and up to seven years before the Revolution the peasants were still paying for their liberty.

The 'Commune' has been mentioned in the last paragraph, and from it comes that potent word 'Communist,' so it is time to see what a Commune was.

A *mir*, as it was called in Russia, is a village community. The land occupied by the village, whoever had the seignorial rights, was considered to belong to the village Commune. Separate members of the community could only claim temporary possession of the parts which were allotted to them by the *mir* in proportion to their working power. After the emancipation each Commune paid into the Imperial Treasury a fixed yearly sum according to the number of peasants it contained and distributed the land among its members as it thought fit. In some Communes the land was divided yearly; in others every two or three years.

A *volost* was a large area of land common to many villages. The village parliament which made the distributions and settled all questions connected with the land was presided over by the village elder, each man and woman in the community had the right to vote, and the headman himself was subject to a peasant's court.

A *zemstvo* was a provincial assembly with representatives of the land-owners, artisans and peasants. It regulated taxation, education, public health, roads, and other matters of local government.

The emancipation of the serfs did not turn out quite all that its sponsors had expected. The majority of the nobility were furious because the compensation money was most unequally. distributed. Those who had large areas of land did fairly well, but those whose main wealth lay in domestic serfs were practically ruined as they had to release them without receiving any equivalent. The peasants felt themselves cheated because, in many cases, only the worst land was sold to them and the nobles reserved the best acreage for themselves. In consequence, the land-hunger of the peasant, far from being satisfied, was stimulated and their hatred of the rich landowners increased to such a degree that the ex-serfs became willing tools in the hands of revolutionaries a generation later.

Some Communes continued on the old lines, but others split up the land permanently among their members. This proved disastrous because once the peasants became private property-owners the inherent and ineradicable inequalities of human nature showed themselves at once. Some worked hard and saved, others were drunken and shiftless, the result being that the thrifty were able to pay the other fellow's taxes, take over his land, and from it earn further capital. These men were known as *mir*-eaters and a new class arose.

The *Kulak,* or rich peasant, was one who exploited his weaker and more stupid brethren after the emancipation; the government of the U.S.S.R. virtually went to war with this element in the population.

From Peter the Great's time onward there began a gradually increasing drift towards the towns. We have spoken of his ordinance allowing serfs to become enrolled as inhabitants of towns for the purposes of trade if they had saved a certain sum of money. Extremely few ever succeeded in doing so, but those who did carried with them the principle of the Commune.

*Artel* was the name of a town commune and it consisted of a number of peasants turned artisan who settled in one house, elected an elder and paid him their quota for sharing at a common table. These town serfs, however, had to pay a tax to their owners in lieu of service.

*Dumas* were granted to the municipalities in 1870, and the citizens having been enrolled, according to property qualifications, duly elected representatives. The wealthier artisans, traders and better educated among the ex-domestic serfs now at last began to form a middle class and rub shoulders with the more liberal-minded among the lower ranks of *Chinovniks*. The Jews who were the deadly enemies of the *Kulaks*, but pursuing exactly the same policy of exploitation which resulted, in their case, in the *pogroms*—hardly heard of before the emancipation—were also moving to the towns when they could afford to do so. Lastly, dispossessed peasants' sons, who had some initiative and could not till the land to their own profit through no fault of their own, were drifting in to work the comparatively few factories which were opening up as a result of the age of steam.

It was from these varied elements that the innumerable secret societies of Anarchists and Nihilists were formed. Practically the whole of the thinking population of Russia, outside the higher official class and wealthier nobility, being anti-monarchist, or at least strongly Liberal.

The peasants had not, and have not yet, learned to think— except in terms of personal greed and vodka. They toiled, mostly for a pittance, and spent the bulk of any savings they had on expensive weddings and funerals. At the burials the women wailed 'O'hone! O'hone!' just like the wild Irish, and some of their keens were very similar; afterwards they stuffed themselves to bursting on the baked meats, not knowing when they would see another square meal. During the winter there was not much work for the peasant to do, except cut a little wood, thresh his rye, or carry grain to town. Most of the time the greater part of the country is snow-bound so he lay on the top of the stove reciting or listening to tales and legends. Abysmal ignorance of the whole world outside the radius of a few *versts* was the rule, and superstition was rampant. Each village had its witch and the lazy, verminous priests did little to counteract her influence. Occasionally, if some rich *Kulak's* crops were blighted he got up an agitation against her, and they chucked her in the pond and prodded her all over with pins to find the devil's mark which is supposed to be painless; sometimes they killed her. Saints' days, a continuance on the same dates of ancient pagan festivals, were celebrated with much junketing and a great deal of drunkenness.

Such was the state of Russia in the year 1881 when Klementy Efremovitch Voroshilov was born.

# 4

# The Pit Boy

Klementy Voroshilov's mother was a servant girl; his father Ephrem, a rolling stone, one of the thousands who had been driven in from the land to the townships through the emancipation of the serfs, which had taken place just twenty years before his son's birth.

Ephrem was a powerful, sinewy man, upright and respected by his fellow-workers, but headstrong, self-willed and independent to a degree. He never kept any job for long as he was constantly at loggerheads with foremen and officials over what he considered injustices, but somehow he gained a precarious living roving from one mine to another and occasionally working as a railway watchman.

Clim, as his son Klementy was called, therefore had little in common with the Lenin and Trotsky type of Bolshevik leader who came of the educated classes; and it was to be many years before he came in touch with the Jews and intelligentsia who, at the time of his birth, were already fomenting revolution. He was a Russian in the very truest sense and all his youth and young manhood were saturated with the life, and hardships and the poverty of the Russian workers in the smoke-blackened Don Basin.

In earlier times the calm waters of the Don flowed like a mirror through untouched steppes with grazing on either shore where shepherds tended their flocks. Long, boat-shaped wagons laden with fish and salt came creeping over the plains through a fair and peaceful landscape before steel and iron were discovered there beneath the soil.

In 1795 an engineer-geologist, named Gascoigne, was brought out from England to build a metal-working factory there. That may have proved an eyesore to the local peasantry, but it did not greatly damage the countryside; neither did the fact that rich veins of anthracite were discovered at Gorodische in 1779; but at last the age of steam came even to backward Russia and in the 1870's the Lougansk railway works were built, thenceforward becoming an important point on the line that connected St. Petersburg, via Moscow and Kharkov, with the Crimea. The huge factory of the Don-Youriev Company was established at Alchevsk in 1895, and a year later the Hartmann locomotive plant at Lougansk. By the end of the nineteenth century the Don Basin could be compared in appearance to one of our own great northern industrial areas.

We have no figures for the population at the time Clim's father came wandering hungrily out of the plain towards the newly risen smoke-stacks that promised bread, but at a census taken in 1897, when Clim was sixteen, it was found that 83 per cent. of the population of the Province of Ekaterinoslav, in which the Don Basin is situated, consisted of new-comers from all parts of Russia brought by want and lack of land to the pits and engine-shops of the Don.

The former ploughmen, fruit-growers and craftsmen did not take readily to their new existence, and the shifting from mine to mine of Clim's father is extremely characteristic of the period. This new class of industrial worker had no means of expressing discontent with the hard conditions imposed upon it. There were as yet no study circles, no mass meetings, no leaflets, no strikes. The only revolt was that of the individual who, having quarrelled with the masters, packed his poor belongings and trudged off to try his luck elsewhere.

Alexander III ascended the throne in the year that Clim Voroshilov was born. The new Czar was an honest man of simple, almost bourgeois tastes. Personally, he was amiable and pleasant to deal with, but all his whole early life he had been a prey to fear and anxiety through the almost unceasing conspiracies to murder his father. He lived in the depths of his palaces hedged in by innumerable officials, whose very livelihood depended upon his autocratic will, and who therefore, for their own ends, spared him from every possible unpleasantness; so he could have had little conception of the actual state of things in his vast dominions.

Not unnaturally he regarded the shabby people who plotted in cellars and had just succeeded in assassinating his father as no better than murderous bandits to be seized and eliminated whenever his police could lay hands upon them. He probably believed in all honesty that the bulk of his people were per-

fectly happy and contented and would continue so were it not
for these accursed agitators, and he therefore placed himself
entirely in the hands of reactionary ministers.

He actually began his reign by attesting his 'belief in the
reality and strength of the autocratic power which we are
called upon to secure and maintain *for the good of the people*
against all aggression,' and passed a measure for strengthening
the hand of his Government against revolutionary activity,
whereby Governors or Prefects of Police were empowered to
prohibit at will all meetings and assemblies; to arrest, dismiss
from office or position, court-martial and exile any individual;
and to close down universities and schools.

All citizens and institutions of Russia were therefore now
placed under the absolute control of single administrators.
This measure, which was at first put into force for one year
only, was automatically renewed from year to year in many
Governments right up to 1905. The freedom of the press and
the independent course of justice were especially restricted.
An elaborate espionage system was already in operation, but
this was increased to an extraordinary extent and no one was
safe from denunciation. New university regulations in 1884
brought an end to the independence of the professional body
in Russia. The Government henceforward appointed its own
professors and also special inspectors, whose duty it was to
keep the students under close observation. A special factory
police-force was organised and spies were placed among the
workers. The local prefects assumed extraordinary powers.
The provincial *Zemstvos*, which were showing a strong liberal
tendency, were reorganised in order that the State might control their powers of local government, and a genuine reign of
terror set in. Countless thousands of people, many of them
completely innocent of even the mildest political activities,
were imprisoned or sent to Siberia during Alexander's reign.

From the time of the Dekabrists liberal feeling had never
altogether died in the upper classes; news of the French Revolutions of '48 and '71 had kept it alive and in the 'eighties it began to gain ground rapidly. Alexander's tyrannical measures
only resulted in estranging ever-growing numbers of the more
liberal-minded nobility, gentry and official classes from the
autocracy, and such revolutionary organisations as 'Land and
Freedom' and 'The People's Will' included many educated
people among their members. 'The Union of Struggle for

Liberation of the Working Classes,' founded by Lenin and Martov in the 'nineties, soon gained many adherents. The object of all these early secret associations was not to dethrone the Czar, but to force him into giving the country a Constitution.

As we have said the age of steam and steel was now creeping out of Western Europe over Russia. In 1881 the Trans-Caspian Railway to Samarkand was opened and ten years later the heir-apparent, afterwards Nicolas II, cut the first turf for the construction of the longest railway in the world, the Trans-Siberian, the first portion of which, from Chelyabinsk to Tomsk, was opened in '94.

In 1883, Germany, Austro-Hungary and Italy signed a defensive treaty, thereby forming the combination afterwards known as the Triple Alliance. Russia found herself isolated and so looked to France. The French, still smarting under their defeat in the 1870 war, readily agreed to an alliance, so the Franco-Russian Entente was established and visits of the two fleets were exchanged in 1891 and 1893.

In the 'eighties the first Marxian revolutionary organisation was formed abroad under the leadership of G. Plekhanov, while at home the activities of the Nihilists continued unabated and many Russian officials of high rank were assassinated. The *Zemstvos* implored the Government in vain to grant some concession whereby the autocracy might be limited by a Constituent Assembly. The words of the Kharkov *Zemstvo* sum up the situation: 'Grant, oh Most Gracious Czar, to your faithful people what you have given to the Bulgarians.' But pleading and wise counsel alike continued to be ignored.

Up to the 'eighties there existed no definite regulations for protecting the interests of labour or for controlling relations between employers and employed, and there can be no question but that the workers were mercilessly exploited. Wages were paid with the greatest irregularity. Less than 20 per cent. of the workers were paid weekly or fortnightly; 40 per cent. about once a month, and over 40 per cent. less regularly. This policy was deliberate as by keeping their employees in a constant state of want the factory owners virtually compelled them to purchase their necessities from the factory stores on credit; and from this system made an iniquitous profit out of their labour by charging from 20 per cent. to 100 per cent. more than the ordinary retail price for the goods supplied.

There was further an almost unbelievably harsh system of fines by which as much as 40 per cent. of the workers' wages were at times deducted when their pay-day at last arrived, and the hours that men, women and children were compelled to toil for a mere pittance would fill the least humane with horror.

Such were conditions when Ephrem Voroshilov was picking up a living as best he could in the Don Basin, and when his son Clim first came running on childish feet to the foreman's shout.

As soon as they could stand Clim and his sister Anna were sent out to beg their bread. At the age of seven, a ragged urchin, he was actually employed as a boy mine-worker gathering pyrites in the pits at ten kopecks, about 2d., a day. A little later he was made a lamp hand, next he put in twelve hours a day slaving for a rich peasant and then, being a bright lad, got himself a softer job as herd boy to a squire.

It was an accidental acquaintance with a member of the first *Duma*, the schoolmaster Ryzhkov, which brought the boy to light. Ryzhkov arranged for him to go to school, where at the age of thirteen he acquired an accomplishment extremely unusual among the contemporaries of his class and learned to read.

In the year 1894, the Czar Alexander III died, and was succeeded by his son, Nicolas II, who twenty-four years later was to be done to death by the Bolsheviks.

Nicolas had a great advantage over many of his predecessors in that he had travelled widely before his accession to the throne, visiting many parts of Europe and Asia, including India and Japan; yet he seems to have derived little benefit from this more liberal education. He was a family man, a devoted husband and a good father, he was also extremely religious in a primitive, superstitious way, but it would be difficult to name a ruler who took less interest in the welfare of his people. Nicolas's marriage had been a genuine love match and, in the face of great opposition, he had courted Princess Alix of Hesse for five years before winning her. She had a stronger personality than her husband but the same narrow, religious outlook, and he devoted himself to her entirely. His private diaries, which have been preserved, show the hopelessly low state of his mentality for the position he occupied. They contain little but trifling pieces of gossip about his numerous relatives, which appear to have interested him exceedingly, and to have absorbed the time which he should have given to the vast responsibilities of State. A letter to his mother, the Empress Marie, shows him to have been far more concerned about the death of his pet dog than a major crisis which occurred at that time in Finland.

His reign opened badly with a terrible disaster, which occurred on the Khodinski field at Moscow, during the celebrations for his coronation. Owing to bad organisation, the peasants who had flocked into the city, and large numbers of the citizens, were so crowded by the soldiers that they panicked. The authorities, who were in constant dread of anarchists, believed it to be a planned revolt, and in the terrible scene that followed, many people were wounded, killed and trampled to death.

The new Czar continued, and even extended, the repressive policy of his father against all elements in the Empire which were likely to become foci for trouble. The Finns, who had previously enjoyed a certain degree of independence, were curtailed of many of their privileges, and General Bobrikov was sent to Helsingfors, in 1898, where he acted towards the Finnish people with the greatest brutality. Further measures were also taken against the unfortunate Poles in a fierce but fruitless attempt to stamp out the last vestiges of their ancient national culture. The 8,000,000 Jews in Russia at that time continued to suffer under Nicolas as they had under his father, and *pogrom* after *pogrom* brought slaughter and despoliation to their villages, but this, as has been mentioned earlier, was not in any way a religious persecution. It was inspired by a jealousy in the Russian agriculturists, which found sympathy in high quarters, of the Jews' rapid advancement and was an arbitrary and barbarous method of keeping them down and in addition an endeavour to terrorise them on account of the fact that the Government found such a large proportion of Jews among the secret societies whose members were constantly being arrested by the police.

After two years of elementary schooling, which was all he ever had, Voroshilov went to work in earnest. The friendly schoolmaster Ryzhkov obtained a job for him at the Lougansk metallurgical works in the department of iron-casting. The boy showed unusual gumption, and was soon made assistant locksmith, then smith, from which he rose to be engine-man on a crane. The veteran worker Tolstorebrov, speaking of this period, says: 'Before becoming a crane engine-man, it was usual to be an assistant for two or three years at least, but Clim Voroshilov was assistant for only six or seven months.'

It was in the factory that Voroshilov's revolutionary career began. A man named Grekov was appointed Chief of Police for the Alchevsk district, and he introduced an unwritten law that all hats should be removed in his presence.

One day the strictly observed law was rudely broken. The burly, smart, uniformed Grekov, with his fierce moustache and clanking sword, was standing at the factory gates. A group of workers came hurrying out, all submissively doffed their caps except young Voroshilov, who deliberately kept his on. The Police Chief seized him by the collar, Clim hit out at him, the ordinary police ran up, the workers scattered and the lad had his first thrashing from the police.

As a form of revolt it was superior to his father's sullen throwing up of a job to go out seeking another, because it was an open demonstration against tyrannous officialdom, and next morning the whole factory was abuzz with talk about it.

They began to ask each other: 'Why was Clim beaten up? Because we other fellows ran away. But if we had all acted together? The whole shop? The whole factory? Then those brutal policemen wouldn't have been so ready to lay hands on any one of us.' Voroshilov's brush with the police, when a lad of sixteen, sowed the first seed of collective action in his district.

# 5

# The Young Revolutionary

From the time of his first scrap with the police Voroshilov's
path was set as a revolutionary. In 1898, at the age of seventeen, he was a good-looking, strong-limbed young fellow en-
dowed with tremendous vitality. He was excitable, and easily
roused to flaming anger, but his actions were governed by a
cautious, extraordinarily well-balanced brain. Quite unlike the
pale studious youths of the intelligentsia, who were taking the
burdens of the toiling millions on their shoulders at that time
and crankily despised pleasure as a bourgeois drug which
diverted them from their purpose, Voroshilov lost no opportunity of indulging in the lusty recreations common to virile
youth. Love does not have to be paid for by an attractive
young man however poor he may be, vodka was cheap, and
singing cost nothing at all; Clim racketed round with the boys
and girls of the factory township and played the devil with the
best of them in many a wild party. But women and wine and
song were not enough to occupy his active mind.

His two years at school had fired in him an insatiable desire
for knowledge; he craved for it as others crave for drugs. In
consequence he read everything he could lay his hands on and
contacted all the factory workers who either had some smat-
tering of education or were ambitious to learn like himself.
From this sprang the first revolutionary organisation in his
factory; it started as a study circle for the exchange and discussion of those rare, precious things, books; almost insensibly
it passed to a debating society where such subjects as the
'rights of man' and the appalling conditions of the workers became the foremost topics.

There is little doubt that Voroshilov's early revolutionary
activities were largely governed by a craving for adventure.
Had he been an English boy he would probably have run
away to sea or faked his age to join the army and go off to a
war. As it was the 'police' became the 'enemy,' the 'big bad

wolf,' to be tricked, and fooled, and stung up with a pellet
from a catapult whenever possible. This is quite obvious because, owing to the ubiquitous censorship at that time, the
workers in the Don Basin knew nothing of the intelligentsia's
activities or the theories which were being propounded by
them. It is also seen in his irrepressible desire to stage exciting
*coups* such as setting the gaol on fire in order to rescue imprisoned comrades and the enthusiasm with which he set about
organising secret meetings. At those early meetings there was
little to discuss except quite harmless books that had been read,
but it was a thrilling business to plan and hold them in defi-
ance of the police.

The first revolutionary literature he ever saw was brought
back to Alchevsk by a caster named Galouska, who had been
in prison at Rostov. Clim spoke from it, made copies of it,
and distributed these among the most dependable of his associates. Secret printing presses were at work in the larger towns
and bundles of these revolutionary tracts were also being
smuggled across the frontier in ever-increasing quantities.
They began to filter through to the Don Basin and Voroshilov
organised their distribution. During the night shift they would
be stuck up all over the factory and put into the men's lockers
in all the shops.

While this early work was in progress the *entente* with
France was strengthened by a visit of the French President,
Monsieur Faure, to Russia in 1897. The Trans-Siberian Railway was also creeping across the great plains towards the
East. It was carried on to Irkutsk and completed to Vladivostok in 1898. In the same year Russia leased Port Arthur
from the Chinese for a period of twenty-five years, and this
brought her face to face with the Japanese in a struggle for the
supremacy of the North Western Pacific.

Voroshilov's activities soon bore fruit. His meetings increased from the old handful that had formed the original
study circle to scores of workers eager to learn how they might
better their condition. He spoke with fiery logic in the debates
which they held at night-time behind the closed doors of some
abandoned shed near the works or in cellars of the dreary
factory town.

At the age of eighteen he organised his first strike which was
ever declared in his part of the world. None of the strikers
had ever participated in a strike before, and many of them

were filled with trepidation as to where it would land them, but without the least idea of how to conduct such an action Voroshilov urged them on with the impatient words which were ever afterwards to be his battle cry: 'What are we waiting for?'

The point of issue between the workers and the management was the favouritism shown to a body of French machinists who were employed at the Domeau works. The foreigners were being paid from 12 to 25 roubles a day, while the local men were only receiving 80 kopecks to 2 roubles, and this very naturally caused great soreness among them.

This strike was one of a great number which took place at about the same time in nearly all the labour areas in Russia and resulted, among other things, in a law being passed which limited working hours to $11\frac{1}{2}$ per day. Regarding this reduction we have the amazing comment of the Finance Minister of the time, who stated that *the $11\frac{1}{2}$-hour day established the limit beyond which the exploitation of the worker was useless to the employer!*

Encouraged by his success Voroshilov organised, in 1899, the first strike of the crane men at Alchevsk. It resulted in the management making partial concessions and some improvement in conditions but, on balance, the strike ended in disaster, since the secret police managed to get spies in among the workers and, when the strike was over, had marked down Voroshilov's group.

The ringleaders were turned out of the factory and there began for Voroshilov three years of wandering, police oppression and interference. He was driven to become an underground agitator moving about the country under the assumed names of Volodka or Plakhov, but he always managed to keep in touch with his friends at Alchevsk, and during this period made contact with many other revolutionary circles in the Don Basin.

In 1902 his old friend, the teacher Ryzhkov, was invited to the Hartmann factory at Lougansk, and by his intervention Voroshilov was taken on there in the electrical department.

The report of Moses Benderovich, who took him on, is interesting because it shows that Voroshilov was no hooligan out to wreck plant, loot shops, and make trouble for trouble's sake; but a steady chap of decent instincts who only demanded for himself and his fellows the right to work on honourable terms and live decently in reasonable freedom.

Benderovich says: 'I was a master workman in the electrical department of Hartmann's factory and I had a friend named Ryzhkov of whom I had a great opinion. One day Ryzhkov brought me a young fellow, he was very young looking, almost a boy, and Ryzhkov said: "Mosesovich, take him on."

' "Who is he?" I asked.'

' "You know me," replied Ryzhkov.'

' "I do."'

' "Well, he's like me. He's my pupil."'

'I said no more and took the young man on. It was Klementy Efremovich Voroshilov.

'For two or three weeks he worked as a pupil under the charge of an old skilled machinist, but he proved to be clever, handy and full of gumption so I put him on to drive a crane.

'What always struck me about him was his reliability, and as far as work goes it would have been difficult to find a more disciplined hand.

'Iron-casting is a ticklish job, but he managed his part excellently. In politics, however, he was as untameable as he was reliable at work. He immediately became the centre of the revolutionary forces in the factory. This combination of good worker and leader of revolutionary thought made the administration of the factory respect him, and when there was talk of the workers taking over control, the director, who was a bit of a liberal, said: "If they were all like Voroshilov I should have nothing against the workers running the factory." He became my favourite and I followed his development with the greatest interest.'

There had been a Social Democrat group at Hartmann's from May, 1901, and by the time Voroshilov arrived there, they had acquired a considerable influence in the factory. Soon he was playing a great part in the organisation as a committee member, propagandist, and speaker at meetings. Whatever he took on he carried through.

An old comrade says of him at this period: 'He knew how to inspire us; we submitted to him and did whatever was required. His great qualities were independence, decisiveness and courage, but a mature courage. He never ran silly risks. He was brave when necessary but otherwise cautious. The men trusted him absolutely, and for that reason did all that he asked of them. At that distant time he did not make two-hour speeches, but none the less was a strong persuasive speaker who spoke so that the workers could understand.'

Another worker, Zveriaka, says of him: 'Small groups of us used to meet and spend the evening together. We also met at mass meetings where we had three or four speakers, but the outstanding one was always Voroshilov.

'He was both determined and courageous. On one occasion one of our workers shot at the director of the Hartmann factory. A number of men were arrested and the crowd swept down to the police station. Voroshilov then appeared and began to address them, but almost at once the police set about the people and they began to run. One policeman seized Voroshilov by the hair, but he tore himself away so violently that a tuft of his hair remained in the policeman's hand.'

In 1903 Voroshilov entered upon a new stage of his career. Up to that time the young provincial metal worker had never been outside the Don Basin, but as Chairman of the Committee of the Workers' Movement in Lougansk, he was elected to represent his area at the second All-Russia Conference of the Social Democratic Party in St. Petersburg.

The emotions of this young man of twenty-five, who up till then had known nothing but the dreariness and sordid poverty of a great industrial area, yet who loved pleasure and vodka and songs and dancing, can well be imagined when he saw the richness of the palaces, the shops, the costumes and all the splendour that went to make up the life of Czarist St. Petersburg.

The year 1903 was a critical one in the history of the labour movement and to appreciate the importance of the happenings which occurred at the Conference of that date it is necessary to outline the progress of the movement up to that time.

Karl Marx, the son of a Jewish lawyer, was born in Germany in 1818. From 1842 he devoted himself to the study of social economics and published his conclusions which were strongly influenced by the work of the philosopher Hegel. In Paris he met Frederick Engels, a German manufacturer whose business was in Manchester. Engels had also been influenced by Hegel's writings and further was a close friend of Robert Owen, the pioneer of the British working-class movement and the founder of the co-operative societies.

Marx and Engels worked together for many years and their

work resulted in the formulation of a Socialist theory which forms the basis of what we know as 'Communism' of the present day.

Their principles were adopted by the First International Socialist Congress, which was held in London in 1864. There were seven other congresses held between that year and 1889, when there occurred a split in the party. From that time the First International continued to hold its meetings regularly every three years, but another group, the International Socialist Bureau, which was more strongly Marxist, mainly composed of German Socialists under Rosa Luxemburg, and known as the Second International, met at more frequent intervals.

The Russian Socialists, while participating in these International Conferences, held a first Congress of their own at Minsk in 1898. Only eight delegates attended, but they founded the Russian Social Democratic Party.

Lenin, who was later to become the most important of all their members, and, when he achieved power in 1917, the founder of the Third International, was then in exile in Siberia. The time has come to give some particulars of this remarkable man.

He was born on April 10th, 1870. His real name was Vladimir Ilyich Ul'yanov. His father held a position in the educational service of the province of Simbirsk, while his mother came from the land-owning class, her family owning a small estate in the province of Kazan.

Ilyich, as he was called, was educated at the High School of Simbirsk on the middle Volga, up to the age of eighteen, under the father of that Kerensky, whom he was afterwards to drive from the office of President of the Russian Republic.

At the age of seventeen Ilyich was studying Marx, and in that year, 1887, his elder brother Alexander died on the scaffold for participation in an attempt on the life of the Czar. In consequence it was only as a special concession that Ilyich was allowed to sit for his final examination. He had shown outstanding brilliance throughout the whole of his school career and took first place in his finals.

In the autumn of 1887 he was sent to the University of Kazan, but only remained there for one month as he was expelled among others on account of an anti-Monarchist students' demonstration. However, he took the full university course in his own home and was granted the concession of being allowed to sit, as an outside student, for his examinations at the University of St. Petersburg in 1890, where he took his degree in Law.

He then went to Samara where he practised as an assistant barrister for the space of a year, but his whole interest was wrapped up in the revolutionary movement, and in 1893 he moved to St. Petersburg; henceforth he devoted himself to the revolutionary cause entirely. It was at this time that he met Leonid Krassin who was afterwards the first Soviet Ambassador accredited to the Court of St. James. Another of his earliest contacts in the city was Nadezhda Konstantinova Krupskaya who later became his wife.

In 1895 he had a serious illness and obtained permission to go abroad on account of his health. He visited Berlin, and in Geneva met Plekhanov—the recognised leader of the Russian revolutionaries who had lived in exile since 1883. When Lenin returned to Russia in the autumn he had completed all the necessary plans for producing a secret revolutionary newssheet which was to be called *The Workers' Cause*. The paper was printed and the proofs had actually been corrected when he and his helpers suddenly disappeared in December, 1895.

His imprisonment or preliminary detention, as it was then euphemistically termed, lasted for one year. The Czar then pronounced sentence which took the form of banishment to Siberia for three years. During his solitary confinement he had been allowed books, and found a prison cell not a bad place for work of a serious literary nature. When he heard his sentence, he remarked in jest: 'It is a pity they let me out so soon. I would have liked to do little more work on the book. It'll be difficult to obtain books in Siberia.'

It should be noted here that exile to Siberia did not necessarily imply a prison cell in some grim building. There were prisons in Siberia and many prisoners were detained in them, but these were mostly dangerous convicts. The bulk of the political prisoners sentenced to exile were only ordered out of European Russia and assigned some town or village in which they must live, reporting to the local authorities at stated intervals. Hence the comparative ease and frequency of escapes.

The worst horrors of exile were in earlier times, before the railways had been constructed. Then political and convicted criminals alike were chained together in gangs, women and children too, and marched for weeks on end through the bitter cold and glaring whiteness of the Siberian snows, by soldiers who had orders to shoot them on sight if they attempted to escape. The endless marches, the filthy, verminous rest houses in which they were herded together and locked up each night, and the meagre rations, quite insufficient to support such exertions, were responsible for great numbers of the poor wretches never completing their journey. If they were sick, constitutionally weak, or had had their health undermined through the privations of a previous spell in prison, a sentence of exile was tantamount to one of death. A very great number of those ordered into exile died in this way.

With the coming of the railways, however, the majority of the political exiles were spared this terrible march, allowed to have their families and belongings sent after them, and to practise their ordinary avocations in their place of exile. Irkutsk, on Lake Baikal, became a great and flourishing city, almost entirely for this reason. Most of its citizens were originally political exiles, but having established themselves there in their trades and professions they decided to remain on even after their period of exile was over and they were free to return to their old homes. The intelligentsia were to be found there in great numbers and by a curious anomaly there was much more freedom allowed in Irkutsk, the city of the exiles, than to dwellers in Moscow or St. Petersburg. By 1914 it had the most brilliant intelluctual society and the most advanced population of all the cities in the Russian Empire. Dangerous politicals were, however, sent to tiny villages in the far north where they were completely isolated and snowbound for seven months of the year.

Lenin was ordered to the village of Shushenskoye near the River Yenisei. He proceeded there in January, 1897, and took rooms in a peasant's house. A little later Krupskaya was allowed to join him on the plea that she was his fiancée. He employed himself with his writing, and for recreation went out regularly to shoot hares and wild duck with a Gordon setter which he himself trained as a sporting dog. In February, 1900, now a man of thirty, his exile was at an end and they returned to Russia. It was at this time that he assumed the name of N. Lenin as a *nom de guerre*.

He was not allowed to return to St. Petersburg and it was decided that, with another prominent revolutionary of the early days named Martov, he should go abroad to re-establish contact with Plekhanov and the group in exile. From this time on Lenin lived in exile until the coming of the Revolution seventeen years later, with the one exception of a comparatively brief return to Russia between 1905–1907.

Munich was his first place of residence for any length of time, and there he got going on the old project of a revolutionary paper, his wife acting as general secretary to the organisation. By that time revolutionary sympathisers in Russia were so numerous that in spite of the activities of an enormous force of Secret Police, the dreaded *Okrana,* Lenin's paper was smuggled over the frontier in considerable numbers.

Early in 1902, however, the Munich printer feared arrest by the German authorities, and so a new headquarters had to be found. Lenin and his wife moved to London in the April of that year. They occupied two rooms of a house at No. 30 Holford Square to the north of the Euston Road, and his wife records, rather unhappily: 'We found that the Russian stomach is not easily adaptable to the ox-tails, skate fried in fat, cake and other mysteries of the English fare.' They were at that time without resources other than what they drew from the Party funds and lived on thirty shillings a week.

During his stay in London, Lenin's one refuge was the reading-room of the British Museum, where Karl Marx had also done much of his work at an earlier date, and it is interesting to observe that a good proportion of the theory and planning for the World Revolution should have been carried out in this secure sanctum at the very heart of the British Empire.

Richter was the name that Lenin and his wife chose to live under while they were in London, although, of course, they need not have bothered their heads to try and conceal their identity as far as the British authorities were concerned. Finding their book-learned English insufficient for getting about conveniently, they chose a peculiarly strange method for improving it, this being to listen attentively to the orators on the soap-boxes in Hyde Park. They were crusaders burnt up with a mission in life, and doubtless what they lacked in acquiring a good accent was more than compensated for, to them, by interest in the matter spouted by the soap-box orators.

In October, 1902, Leon Trotsky arrived in London still full of nervous excitement after having escaped from Siberia. So wrought up was he that he took a cab straight from the station and knocked Lenin up at some godless hour on a Sunday morning, this being the first meeting of the pair who were afterwards to rule Russia between them.

Lev Davidovitch Trotsky's real surname was Bronstein. He was at that time twenty-three years old, nine years younger than Lenin, having been born at Elizavetgrad, the son of middle-class Jewish parents. His father was a small merchant and had him educated at the Paul Real Schule and the University, both in Odessa.

In 1902 so loose was the revolutionary organisation that it was virtually centralised in the committee that ran Lenin's paper the *Iskra* in London, and when it was decided to hold a formal conference of the Russian Social Democratic Party, the principal work of organising it fell upon this group. One conference, the first, had been held at Minsk in 1898, as has been stated. A second congress was now planned for the year 1903, and in April the revolutionary group left London for Switzerland.

The second congress of the Social Democrats was held in a flour warehouse in Brussels; fifty-seven delegates appeared, but the Belgian authorities took exception to the red bunting with which the place was decorated, and so the conference was moved to London.

In the preliminary work of organising the conference some disagreement had already arisen between Lenin, who drafted the programme, and the veteran revolutionary, Plekhanov, who stood at his elbow. Lenin was all for directness in both speech and work; Plekhanov for the continual insertion of qualifying phrases such as politicians have at all times found so useful.

This difference of opinion about words developed at the conference into an open feud upon the policy and actions of the Party. Plekhanov and the more liberal delegates were for reform; for bringing pressure to bear upon established governments in order to force the alteration of the law and achieve their aim by evolutionary revolution. His followers were termed the Mensheviki, from *menshe* meaning less. Lenin, on the other hand, seeing how the Russian Government had so consistently gone back upon their promises and how, even when concessions to the working classes had been secured, these were made inoperative and useless through special measures taken by the rulers to nullify them, was most strongly of the opinion that no lasting good could ever be achieved in this manner. He declared that their policy must be one of action—with bloodshed if necessary—but action without compromise to root out the whole system and start again with a clean slate, the workers of the proletariat constituting the new Government. His followers were called the Bolsheviki, as a result of obtaining the majority vote, from *bolshe* meaning 'more'.

When Voroshilov got back from the All-Russia Socialist Conference in the same year, the question was put to him as to which side he took in the now famous schism between the Plekhanovists and the Leninists; he answered unhesitatingly: 'I belong to the Lenin group.'

With money collected from the workers he had brought back about twenty large-calibre Smith and Wesson revolvers to St. Petersburg, and managed to get them safely into the hands of his most trusted friends. The revolutionary spirit was growing stronger every month and with Lenin's new doctrine of action pointing the way to the future, Voroshilov was now preparing for a clash; he began to organise fighting squads among the workers.

The purpose of these squads at first was to protect the mass meetings which took place at secret rendezvous away from the factories in the country. Often the police got wind of these and the Cossacks came charging down to break up the crowds of workers, upon which the meetings ended in a bloody affray.

In 1904 he made a journey to Finland and managed to bring back a further eighty Brownings and other types of automatic, 400 rounds of ammunition, and a great stack of Leninist literature; smuggling the whole lot through the Customs in ornate ladies' dress boxes. A steady traffic in arms was now arranged between Finland and the Bolshevik groups in the Don Basin. Voroshilov's organisation kept an Esthonian Anarchist who furnished bombs; dynamite was obtained from the mines, and other explosive materials from chemists who were secret sympathisers. Nearly all his followers now had some illegal arm carefully hidden away, but it was agreed that they should not be used until the general signal for insurrection was given.

Strike fever was spreading again all over Russia, and Voroshilov prepared one to force the release of some of his comrades who had been imprisoned. He coupled with this demand

the points that the right of the police to make household
search should be abolished, that an eight-hour day should be
established and a general improvement in the workers' conditions arranged by negotiation. Measures were taken by the
police and he was compelled to hide, but they knew he was
still in the district and continued to search for him.

His comrade, Shcherbakov, tells us: 'Some of us went to the
Alexeiev railway and I saw some police hurrying along. We got
a boat and started across the river, but the police sent us back
and cross-questioned us as to where Voroshilov was. I crossed
myself and swore I did not know, and when I got home my
mother, having heard of it, said that we were a lot of wastrels
and didn't want either God or Czar. The police were still not
content and they even combed the hills for him, but he was no
longer there, having succeeded in escaping to Lougansk. He
had fighting squads but not everybody knew of it, and he
used to tell the members that if an attempt was made to arrest
anyone, efforts to get away must be made, but that no blood
was to be shed. His advice was to always carry sand in our
pockets with which to blind any attacker. From among the
fighting squads flying detachments were organised, and we
even had two machine-guns which we kept hidden in the pits.'

Voroshilov returned later and in an attempt to rescue the
imprisoned men, ordered his groups to set the gaol on fire. The
police arrested him and thrashed him senseless; then beat him
up from day to day in his cell. But the strength of the workers
was growing. Every man in the district declared they would
down tools if he was not released. His friends threatened to
call a general strike. The police for once funked having to face
further trouble, gave way and let him go.

At this time he was twenty-three, a big-boned, sturdy, well-
knit fellow, popular with the girls and well liked by the men,
always ready for a jollification when there was no Party work
to be done, but he kept his cause ever before him and at all
hours of the day and night his sturdy figure in greased top
boots, cap and Russian shorts, worn under a cheap jacket,
could be met with moving on his mission throughout the district.

At meetings his favourite wind-up of a speech used to be: 'If
a broody hen has laid an egg, and in that egg there is a germ,
then under all normal conditions there is bound to be a

chicken. Well, here's the germ of the Revolution, comrades. Come on. What are we waiting for?'

At one meeting, in no way differing from the others, except that it is well remembered now by a number of his contemporaries who were present, he said:

'Comrade Lenin says that one must learn to direct the masses. That is quite true, and anything, a revolver, a stone or a bolt will serve our turn. But, comrades, don't forget that in the Revolution the masses will be armed, and it is then that we shall have to have our commanders.'

One of the workmen called out: 'We'll appoint you our general, Clim.'

'Don't talk rot,' Voroshilov answered with a laugh. 'What sort of a general would I make? I know nothing about such things.'

By carrying forged papers he had even evaded being conscripted as a private, but fifteen years later he did become a general, and has since risen to be the War Lord of All the Russias.

# 6

# The First Revolution

The years 1904 and 1905 were fateful ones for Russia. The whole vast Empire was seething with trouble from one end to the other. Even the majority of the upper classes were now arrayed against a continuance of the autocracy. The intelligentsia ceaselessly demanded that the Czar grant a Constitution. The Provincial *Zemstvos* were packed with Liberals and exerted their limited powers to spread education as widely as possible, which brought greater and greater numbers of malcontents into the political arena. Mensheviks and Bolsheviks alike deluged the country with illicit literature; Lenin and the other exiles worked like furies. The peasants were still hungry for the land; the factory workers were preparing in secret for armed revolt.

In February, 1904 the Russo-Japanese war broke out. The people's thoughts were entirely concentrated on the ever-growing tension at home and they had little interest in the distant East. The great bulk of them was still concerned with the tillage of the soil; 82½ per cent. of Russia's total population still lived *outside* the cities even in 1914, and the country folk had no interest whatever in foreign conquests or securing fresh markets for Russian manufacturers. Even the hearts of the soldiery were not in the campaign, and from the very beginning the Russian general staff were beset with anxiety from their knowledge that they were expected by their ill-informed and autocratic master to conduct a successful war with their main bases six thousand miles away at the end of a single track railway line.

The Japanese on the other hand were on the spot and imbued with all the vitality of a renaissance which had brought their fighting arms up to European standard. Their army had been trained by German experts; their navy in the tradition of the British. No expense or labour had been spared to equip both arms with the very latest fighting devices and materials.

The Japanese people were ready for war and behind their leaders.

The conflict opened by the Japanese sinking two Russian warships before war was officially declared. They then proceeded to disembark their expeditionary forces upon the mainland. General Kuropatkin, who commanded the Russian troops, was an able man, and he records that the single line of the Trans-Siberian Railway did everything that could possibly be expected of it, but he was up against a machine rather than an army. Faultlessly trained by high German staff officers, the Japanese functioned like clockwork. The Russians fought bravely, but position after position was taken from them with merciless regularity and in absolute keeping with the Japanese schedule. Few campaigns can be more instructive to the student of military affairs than the perfect timing which distinguished the Japanese operations in the virtually decisive battle of the Yalu River. From that time the Russians were continually upon the defensive and the war dragged on drearily, its effect upon the Russian people at home being only one more irritant added to their many troubles.

The Nihilists were very active and a series of political murders took place, including that of the Minister of Public Instruction, Plehve, who was killed in St. Petersburg on June 28th by a bomb.

The ill-fated Czarevitch was born on July 13th. This was a great relief to Nicolas as the heir apparent up to that time, his younger brother the Grand Duke Michael, was desperately in love with a Madame Natalie Marmontov. She was a lady of great beauty, clever and extremely well educated; in fact eminently fitted in every way to be a ruler's consort *except* for the fact that she was of noble birth and was twice divorced.

The Grand Duke, who was handsome, popular, intelligent, and had strong democratic leanings, declared his intention of marrying the lady. Nicolas and his family, governed by age-old custom and entirely dominated by the pontiffs of the Church, were utterly aghast. The Czar threatened, pleaded and finally confined his brother; the struggle continued for seven years during which, the poor little Czarevitch being a chronic invalid, Michael continued as the likely Regent, or even possible successor to the throne in the event of Nicolas's death. In 1912, Michael at last married the woman he loved, in 1914 he went back to fight for Russia, and in 1917 his friend

Kerensky, who knew that he would make a splendid Constitutional Monarch, offered him the crown. Had fate cast the cards a little differently and made Michael Romanoff the elder brother, he would certainly have granted a Constitution soon after he came to the throne, and it is very doubtful if there would have ever been any Bolshevik revolution.

The Provincial *Zemstvos* became extremely active in war work in 1904–5; collecting comforts for the troops, arranging hospital accommodation, etc. They decided it would be a good thing to have a central committee in the capital to co-ordinate their efforts and so sent representatives to St. Petersburg. This body did the most splendid work in organising civilian war services, but since politics were so much in the air and most of its members would have been the very people elected to represent their districts in a National Assembly, had such a thing existed, it automatically became a sort of 'shadow' Parliament, although without a vestige of actual power.

There was no Parliament, in Russia; nor was there any machinery to make one. The vote did not exist as an instrument for ascertaining the national will. None except the Czar and his ministers had any say in such vital matters as finance or foreign alliances, which might plunge the country into war. There was not even a Prime Minister. All ministers ranked as equal; the advice of one being taken one day and of another the next.

The Czar was warned again and again that this state of affairs could not go on, and the disaster was impending, but he continued to be utterly blind and senseless beyond all reason. Even the highest people in the land realised that the Monarchy was doomed unless it allowed a check to be placed upon new measures affecting the whole people, and ceased issuing ill-considered commands at the instigation of anyone, competent or incompetent, who happened to have been the last to have the Monarch's private ear.

Count Muraviev, the Minister of Justice, writes in his diary at this time: 'The general dissatisfaction with the existing régime has seized all sections of society. Things cannot continue in this way for long,' and General Kuropatkin wrote in his diary just before he left to take command of the forces in the Far East: 'The people will understand the danger of leaving the destinies of one hundred and eighty millions of a population in the hands of an autocratic power, when the autocrat's decision may at any time be influenced by such crooks as Bezobrazov' (a general who had been lining his own pockets out of the Czar's Manchurian possessions).

That this fear of the autocrat committing some incredible folly which might land the nation in a most grievous pass without the least warning had real foundation, is instanced by Nicolas's correspondence at that time with Wilhelm II of Germany.

The Kaiser and his able Chancellor, Prince Bulow, sought to inveigle the Czar into a secret treaty against England. Russia had nothing whatsoever to gain from this and, by it, stood to lose the friendship of France, her only really powerful ally in Europe, who was then giving her the most valuable financial aid. Nevertheless, a few months later the astute Kaiser went on a Baltic cruise and visited Nicolas in his yacht, upon which, the Russian Monarch allowed himself to be persuaded into committing the crass stupidity of actually signing a secret treaty on these lines.

The Russian Foreign Office had not been consulted about this complete reversal of a policy which they had so laboriously built up and, when it leaked out, were absolutely thunder-struck. It took them many months of arduous work to undo the damage that had been done and reassure the naturally infuriated French. No one to this day knows exactly how, by the burning of much midnight oil, they at last succeeded in relieving their foolish master of the obligations with which he had saddled himself by his criminally irresponsible action.

In January, 1905, Port Arthur fell to the Japanese and General Kondratenko, who had defended it so gallantly for many months, was killed. By this time the whole of Russia was in a turmoil with strikes breaking out in every direction, and constant demonstrations demanding that the war should be stopped and a Constitution granted. A third Social Democratic congress was held in London in 1905, and partly as the result of the activity of its members a general strike was declared in Russia.

As can be imagined, young Voroshilov was not inactive at such a troublesome time. His friend, Saltykov, tells us: 'We were preparing for the coming Revolution, but all our work had to be carried on secretly. We used to collect, lie down on the grass, post sentries and start work whispering. We were all tense to the limit and the least rustle made us look round.

C

At times it used to seem that the very moon was spying on us. Our sentries would lie, peering intently into the darkness, then suddenly it would seem that a Cossack patrol was coming. "Cossacks!" someone would cry, and we would all jump to our feet only to find that it was a false alarm.

'The local Party organisation declared a general strike, and the Lougansk strike began at the Hartmann cartridge factory. It was from among these workers that delegations were formed to bring the men out at other factories. Voroshilov was the man who managed that.

'A general meeting was called in the hall of the Botanical Gardens. All workers marched there in a great demonstration: the first to speak was Clim Voroshilov, who spoke for two hours, summoning us to the struggle. After the meeting some-one proposed that we should go to the prison and demand the release of the political prisoners. We made off down the Louganski Pereoulok towards the prison, but we were met by Cossacks and there was a bloody clash in which many of us were wounded.'

But that Voroshilov was no hooligan is instanced again by another worker, Poushkarev, who tells us:

'At the factory, if the workers knew there was to be any sort of meeting they were never keen and never more than a third stopped, but if they heard that Voroshilov was to speak they would all stop and listen to him with the greatest interest. We had a factory manager then who, if he saw Voroshilov at a meeting, was beside himself with rage because all the workers listened to Voroshilov, but at one meeting, when it looked as though the men were going to get out of hand, Voroshilov calmed them down and behaved so wisely and quietly that in the end the director was on his side.'

It was on January 22nd, 1905, afterwards known as Red Sunday, that a South Russian priest, one Father Gapon, led a demonstration of an immense number of men, women and children of the working classes in solemn procession through St. Petersburg. They carried their sacred banners and *ikons* and sang hymns as they marched, making for the great square which lies outside the Winter Palace. Their object was to lay a petition of their grievances at the feet of the Czar.

This great unarmed and perfectly peaceful crowd was met at the approaches to the Winter Palace by armed police and troops, but the concourse was so great that through pressure of those behind it was impossible to stop them breaking through the cordons, and they soon filled the great square in a solid mass. The Cossacks used their knouts, the soldiers the flats of their swords and the butts of their rifles, beating the wretched people in an attempt to disperse them; although, such was their misery, that they stubbornly knelt there fingering their rosaries before the blank windows of the Palace.

The responsibility for the terrible order has never finally been settled, but finding that the crowd refused to budge someone in authority ordered that the square should be cleared by force of arms. The Cossacks began to wield their sabres in earnest and the infantry fired volley after volley at close range into the densest portion of the mass without discrimination. They then chased the screaming people away through the surrounding streets and a massacre ensued which lasted for several hours.

In February the Grand Duke Serge was assassinated in Moscow, and in February, too, Voroshilov at last launched his first armed uprising at Lougansk. When the first revolutionary war began he was already the President of the Lougansk Workers' Soviet, and the revolt showed him to be a first-class fighting leader as well as a skilful political organiser.

P. Maltzev, who worked and fought with him at that time, tells us: 'I remember an occasion when we were expecting trouble and were forging pikes. There was a meeting in the square at Lougansk. After the meeting I went with some of the lads to the Botanical Gardens to have a read at illegal literature in the thickets. The Cossacks were not far away and soon somebody told us they had ridden into the Gardens.

'I said to the boys, "Let's go and have a look," and I walked right into the arms of a party of Cossacks. They seized me, tied me up, brought me out on to the road and beat me. I held my arms over my head to protect myself from their whips, but I got it badly. Just as they were leading me off up came Korolkov, the master of the Botanial Gardens, who was an old friend of mine. He spoke to the Cossacks, telling them that I was all right, and so they let me go; but my arms were black and blue and very painful.

'There was a meeting at the factory that evening. As a member of a fighting squad I had some bombs, so I took one with me. I said to myself: "If any of these blasted Cossacks come riding up in the direction of my squad when we are protecting the meeting I'll give them something to think about."

'My squad was posted at a little bridge and I felt that I had to tell someone of my intention. I did so, and somebody must have passed it on for I hadn't gone a further fifty paces before I heard Voroshilov's voice:

' "Maltzev, come here."

'I went up to him and I saw at once he was furious.

' "What nonsense are you up to?" he snapped at me.

' "I want my revenge," I said.

' "I'll give you revenge! You must not upset the whole business on account of personal trifles. You ought to be utterly ashamed of yourself."

'And so on and so on. He stormed and swore as he always did when he was angry. At last he said: "If they shoot you may throw your bomb, but not unless."

'The Cossacks charged down on our squad and broke us up, but they didn't begin shooting till they reached the Louganski Pereoulok, where they wounded a girl named Lourier and some other people, but they were a good way off then, so I was unable to throw my bomb after all.

'I remember another dressing-down that Clim Voroshilov gave me. There was a lot of fighting going on and three of our workers had been condemned to be hanged. That night I was with a fellow called Sava Batinov and a couple of girls. We were very wrought up about our friends and Batinov had the gift of the gab. Once he started philosophising about how future life would be organised you quite lost yourself listening, so it was pretty late when we set off to see the girls home.

'All of a sudden from the other side of the street some hooligan flung a big stone and it struck the wall just over my head; if it had hit me it would have killed me on the spot. As a member of one of the fighting squads I had been issued with a Browning and I was carrying it at the time. Another stone sailed by and just missed me. I was young and hot-tempered so I pulled out my automatic and fired.

'I didn't aim really, but I got him by luck, I could see, in the leg and he went down with a yell. I was pretty scared then, as I realised that I had let myself in for something serious. Batinov and I sent the girls home, then hurried round a block of houses and so back by the next street. We found the wounded man in the gutter and asked who had shot him.

'It was quite dark, of course, and it appears that he had mistaken us for the Cossacks. We called a policeman and a doctor. A protocol was made on the spot and in it the police-man wrote "wounded by rifle bullet". I felt that let me out, but I passed an anxious night and by morning I was in a stew again. When I got to the factory I passed my Browning to another squad man for fear they'd pinch me and search my lodging.

'This was reported to Voroshilov and he came to see me at once, questioning me as to what had happened. I told him the whole story, but he flared up and gave me a lecture. Oh, what a lecture! He thoroughly turned me upside down and called me every possible name he could lay his tongue to.

'He said: "You have no right to draw that Browning and use it for your own affairs. Such conduct is not worthy of a member of the organisation. You might have given us all away."

' "Don't get worried, Clim," I pleaded. "You mustn't forget that the protocol they made says it was a rifle bullet, and even if they did suspect that we had illicit arms I'd never say a word. I'll take it all on myself. They won't get one word out of me. Surely you know the sort of stuff I'm made of."

'All the same he kept on cursing me. I shall never forget the drubbing he gave me, but that was his way; as brave as they make them when it came to the real fighting, but an absolute martinet about any of us causing unnecessary trouble which might prematurely wreck our organisation.'

The means of battle in those days were the revolver, the shot-gun, and the home-made bomb, rarely the rifle, and the fighters were groups of five or ten, rarely hundreds. This first revolutionary effort acted as a testing fire and proved to Voroshilov which of his comrades were courageous and which not to be relied upon.

The February revolt ended in a workers' victory, as according to the law passed in the following March, it was at last made legal for each factory to elect an acknowledged Council of Delegates. This council had an executive committee of four, and at the Hartmann Works Voroshilov was chosen as chairman.

In March the Japanese drove the Russians out of Mukden, and in May the so-called Second Pacific Squadron, really consisting of the Main Russian Fleet which had sailed half round the world from the Baltic, arrived at the scene of conflict. On the 27th of that month Admiral Count Togo of the Japanese Navy, who had been educated as a boy in His Britannic Majesty's training ship *Worcester,* sank or captured the whole Russian squadron; thereby distinguishing himself as being the only admiral of any nation, not excluding those who fought in the Great War, who has ever completely annihilated an enemy fleet of steam-powered, steel-armoured warships.

In June there was grave trouble in the principal Russian Black Sea port Odessa, and also in Sevastopol. The workers in the dockyards, and the sailors in such ships of the Russian Navy as had not been sunk by the Japanese, mutinied. Terrible scenes of brutality were enacted, and we have a foretaste of the horrors which the Great Revolution was to bring in the manner in which these sailors treated a number of their officers. Many of them were handcuffed and thrown overboard, and others were thrown alive into the red-hot boiler furnaces. One of the principal ships, the *Prince Potemkin,* refused all negotiations with the authorities on shore and only surrendered some time afterwards to the Roumanian Government.

The situation was critical and on August 6th the Czar at last gave way; agreeing to summon the elected representatives of all Russia to a State *Duma.*

Discerning observers, such as Lenin, must have seen that this almost certainly foreshadowed the complete doom of the Monarchy. When Louis XVI was similarly pressed by his people he resorted to this expedient and summoned the States General, a step no French monarch had taken for 179 years. Now, after a lapse of 207 years, a Russian Emperor fell back upon an ancient institution which his ancestors had used occasionally to gauge the feeling of the nation.

This was no surrender of the Autocracy, of course, as the Czar's '*Ukase*' declared that 'while preserving the fundamental law concerning the autocratic powers' he had in accordance with the policy of his predecessors decided to 'summon elected representatives ... to be entrusted with the preliminary discussion and elaboration of measures and with the examination of the State Budget'. So it was quite clear that the *Duma* was to be given no other right than that of expressing opinions which would be in no way binding on the Government.

However, in an autocracy which is losing its grip the summoning of such bodies is invariably a fatal step. Concessions can be granted from the throne to alleviate ill-feeling and tide over a period of trouble; ministers who have failed can be dismissed and fresh advice taken, but once a representative assembly is brought into being after a lapse of centuries all authority must finally fall into its hands. The monarch may disregard their advice or even dismiss them, but its members will consider that from the time of their election they have a right to voice the opinion they were elected to express. If they can meet in no other way they will meet even against the monarch's orders, and the people who have elected them will support them against the monarch.

In the same month the Czar's minister, Count Witte, brought the war to an end by concluding the treaty of Portsmouth, U.S.A., with the Japanese. Russia was unquestionably the defeated nation, but Witte proved himself a most able diplomat, as he ceded only the northern half of the island of Sakhalin, the peninsula of Quantung, and a part of Manchuria to the Japanese, and got away without having to pay them any war indemnity at all.

On his return from America Witte, who had Liberal sympathies, found Russia in a frightful state. The enormous work of constructing electoral machinery made it impossible for a *Duma* actually to assemble before January; the State was practically bankrupt owing to the great expense of the war, yet the Czar had hopelessly compromised Russia with her principal banker, France, owing to his fooling with the German Emperor; and the half measure of calling a *Duma* yet proposing to treat it merely as an advisory body, instead of appeasing public opinion only fanned the flame of revolt. An armed rising in St. Petersburg was only suppressed with difficulty and much bloodshed.

In a frantic endeavour to save the situation Witte advised his master to issue a manifesto, and this was done on October 17th. Its principal points were the grant of civic liberty based on the inviolability of the person and freedom of conscience, speech, union, and association.

This was a concrete victory for the revolutionaries; at one sweep they had gained half the things they had been striving to get for over three-quarters of a century. They instantly made use of their new-found rights. The conspirators came up out of their cellars and every class of people in the larger towns and labour centres began at once to form unions. In St.

Petersburg a union of all these unions was created which later became the Central Soviet of Workers' Deputies; one of its leading members was the fiery orator Leon Trotsky. Lenin now decided that it would be safe for him to return to St. Petersburg and reached there in November.

The atmosphere was tense and threatening. However autocratic the rule of the previous Czars they had, almost without exception, been able to stand before their people as victorious conquerors at least, but now even that bulwark of glamour had been destroyed by the successive defeats which Russia had sustained in the war with Japan. Soldiers returning from the front spread rumours of ill-management and bribery by the organisers of the campaign, and from municipal bodies the *Zemstvos* were rapidly becoming a Liberal political organisation.

Lenin duly registered and lived openly in St. Petersburg for some time, but he was so harassed by police spies that he soon disappeared underground again and reassumed illegal status. Maxim Gorky, the famous writer, was one of his principal companions, and Lenin wrote such uncompromising articles in Gorky's paper, *New Life,* that it became the organ of the Bolsheviks.

Trotsky was then neither a Menshevik nor a Bolshevik, but hovered somewhere between the two parties, although his St. Petersburg Soviet of Workers' Deputies consisted of real working men and not the intelligentsia. Lenin attended several of its meetings in disguise to gauge its possibilities and soon urged his own followers to link up with it, but in spite of these activities he found St. Petersburg unripe for further open effort at the moment as the heart had been taken out of its citizens by the quelling of a long series of sporadic risings.

After his great effort of persuading the Czar into signing the manifesto of the previous October, which appeared to grant most of the things the country asked for, Count Witte suddenly weakened in his policy. The reforms proposed were so sweeping that he lacked the courage to endeavour to carry them through. Actually he was not trusted by the Court and only tolerated because of his great influence in financial circles, and the Czar was depending on him to negotiate the French loan, since the Treasury was now empty after the colossal but useless expenditure upon the Russo-Japanese War.

In consequence, immediately the loan was safely negotiated

the Czar felt himself strong enough to take repressive measures and Witte bowed to the decision. The arrest of Nosar, the President of the St. Petersburg Soviet, was ordered, and the revolutionaries being too exhausted to stage any reprisals, all the members of the Soviet were arrested soon after.

The Czar, evidently in the most abysmal ignorance of the nation's true feeling, wrote to his mother: 'Every one was delighted when 250 important leaders of the Workmen's Committees and other organisations were arrested the other day. Furthermore, twelve newspapers have been suppressed and their editors will be prosecuted for the odious things they have printed.' He attributed the state of things to not having enough troops, and in a a further letter states: 'Many seditious hands have been dispersed, their homes and property burnt. Terror must be met by Terror.'

The proletariat of St. Petersburg cursed and threatened, but weakened as they were and robbed of many of their most fiery leaders by this wholesale arrest, they could do nothing. The Czar dismissed Witte and replaced him by the reactionary minister Stolypin.

The next step was the promulgation of 'fundamental laws' which could only be altered or amended on the initiative of the Czar in direct violation of the principle laid down in the manifesto of October 17th. The Czar announced his right to enact any law during the intervals when the *Duma* was not sitting. These edicts virtually put the state of things back to where they had been the previous September.

A new series of strikes began to paralyse the country, Lenin moved to Moscow, where revolutionary feeling was at feverpitch, and Labour had not yet attempted any full-dress attack upon the Government.

The Moscow Soviet declared a general strike, the soldiers on duty in the city showed no antagonism, so the strike was converted into an armed rising, and the revolutionaries visited the rifle dealers to commandeer all their stock. Next they seized the station and, without protest, the troops returning from the war handed over their ammunition to them. Special troops were then called for by the military governor from the capital, including artillery, and for five days shells were poured into the strongholds and dwelling quarters of the strikers. The Moscow revolt came ten months after the armed rising in St.

Petersburg. It was too late and could not be supported. The abortive revolt collapsed.

Stolypin, the new reactionary minister, and the Czar now took their vengeance. A thousand people were put to death and over 70,000 imprisoned, in addition to a further 14,000 who had died during the five days' street fighting. Moscow was now bled white like St. Petersburg. The first Revolution was over.

# 7

# The Unquiet Lull

The defeat of the 1905 Revolution gave rise to pessimism in many of those working for the granting of a Constitution and the freedom of the workers, alike. The Mensheviks gained a tremendous ascendancy among the labour groups and everywhere Plekhanov's words were repeated: 'Armed uprising is stupidity. Arms should never have been used.' The main tendency of the movement swung round once more towards the theory that the autocracy would eventually be persuaded to see sense, and give way to sweet reason.

Lenin and his immediate supporters alone remained absolutely uncompromising in their belief that arms must be used against arms, and that by these alone could Russia eventually secure a democracy. Voroshilov and his most trusted comrades were Leninists. They buried their guns, hid their bombs and prepared themselves to wait, filled with the conviction that the *Duma* would be tricked by the Government, and that public opinion would swing to the support of their own views once again.

After the crushing of the Moscow rebellion, Lenin established himself in Finland, just over the border from St. Petersburg, to get clear of the police, who were hot on his trail, yet remain within easy contact with his followers.

Writing of their life at Kuokalla, in Finland, his wife says: 'The door of our house was never bolted, but always open either for messengers or refugees. A jug of milk and a loaf of bread were left in the dining-room overnight and bedding spread on the divan, so that in the event of anyone coming in on the night train they could enter without waking anybody, have some refreshment and lie down to sleep. In the morning we often found comrades in the dining-room who had come in the night.'

In February, 1906, the new Constitution was finally approved. The method of election had been so arranged that the

bulk of the members would almost certainly be people of
property and by no means a proportional representation of
all classes; the result of the polls proved that the reactionary
minister, Stolypin, had done this work efficiently.

When the First *Duma* met, on April 27th, there were 172
Liberals opposed to 92 representatives of the Labour and Toil
group. The majority of the latter being returned by the peasant interests, the proletariat was hardly represented at all.
Yet all classes in Russia, with the exception of the great landowners and high officials of State, were united in the common
aim of securing definite civil and political rights.

A great uprush of Liberal sentiment had seized the country
and practically every member of the First *Duma* came to it
with a vast sack of memoranda, in which his own particular
theory as to how the country should be run was worked out to
the last detail. This was the inevitable result of all the previous
expression of opinion in public having been bottled up. For
the best part of two generations small groups of people all
over the country had been threshing out political questions in
private, and by these means had reached various hard-and-
fast conclusions.

In consequence, the wildest possible divergence of opinion
prevailed; an incredible amount of nonsense was talked and
the majority of the members endeavoured to run before they
could walk, by proposing such extreme measures as the abolition of private property in land, and of capital punishment for
any offence whatever, instead of settling down to discuss practical fundamentals.

Political parties were, however, now able to exercise their
influence openly. The great nobles proceeded to organise the
'Black Hundreds', as the society of 'True Russian Men' was
called; gangs of toughs who at the instigation of the secret
police, now no longer entitled by law to break up meetings
themselves, did this work for them; but there did not exist any
body at all which could be likened to a Conservative Party.

The nearest to this was the Party of Constitutional Democrats, known as the Cadets, but we still refer to them as
Liberals, since the word 'Cadet' has a slightly military flavour
and they were in no way a military party.

The Liberals were mostly drawn from the higher classes of
society and numbered many nobles among their members. The
great majority of them had been respresentatives in the Provin-

cial *Zemstvos,* the only governing bodies outside the autocracy which had any powers at all, and had been doing much
fine work in the way of increasing education, health facilities,
ameliorating the lot of the peasants and so on. They were all
strong Radicals, who wished for Constitutional Monarchy,
based in its general principles upon that of Great Britain, but
they were not necessarily anti-Monarchist. Later, however,
owing to the violence of the Socialists and Communists, quite
against its will this party took on a somewhat Conservative
appearance, because many members of the Court joined it,
seeing in it the only defence against complete abolition of the
Monarchy.

The Opposition consisted of several groups of Socialists,
the principal among them being the Mensheviks, whose
avowed aim was to turn Russia into a Socialist Republic without resorting to a class war.

The Bolsheviks were die-hard Communists governed entirely by the Marxist ideal and determined to root out altogether not only the Monarchy, but the powers and privileges
of the whole of the upper classes. In accordance with their
policy of 'action not words', initiated by Lenin, they boycot-
ted the *Duma* and refused to put up candidates of their own
to vote for others at the elections.

Early in the year Voroshilov attended a conference in St.
Petersburg and it was on this occasion that he first came into
personal contact with Lenin. He says himself of the meeting:
'That remains the most vivid impression of my whole life.
Everything about Lenin seemed to me extraordinary, his manner of speech, his simplicity and above all his piercing, soul-
uncovering eyes.'

On his return from St. Petersburg Voroshilov reformed his
old fighting squads into a Red Guard consisting of 700 to
800 workers in the Hartmann factory. This numerically small
force consisted of tried men, who had been tempered in the
revolutionary struggles of the preceding years, and it formed
the nucleus for the much larger force which was to be Voroshilov's first command when the workers of the Don Basin
actually took the field in the Revolution.

In March a law was passed by the First *Duma,* permitting
the formation of Trades Unions. A union was immediately
formed at the Hartmann works consisting of nearly 4000 members. Its organiser and chairman was Voroshilov and it was

soon known as the largest and best organised in the whole of
the Don Basin.

He next made his first trip abroad; this was as a delegate to
a full Party conference, which included both Mensheviks and
Bolsheviks, held in Stockholm. Lenin was also there and after
his return to his hide-out just over the Finnish border he
visited St. Petersburg frequently, both openly and in disguise.
On May 9th the future dictator made his first public speech in
the capital at a huge mass meeting.

After a great deal of talk the *Duma's* first concrete act was
an attempt to amend the existing electoral law on the basis of
universal suffrage, but the Czar refused to receive their deputation, and on July 7th summarily dissolved the First *Duma*
by *ukase* after a session of only ten weeks.

By this fatal step he alienated from himself the support of
the Liberals and even they now decided upon revolutionary
action. Assembling unofficially at Wyborg, in Finland, just as
Louis XVI's Third Estate met after their dismissal, in the ten-
nis court at Versailles, the members of the ex-*Duma* drew up a
proclamation enjoining the people of Russia to refuse the payment of taxes and the fulfilment of military obligations as long
as the promised constitutional reforms were not carried out.

Nicolas II, weak-willed, obstinate as ever, silent, suspicious,
immersed in the trivial life of his immediate family and superstitious practices of a semi-religious nature, was steadily bringing down his doom upon himself.

In February, 1907, he was forced to summon a Second
*Duma,* but feeling had grown to such an extent throughout the
country that it showed the strongest revolutionary proclivities;
in consequence he decided on another dissolution and wrote
to his mother on March 29th: '. . . but it is too early for that.
One must let them do something manifestly stupid or mean,
and then—stop!' He had not the least intention of trying to
co-operate and dismissed it in June after a sitting of five
months.

Lenin now showed one of the qualities of great leadership;
the courage to go back upon a majority policy that he had
initiated himself. He saw that no hope from revolutionary
action could be expected for some time to come owing to the
firm stand the Government was taking, and in consequence
now urged his followers to take part in the elections of the
next *Duma*.

Stolypin, however, although a whole-hearted reactionary, was a man of great ability. On his advice the Czar altered the electoral law with a view to depriving as large a percentage as possible of the discontented elements in the nation of their vote. A Third *Duma* was then called in the autumn. When it met, as was to be expected, it had been purged of its most violent members and consisted almost entirely of mild, academic Liberals drawn from the Right Wing of the intelligentsia.

This was a heavy defeat for the extremists. The police began to ferret for Lenin in Finland and, seeing the apparently hopeless state of affairs, he again moved outside the Russian Empire to wait for more promising times during his second long period of exile.

On his way through Germany he stayed for a day or two in Berlin to renew his acquaintance with the famous German Communist leaders Karl Liebknecht and Rosa Luxemburg; he then attended the 1907 Party conference in London. Voroshilov, undismayed by the set-backs they had sustained and utterly devoted to Lenin, travelled from the Don Basin to support him there.

Meanwhile Stolypin was making a big bid for the support of the peasants. He established monarchial organisations in the provincial centres and used the police to the utmost possible extent in stimulating a bogus loyalty. He then brought in a measure for land reform, by which communal holdings could be converted into homestead property actually owned by individual land workers. Between 1907 and 1914, 2,426,000 properties changed hands in this way. The measure was of the greatest assistance to the land-grabbing *Kulaks* and it enormously increased their power as wreckers of the State when the Central Government found itself, both in the War and after the Revolution, unable to cope with their greed during times of crisis.

The Co-operative movement showed a great increase during these years. It raised the standard of agriculture and helped in the cultural development of the peasantry; by 1911 it was sufficiently strong to establish its own bank in Moscow. The *Zemstvos* were also extremely active, bettering the condition of the people in every way which was possible in view of their limited authority, but the work of both was continually handicapped by the Czar, who would not even adhere to the partial

Constitution which he had granted. He instructed his ministers
to push the estimates for the upkeep of the Court through the
State Budget without any mention being made of them, hampered the operations of the *Duma* and overrode its advice in
every direction.

When Voroshilov returned from London the police were
watching for him. He was warned in time and was at first kept
in hiding by his friends, who moved him about among themselves. He had to live for weeks in secret cellars or hidden in
the reeds on the river bank, where his vodka and *zakusska*
were smuggled to him.

On one occasion, during this period that he was living in
hiding, some amateur theatricals were got up for the benefit
of elderly workers, who, of course, in Russia had no old age
pensions. They put on a play called 'The Worker's Quarter' in
the Public Gardens and Voroshilov took part in it disguised as
one of the actors. He took the opportunity to break out of his
part into a rousing revolutionary address. The watching police
immediately took action and broke up the audience. Voroshilov had been recognised by his voice and manner of speaking.
They gave chase but his friends threw them off the scent and
he escaped to Kiev. Soon after, however, an information was
laid against him with the police by a traitor in the group who
gave away his hiding-place. He was arrested in June, 1907, and
sentenced to three years' exile at Archangel.

At the railway station many of his friends came to see him
off and with a cheerful smile he called out to them: 'Don't lose
heart; I'm coming back; our time will come and we'll show
them yet.' We next hear of him in Baku, where he worked in
secret after escaping from exile.

By January, 1908, Lenin was settled at Geneva again and it
was soon after that he made his first appearance at an International Socialist Conference. He continued to write furiously
although his health had temporarily broken down during the
latter part of his stay in Finland. His extremist views caused
him to quarrel with nearly all his associates and he left Geneva
in disgust to go on a hiking tour through the mountains. This
set him up again so thoroughly that he reanimated the faint-
hearted on his return and even in his periods of poor health
rarely failed to dominate the councils of the exiles.

On September 1st, 1911, the reactionary Minister Stolypin
was assassinated by one of his own police spies, at a theatre

in the presence of the Czar; but revolutionary work in these years continued to be mainly underground as the ardour had been taken out of the movement by the reprisals for the armed risings of 1905.

At a congress in Paris an attempt was made to bridge the gap between the Liberal and Socialist parties, but this ended in complete failure, and in January, 1912, under Lenin's leadership, the Bolsheviks at the Prague Conference broke completely with the Mensheviks.

In April of that year two hundred strikers in the Lena Gold Fields were shot down by the police, which resulted in a fresh crop of strikes and a more fiery spirit becoming apparent again among the workers. Lenin seized upon this revival of antagonism to the autocracy and fanned its flame by the production of a new paper called *Pravda* or *Truth*, which from that time on appeared daily in St. Petersburg and has since become the official organ of the Communist Party. To be nearer Russia and facilitate the despatch of copy to the capital, he moved to Galicia, and settled near Cracow at a place where he was within walking distance of the Russian frontier.

In the Fourth *Duma*, elected in this year, six Bolshevik deputies were returned, thus for the first time forming a little independent Communist party, but their leader, Malinowsky, was discovered to be a police agent, which was a sad blow to Lenin, who had regarded him as one of his closest friends.

The Czar, however, was much too busy with other affairs to pay great attention to the deliberations of the *Duma*. In August, President Raymond Poincaré paid a state visit which materially strengthened the Franco-Russian Entente. In October the young Czarevitch went down with his first attack of hæmophilia and was nursed most devotedly by his parents. Nicolas II wrote to the Dowager Empress:

'Documents were brought to me twice a week in spite of everything, but in my free moments I wanted only to go and sit by his bedside—that is how all my time was spent and I could not even find a moment to write to you, dear Mama.'

It might well be asked: How is it that Stalin's name has not so far appeared in this chronicle? Why is it that he is never mentioned in accounts of all these innumerable Socialist 'pow-wows', where revolutionaries were seeking to reshape the destinies of Russia, and yet achieved absolute power among them later on? What was he up to all this time? The answer is that

Stalin was no talker in those days; only the inner ring of the revolutionaries even knew of his existence, but he played an extremely important part in the Bolshevik organisation, all the same.

His real name was Joseph Djugashvili and he was born in the little town of Gori, Georgia, in 1879. His father was a poor cobbler who worked in a factory at Tiflis, no great distance away. Stalin's childhood was spent in a tiny slum house built of cheap bricks with a plank roof. The front door gave on to a rough cobbled alleyway and down the middle of this alley ran a trickle of foul water collecting some of the filth and refuse as it went. Round about was a collection of tumble-down shanties where families as poor, or even poorer, than the Djugashvilis dragged out a miserable existence.

Joseph's childhood was one of great misery. His mother was a poor half-wit creature and his father, Vissarion, a drunken brute who constantly thrashed his wife and child; he died in a fit of delirium tremens when his son was nine. Little Joseph was then rescued from the gutter by a distant relative named Catherine, a small shopkeeper, who adopted him, sent him to the Gori school and later to the Seminary at Tiflis. The old lady's reward was to die mistress of the Palace of the ex-Viceroy of the Caucasus.

Stalin was known as 'Zozo' in those days and was a dark, rather frail-looking boy. Revolutionary literature was already dribbling into Georgia and the students used to smuggle it into the Seminary, preferring such illicit studies to those of archaic Orthodox Church liturgies. At the age of fifteen young Stalin was reading Marx; at nineteen he became one of the founders of the Tiflis branch of the Russian Social Democratic Workers' Party, and devoted himself henceforth entirely to revolutionary work.

His education and insatiable passion for exact knowledge made him an interesting companion to intellectuals, yet coming from a working-class home he never lost an easy familiarity with the poorest labourers. A small beard, inky black hair and languid, laughing eyes made him a striking personality, but he soon became of necessity an adept at disguise.

On March 1st, 1902, he led a great demonstration of Batum workers. There was a violent clash with the police, fourteen of the rioters were killed, forty wounded and nearly five hundred arrested, but Stalin managed to get away. Afterwards he had to hide a secret printing press he had been using and he buried it in a Moslem cemetery with the help of a grave-digger. He was arrested many times but used his periods in jail to form fresh cadres of revolutionaries among his fellow-prisoners.

His first meeting with Lenin was in Finland in 1905, and his position among the revolutionary exiles later became a very curious one. The workers in Russia were so miserably paid that with the best will in the world they could not afford contributions of more than a few kopecks a week to the secret Labour organisations. Most of this went in the support of leaders on the spot who were temporarily in hiding or to purchase arms aganst the day of revolution; very little of it found its way abroad to headquarters. Yet the exiles had to live while they wrote their polemics against the capitalist system and thundered abuse at the Czar during the conferences; moreover there was the much heavier expense of keeping the secret printing presses going and smuggling tons of illicit literature over the frontier. The Bolsheviks were particularly hard pressed in this way as in 1914 the registered members of their party numbered only round about 20,000, an infinitesimal proportion of the workers contributed to Socialistic organisations as a whole. Money had to be found somehow during the pre-war years otherwise Lenin's activities would have been brought to a stop. Stalin took upon himself the by no means easy task of finding it.

Whether you regard him in the same light as the late John Dillinger, America's first Public Enemy No. 1, or place him in the same category as our national hero Robin Hood, depends entirely on your point of view. Russian youth of future generations may well be thrilled by the stories of his exploits when these come to be written. In any case, Stalin employed himself visiting certain banks and wealthy capitalist concerns on the lines indicated above. He continued to live with almost Spartan simplicity himself, but the Bolshevik Party did *not* run out of funds.

On June 28th, 1914, the Archduke Francis Ferdinand, the heir-apparent to the Austrian Empire, was assassinated by a Serbian anarchist in Sarajevo. The Austrian Government accused the Serbian Government of instigating the murder, pressed for satisfaction and, in spite of Serbia's almost entire compliance with its demands, declared war on July 28th.

Russia mobilised on July 30th in support of her small ally

Serbia. Germany took the Russian mobilisation as a threat against herself, and, on August 1st, declared war against Russia. On the following day the Germans also moved against France and notified the Belgians of their intention to march through Belgian territory. The Belgians refused to permit this and, with France, called upon Britain to acknowledge her treaty obligations. Great efforts were made by the Foreign Secretary, Sir Edward Grey, to prevent hostilities, but things had gone too far, and upon Germany refusing to withdraw her troops from Belgian soil Great Britain declared war upon her at eleven o'clock on the night of August 4th.

For the Western nations it meant the end of an era. As Sir Edward Grey said so truly on that fateful night, 'The lamps are going out all over Europe ...' Such freedom of speech and action as existed then was never to be known again, even by the children of that generation, nor were they ever to know again the same comfort and security in their daily lives. The peoples were given over bound hand and foot by their national patriotism to the politicians, the swashbucklers and profiteers so that even fifty years later they are still in a state of bondage to which they would not have submitted for a single month in the Victorian age.

A state of constant anxiety as to when the next holocaust may be decreed gnaws like a rat at all planning for the future; a vast treasure, with which infinite good might be done, must be expended on fresh armaments; in many countries the people are reduced merely to the puppets of the men of destiny. Even in Britain the old freedom is now only a myth, dozens of war measures still circumscribe our actions and our only right is to re-elect a new House of Commons every few years which may voice our grievances but it is not consulted by the little clique of Rulers in the Cabinet on a major crisis.

The right of people to move freely, without qualifications, from one country to another is now denied them. In the majority of countries they may no longer write or speak their true thoughts without risk of imprisonment and must even order their lives in accordance with their Government's will. Most tragic of all, that free intercourse between peoples of different countries and the independence of the individual, which begot mutual respect and chivalry and seemly behaviour, ceased to be when the warring nations went down into the pit.

# 8

# The Beginning of the End

In Russia, where personal liberty had always been restricted, the effect of the war measures did not bring about the same radical change in the lives of the people as occurred in other countries, and in the first year of the conflict there was a definite slackening of revolutionary activity owing to a widespread patriotic feeling that it was unfair to stab the Government in the back now all its energies were needed to conduct an enormous campaign. Even Voroshilov went into a cartridge-making factory at Tzaritsyn although he also employed himself in converting many of the troops stationed there to his ideas, against the day of action which he was convinced would come.

In the first clash at the frontier with Germany the Russian troops were successful and overran a considerable portion of East Prussia. This was not owing to any lack of courage in the Germans, but their major strength was concentrated in the west for von Kluck's 'wheel' through Belgium, which had for its objective the encirclement of Paris and the seizing of the Channel ports. In consequence, the German eastern front was considerably under-manned and their troops there were quite unable to put up a successful resistance against the enormous number of Russian divisions which contained many of the picked regiments of the Czar's army.

The Allies received the news of these successes with delight. As the Germans were so heavily engaged in the west it did not look as though they would be able to spare many divisions from the theatre, or organise enough reserve divisions in time to fill the gap. Berlin was only a little over a hundred miles from the advancing Cossacks and there seemed nothing to prevent the Russian masses pressing on to a decisive victory. There entered into the situation, however, one factor that nobody had reckoned on.

This was an elderly gentleman; a retired officer, whose principal occupation for some years had been sitting at a marble-topped table outside a café in Hamburg, making puddles with his beer and, to the amusement of young German military cadets who regarded him as half-witted, explaining that these puddles were the Masurian Lakes in which he would drown the enemy if he ever had the good fortune to command an army in that area.

The portly gentleman concerned had entered the Army in 1865, had achieved the rank of General after a not particularly distinguished career, had never been very popular with the Kaiser and the High Command, and had retired on reaching the service age limit in 1911. He was obviously due, in the normal course of events, to live on for a few years in retirement and then die without anybody except his immediate associates ever having heard of him. As it was, he started off on a completely new career at the age of sixty-seven, lived for another twenty years shouldering the greatest responsibilities that any man has ever been called upon to undertake, and became the President of the German Republic. His name was Von Hindenburg.

The story of this half-pay officer's metamorphosis, literally overnight, into one of the spectacular figures of the war is more dramatic than that of any fiction character that an author would dare to put into the wildest romance.

At the outbreak of the War he had immediately volunteered to serve with the army. They didn't want him. He then applied to be taken on to train fresh levies or do any sort of war work which might be useful. They told him, in so many words, that they had many far more competent 'dug-outs'. The old man's heart was nearly broken. All his life had been spent in a conscientious endeavour to fit himself to serve his country when the time came, as every German officer of those days knew that it would. The time had come, and they wouldn't even let him train recruits upon a barrack square. All he could do was to sit and mumble over his beer puddles at the marble-topped table in the café while the youngsters mocked at him, believing that he had a bee in his bonnet.

The German eastern front was broken, Berlin, the capital itself, was theatened. Main Headquarters was in a flat spin; no time to bring divisions from the west, practically no reserve troops immediately available; what the devil could they do to save the situation? Suddenly somebody thought of old Hindenburg, a conscientious man, if not brilliant, and he had one quality which all the other Generals lacked; he did know personally every single inch of the country over which the fighting was taking place.

At three o'clock on the afternoon of August 22nd a telegram was sent asking him if he was prepared for immediate employment. His reply ran: 'I am ready,' although he had not the least idea what the employment was to be. Exactly twelve hours later a special train was in Hamburg station to carry him to the scene of conflict. As he stepped on to the train he was informed that the dream of his life had come true and that he was appointed to the Supreme Command of the German armies defending the homeland from the invader.

On the train he met General von Ludendorff, who had been appointed his Chief of Staff. Von Ludendorff had been rushed from Liège in Belgium that day, breaking his journey at Coblentz to receive particulars of the situation on the eastern front from Main Headquarters. While the train roared through the night the two Generals went into conference; next day Hindenburg was in action.

For two days he employed himself stemming the rout and ordering fresh dispositions. Between the 28th and the 31st that is to say within one week of leaving Hamburg, he had planned and fought the battle of Tannenberg, encircled Rennenkampf's army, completely destroyed three entire Russian Corps, severely mauled two others and taken more than 60,000 prisoners. From September 8th to 15th he directed the battle of the Masurian Lakes and its last stages were fought on Russian soil.

When the first rumours of war reached Lenin his hope for world revolution rose high. At innumerable Socialist Conferences delegates of all the leading nations had pledged themselves to resist to the death any new war upon which the capitalist governments might enter. It was to be the signal for a general strike and the great opportunity for the workers to seize power.

His expectations were bitterly disappointed. Karl Liebknecht in Germany and one or two British Socialists stood out, but inherited patriotism had a far stronger hold upon the great majority of Socialists than the doctrines of Karl Marx; almost to a man they threw their theories overboard and rallied to the support of their respective Governments. Lenin was so disgusted that he severed his connection with the Second International and became more than ever convinced that if there was ever to be any world revolution at all he had got to start it himself.

As he was living in Galicia at the time and had an underground network which was smuggling his paper over the Russian frontier, the local inhabitants, not unnaturally, took him for a Russian spy, so he was promptly arrested by the Austrian authorities. Victor Adler, the veteran leader of the Austrian Socialists, came to the rescue, however, and satisfied his Government that, far from Lenin being a Russian spy, he was a more deadly enemy of the Czar than anyone in Austria, upon which he was allowed to leave for neutral Switzerland.

The war severed many of his secret lines of communication with Russia, and as he and his associates were naturally stigmatised by their countrymen as pacifists and traitors, their activities were hampered a great deal. The little group of Bolsheviks in the *Duma* which continued to accept his orders without question were arrested and condemned to penal servitude in Siberia. It seemed that any hope of a successful revolution was farther off than ever and, altogether, this was a very bad period for the Party.

Russia continued to throw vast masses of men into the struggle against Germany and Austria. The Grand Duke Nicolas was the principal Russian commander and Hindenburg pays him the highest tribute as an able general and most dangerous opponent.

The Grand Duke's plan, broadly speaking, was to pin down the German forces in the north and break through towards the south by smashing up the Austro-Hungarians. This was the weak spot in the ring formed by the Central Powers, since the army of the Austrian Empire contained troops of such mixed nationalities, many of whom had been striving to throw off the Austrian yoke for generations and in consequence lacked any enthusiasm for the war. A number of Czecho-Slovak battalions had actually marched over the frontier with their bands playing and their flags flying immediately war was declared to offer themselves for service with the Russian Army. Considerable numbers of men, great stores of munitions and numerous important points had been lost to Austria in this manner, although the Austrians saved the situation by a big frontal attack delivered with great bravery by their own troops and those of Hungary. The Grand Duke well knew the situation, however, and if he could have once broken through, the whole fertile plain of Hungary would have been his for the taking.

He smashed the Austro-Hungarians in the neighbourhood of Cracow, thereby being within an ace of turning their flank at the northern end of the Carpathians. Hindenburg, who had by then penetrated to within a day's march of Warsaw, was compelled to check his advance and hurried south to organise a joint operation with the Austrians and such German troops as could be spared. In the middle of November he fought the great battle of Lodz, thereby relieving the Russian pressure upon Silesia.

In February, 1915, he attacked again; showing the most superb generalship in the face of overwhelming odds. To concentrate his forces at the vital spot he almost entirely uncovered a large section of his line, but in this 'Winter battle of Masuria' he completely annihilated another Russian army, killing 100,000 men and taking a further 100,000 prisoner.

Later in the spring the Grand Duke attempted another break-through to the Hungarian plain, but Hindenburg smashed the Russian line in North Galicia and caught the enemy on the frontier of Hungary in both flank and rear. That summer he captured Warsaw, Vilna and Kovno, although during this period he was fighting with odds of four to one in men against him; and not the ragged, ill-fed troops that were afterwards thrown into the line, but the flower of the Russian Army; brave, well-equipped and well-led regiments.

By this time the effect of the war was beginning to be felt behind the Russian war zone. In spite of Admiral Lord Fisher's scornful tirades, the British Government could never be persuaded into forcing the passage of the Skagerrak, the southern waters of which separate Sweden and Denmark; the Baltic Sea remained, therefore, throughout the war virtually a German lake. The Russian Government had foolishly neglected to develop Archangel and its northern sea route in times of peace, so from the outset of the war, once the land frontiers were closed Russia was to all intents and purposes in a state of blockade.

She had plenty of raw materials, but had never troubled to tap her supplies and now it seemed too late to do so. Practically all machinery had been imported from abroad and she was no longer able to secure the necessary equipment from

Britain or Germany. Such factories as she had were all converted into munition plants, but even so were quite inadequate to produce the great quantities required. The manufacture of peace-time goods came to a standstill and little could be brought in from abroad to make up the deficit; moreover, as she was completely shut off by enemy fronts from Western Europe she could no longer export her principal commodities. The chief concentration of her railways being in the western part of the Empire, they became seriously congested because it was here that the major operations of the war were taking place. A large proportion of the rolling-stock was commandeered for military purposes, goods could not be shipped freely, and even important towns in the interior could no longer get adequate supplies.

In consequence trade suffered severely, the receipts of the exchequer dropped alarmingly, and the rouble began to fall.

In spite of these difficulties the Russians launched another terrific attack in March, 1916. In one sector 128 Russian battalions were hurled against 19 German battalions, but so magnificent was Hindenburg's generalship that even against these colossal odds he was victorious; the Russian losses in this drive exceeded 140,000 men.

Under General Brussilov the Russians attacked once more and succeeded in smashing through the Austro-Hungarian front south of the Pripet. The Germans' main forces were, at that time, involved in the west in the terrible battle for the French fortress of Verdun, but they collected every available division which could be spared and managed to stop the gap.

When the history of the war finally comes to be written, perhaps a hundred years hence, it is probable that Hindenburg will be the only great general to emerge from it. Very few of the high military commanders showed any real imagination and initiative. Many of them had gigantic forces at their disposal, but were hopelessly static in their ideas and seemed to be able to think of nothing but massed attacks against strongly fortified positions in which countless thousands of their men were slaughtered.

Hindenburg, on the other hand, demonstrated again and again how bitterly he was opposed to this mad and wasteful idea of the frontal attack against an entrenched and prepared enemy. Again and again in his own campaigns on the eastern front we see him break off an action immediately it became obvious the enemy could hold their ground and that reinforcements were coming to their assistance. His first action upon being appointed to the Supreme Command at Main Headquarters was to break off the crazy battle for Verdun, where German divisions had been thrown into the mud to rot or be shot to pieces month after month. He had the courage to retreat when necessary and for two years we see him operating with infinitely smaller forces than his opponent, even at times uncovering a large sector of his line, but concentrating the comparatively few troops he had against some vital point in the enemy's armour, and then striking with complete success. That surely is a real general's business.

If he had had his way a decision would have been sought for in the east, in 1916, instead of in the west. Main Headquarters were frightened that if a German army advanced far into Russia the same fate would befall it as befell Napoleon in 1812, and therefore frittered away the main strength of the German nation in their fruitless attacks on Verdun. Conditions, however, were very different to those of the previous century. Then, there were no railways and Russia was not so dependent upon her manufacturing cities to keep a considerable army in the field.

If the divisions which were wasted at Verdun had been placed at Hindenburg's disposal there is good reason to suppose that it would have enabled him to repeat his victories of the previous years, overrun the Ukraine, seize Kiev, Kharkov, Moscow and, with the support of the German fleet, even St. Petersburg, thereby securing the principal industrial centres, the great grain-fields and all the Baltic provinces, which would virtually have put Russia out of the war. This would have nullified the British blockade which eventually brought the German people to their knees, and it is possible that the whole war would have had a different ending.

In Russia things were going from bad to worse. At the munition factories plant was breaking down and the worn parts could not be replaced. As the war advanced soldiers were often sent into the firing-line unarmed and had to wait until one of their comrades was shot down before they could secure a rifle; ammunition supplies began to run short. The troops behind the lines learned this from the returning wounded and naturally began to give trouble. The number of skilled workmen in the factories had never been large; they were hopelessly overdriven, having to do night, as well as day, shifts, and barely getting enough time off for sufficient sleep, let alone a little recreation. Such holidays as they had had before were cancelled or reduced and after two years of such treatment they showed their intense resentment.

The rouble was still falling; the cost of living had increased by leaps and bounds. The middle classes suffered acutely; they had the usual commitments such as rent, clothes and education of their children which they could not escape, yet their earning powers had hardly increased at all.

Over 14,000,000 men were called to the colours but there were not sufficient arms to maintain more than a third of them in the field, so the rest, grumbling and uneasy, were swelling the population of the towns behind the lines. The allowances for soldiers' wives were totally inadequate, and the enormous numbers of these half-starved women added to the general atmosphere of gloom and discontent.

As though impelled by some evil genius to aggravate the situation, the Czar had issued an *ukase* on the outbreak of war prohibiting the sale of all spirits. The Russian people were used enough to hard times, but however bad things were they had always endeavoured to solace themselves with a little jollification, which normally took the shape of singing songs and consuming a good quantity of a very cheap spirit, extracted from potatoes, known as vodka. Now, even this anodyne for their woes was taken from them.

These years were dreary ones for Lenin and the exiles. The total membership of the Party in 1905 was 10,000 and eleven years later, by 1916, it had only increased to 23,000. He could do little except wait and watch, but his hopes gradually increased as his spies reported to him the state of war-weariness at home and the discontent that was leading to the disintegration of the army. Men were already beginning to desert in batches and a renewal of strikes was breaking out.

Soon after the declaration of war the Czar had left St. Petersburg for the headquarters of his army. He was completely useless as a soldier, but apparently considered it his duty to live there during a war. As he was not only useless but dangerous as well when in St. Petersburg, his removal to military headquarters would probably have been a good thing if he had had a different wife or had not been so devoted to her.

As it was, the Empress was virtually in charge of the

Government of Russia, and it happened that she was an extremely dangerous woman. Before her marriage she had been a German, and, unlike Catherine the Great, she does not appear to have changed her nationality in her heart, as well as formally, upon her marriage. That, at least, was the opinion of a great number of Russians and many well-informed persons. Rumours that she intrigued with the German Court to the detriment of Russia and caused patriotic ministers to be replaced by men of dubious honesty were widespread. Be this as it may, one fact is indisputable: being deeply interested in religious matters from a somewhat curious angle she fell under the influence of a man who was to play a terrible part in Russia's story.

This was the monk Rasputin; a very strange and terrible personality indeed. The irregularities of his early life provoked great scandal in the provincial district from which he came, and that is no small testimony to his behaviour since the Russians had never been accustomed to their priests leading the chaste existence which is considered requisite for the clergy of the Western nations.

Rasputin was a fine, well-developed, bearded man with a great big domed head, standing over six feet two in his bare feet. The secret of his power lay in the fact that he was a hypnotist of a most unusual order and, by this force, could bend even strong men who were antagonistic to his will. He was also a clairvoyant and medium of no mean ability and was introduced to the Empress on that account.

If reports are true he very soon had her completely under his domination and had also subdued to his will her daughters and many of the good-looking women attached to the Russian Court. Many of the scandalous stories current at the time regarding Rasputin and the ladies of the Imperial family were doubtless due to anti-Russian propaganda, but his activities in private houses are well substantiated.

A veil must be drawn over the disgraceful scenes that were enacted in secrecy behind the locked doors of numerous palaces in St. Petersburg where Rasputin preached a new cult to certain women.

His message was a masochistic one; all those who desired salvation must achieve it by following in the footsteps of Our Lord and by submitting without question to suffering. Those who gave themselves up to suffering in this life would, by it, expiate their sins and come to heavenly glory in the next. He persuaded these people that because they were used to rich foods they should eat of the coarsest, poorest, and most revolting fare; that because they were used to silken garments they should discard their French lingerie for sackcloth and coarse wool to be worn under their dresses, that because they had the inborn love of cleanliness common to their rank they should submit their beautiful skins to contact with dirt; that because, having been brought up to behave chastely they would suffer by deliberately compelling themselves to be unchaste, they should also seek their salvation in that way, that for them maximum suffering could be achieved by submitting their tender, beautifully cared-for bodies to the embrace of a grimy *muzhik* who stank of stale sweat. He never bathed, he never washed, his straggly beard was matted with filth and his uncut nails were black with grime.

The influence of this 'saint' was immense, and very soon he became absolutely all-powerful. He was the uncrowned Czar of All the Russias. He was a man of tremendous virility and even his almost incredible dissipations did not appear to affect his health in any way. As the 'Master' he was immune from most of the rules of his Order and in or out of the presence of his women disciples he gorged himself with the finest foods and drank incredible quantities of champagne. Into many of his practices Black Magic unquestionably entered and his counsels regarding State affairs were invariably evil. There have been few such monsters in the historic records of the world.

By the end of 1916 the state of Russia was appalling. For two and a half years she had hardly been able to import any goods at all. Ordinary merchandise was so scarce in her village markets that the peasants were sullen and rebellious. In exchange for his corn the *Kulak* was only receiving paper money and now there was no longer anything for him to buy with this. Consequently, instead of continuing to work for the sake of the nation he proceeded to sit down on his job. All over the country peasants reduced their sowing area, so that instead of there being a surplus upon which the army and towns could be fed, little more corn was grown than barely sufficed to feed the villages. The result was bread queues in the cities and immense difficulty in collecting the army rations.

The troops were loyal enough to their country but tired of

fighting an apparently pointless war in which they were under-
fed, underclothed and not even provided with sufficient ammunition to put up a decent show against the well-equipped
Germans. Desertion set in to such an extent that it was quite
beyond the power of the officers to cope with it, and during
1916 over 1,000,000 Russian soldiers just packed up and started
to walk home.

The men of the Imperial Family got together; separately,
and in a body led by the Grand Dukes Nicolas and Michael
they warned the Czar that a time had come when it was absolutely imperative that something must be done. They even
hinted at the conduct of the Empress and demanded that the
evil monk Rasputin should be arrested and imprisoned. The
Czar, however, was still an autocrat. He refused to listen and
remained sitting about Army Headquarters doing nothing at
all. His relatives then decided that if Russia was to be saved
they must take affairs into their own hands.

A number of the great nobles met in St. Petersburg and
organised the last Palace Conspiracy in that long list of bloody
assassinations which makes the history of the Czars such dramatic reading.

Rasputin was very fond of music. One of the Princes invited
him to a party on the night of December 17th, where a
famous violinist was to play. Rasputin arrived after dinner
and found a number of the conspirators gathered at the
Prince's house. The tall, dirty-bearded monk was at least a
man of courage. He knew quite well how much they desired
his death, but he was not afraid to place himself alone in their
hands and so great was his arrogance that he treated them
with open contempt before he sat down to hear a *concerto*.

After it was over they went upstairs. He drank a considerable amount of champagne and was then offered coffee. The
conspirators had put enough arsenic in it to kill ten ordinary
men. Rasputin drank it and never turned a hair.

Covertly they watched him; utterly amazed that he did not
either retch the poison up or collapse and die. He seemed quite
normal and, declaring that he would like to hear some more
music, went downstairs again. Most of the conspirators waited
above, tense and anxious, expecting to hear him suddenly cry
out in agony at any moment, but time drifted on and nothing happened. One of the nobles came up and reported to the
others that the vile monk was quite calm and apparently en-

joying himself. They had all heard that he always carried a charm against poison on him and that he boasted he was immune from death in any form. As educated men they had considered such stories sheer nonsense, but now they were filled with superstitious half-belief.

The hour was approaching when he would be going. It was decided that something must be done; he must not be allowed to leave the house alive. This waiting was intolerable. One of the nobles volunteered to shoot him and went downstairs with a revolver. He walked up to Rasputin and shot him three times through the body.

Rasputin flung over his chair directly he was attacked and stood up. The conspirators crowded into the room expecting him to shudder and die, but he did nothing of the kind. He called them a lot of murderous dogs, but blasphemously declared that he was under the direct protection of Heaven and could not be killed. He proposed to take his revenge upon them for this attempt when he had seen the Czarina in the morning.

The nobles were absolutely aghast. The monk had swallowed enough poison to kill ten men nearly two hours before, and showed no trace of it. He had three mortal bullet wounds in his body, but, apart from a heavy sweat which had broken out on his brow, he seemed to be quite unharmed. As he stood there glowering at them they must have been shaken to their very souls with the belief that they were faced, not by a man but by a demon.

Rasputin turned to walk out of the house. His hypnotic gaze was lifted from the little group of conspirators, but even so they remained as though paralysed. One of their servants who was in the conspiracy seized a dagger from the wall and, as Rasputin passed through the door, drove it into his back.

At last the monk staggered and fell. The spell was lifted. They rushed upon him and tied his hands and legs, yet still, with three bullets, the dagger and the poison in him, he would not die, but lay there blaspheming and glaring at them.

They held a hurried, whispered council, convinced now that the monk was invulnerable, and not knowing what to do with him. Somebody suggested the Neva. They carried him outside, bundled him into a car and drove down to the banks of the river. A hole was found in the ice and they threw him, still alive, into it. He broke the bonds that bound him and tried to struggle out. They forced him back and held his head under the water; the current below the ice caught him and carried him away. Russia was at last free of Rasputin, but it was too late to undo the damage he had done.

At the end of January bread riots broke out in St. Petersburg and the munition workers at the Putilov Metal Works went on strike. Practically the only Bolshevik leader in the capital at that time who afterwards became of any importance was Voroshilov; he had been working twelve hours a day in a munition factory there and employing such spare time as he had suborning the troops of the Ismailovsky Guards. In February he brought the whole regiment out in support of the rioters, proving that the Army could no longer be relied upon by the Government. Nearby, in Kronstadt, the sailors of the Baltic fleet mutinied, murdered many of their officers, and marched upon the Winter Palace.

In the 1905 revolution Moscow had lagged nearly a year behind St. Petersburg, and it had been possible to quell the two rebellions separately, but now, within ten days of the first riots in St. Petersburg, the Moscow workers also declared for a general strike and armed uprising.

The Czar was completely isolated, having now even the great nobles and his principal officers against him, but still he continued adamant to any suggestion of passing measures which would quiet the country. So little did he realise the significance of events that as late as February 27th he telegraphed his categorical refusal to the request of the President of the Council of Ministers for a change in the composition of the Government. The question of his arrest was discussed at Army Headquarters, but the *coup d'état* planned by the aristocracy had come too late and on that same day power was actually assumed by a provisional committee of the *Duma*.

On March 1st the autocracy came to an end by the Czar, under pressure, agreeing to the appointment of responsible ministers, the nomination of whom was to be wholly in the hands of the President of the *Duma*. By March 2nd the Provisional Government under the premiership of Prince Lvov had been formed, and at Pskov, that same night, Nicolas II signed a Deed of Abdication in favour of his brother the Grand Duke Michael.

But the *Duma* itself was losing control because the bulk of

D

the people were now behind the Soviet of Workmen and Soldier's Deputies who would not agree to even a Constitutional Monarchy. The Grand Duke Michael declined to accept power except by the will of the people, and on March 4th formally transferred it to the *Duma*. The Russian monarchy was at an end.

# 9

# Eight Mad Months of Uncertainty

The Revolution was hailed with joy throughout the whole of Russia. A few, a very few, astute men among the nobility and the capitalists may have foreseen that the force of the earthquake was not yet spent and have taken steps to save their families, themselves, and their property; but it can be said that very nearly everyone was filled with delirious happiness.

For a dozen years past various measures had been forced on the Czar from time to time which had foreshadowed some degree of liberty, but in every case the apparent step towards freedom had proved to be an illusion. All classes had come to realise that as long as Nicolas II remained on the throne no promises he gave were worth the paper they were written on and that to act on them was only to lay oneself open to arrest, imprisonment or exile, immediately he felt himself strong enough to go back upon his word. For centuries the whole people of Russia from the highest noble to the lowest serf had lived under a tyranny; never knowing from one day to the next when the dreaded agents of the Czar would appear to spirit them away from their friends and families and charge them in secret with some political activity, or even with having, quite innocently, assisted someone else who was marked down. It was enough; their career was ruined and they were lucky if they escaped with only imprisonment.

Now at last the tyrant was gone. At first they could scarcely believe it, but the joybells were ringing in St. Petersburg and as they streamed out into the streets from the houses, shops and factories it gradually began to penetrate that they were a free people. Workmen and their masters, who had quarrelled for years, shook hands and congratulated each other. Officers and private soldiers drank together to the new régime of liberty and a fair deal for all. Public and private vehicles were boarded by rejoicing throngs; great bonfires were lit and an air of carnival, such as seized London on Armistice Day, ensued.

Even the Grand Duke Nicolas in Tiflis declared for the Provisional Government and announced that he would permit no counter-revolutionary movement in the Army. Even the Allies, still locked in a war to the death with the Central Powers, learnt of the Revolution with satisfaction. The Czarist Government had proved so effete and feeble that for a year past the Northern ally had not been pulling her weight. It was thought that under the new democratic Republic abuses would be stopped, the army reconstituted, and Russia once again become able to renew her attacks on a scale sufficient to absorb enough German divisions for the other Allies to break through in the west.

The upper classes imagined that the country would settle down into a nice, law-abiding republic where they would be able to live free of the irritating restraints which the autocracy had imposed upon them; the working-classes, the soldiers and the peasants that the war was as good as over, and that prosperity such as they had never known before would make Russia a paradise to live in. Everybody was happy—for about two days.

If the Revolution had occurred during a time of peace it is possible that law and order might have been maintained long enough for a Provisional Government to settle the immediate problems with which it was faced to the satisfaction of all but certain small minorities. As it was the urgency of the war brooded over all councils and complicated every problem.

Deserters were still streaming back from the front. The Bolshevik Party, small but exceedingly active, inflamed the passions of the multitude by wild, demagogic speeches in which they insisted that first and foremost, before any other matters were settled, the war must be called off at once. On the other hand the ministers of the Allied Governments sent telegram after telegram to their ambassadors urging them to press the new Government for an immediate advance upon the eastern front.

The great majority of the old constitutionalists and the upper classes that they represented felt that Russia would be dishonoured if she made a separate peace and left the Allies in the lurch. Even the Mensheviks who wanted a bourgeois democratic State as a prelude to Socialism were in favour of a continuance of the war, and wished to fight on until the Germans were driven out of Russian territory.

Two days after the abdication of the Czar the issue of *Pravda* was resumed, but the Soviet called off the general strike and Lenin wrote to a friend: 'The workers have been fighting in bloody battles for a week yet Miliukov plus Guchkov plus Kerensky are in power. The same old European pattern. Well, what of it? This first state of revolution will be neither final nor confined to Russia. We, of course, retain our opposition to the defence of the Fatherland, to the Imperialist slaughter directed by the Kerenskys and Co. . . . We shall see how the "People's Freedom Party" will give the people freedom, bread and peace. . . . We shall see!' He knew that after all the weary years of slaving, poverty and disappointment, his hour was now at hand.

Naturally he was most anxious to get back to Russia as soon as possible; but this was not easy as he had to pass through the territory of one or other of the warring nations and he was far from popular with the Allied Governments. Speed was a most important factor, so he approached the Germans through the Swiss Socialists and received permission to travel via Germany.

We have spoken at the end of a previous chapter of the decay of chivalry and decent feeling which set in with the Great War. This action of the German Government is a typical example. They were fully aware that Lenin was a most dangerous revolutionary who had openly stated on innumerable occasions that he would stop at nothing to destroy existing society. The German High Command regarded him as an untouchable and particularly revolting kind of criminal. They were well aware that Russia was in the melting-pot, and it was a toss-up whether an orderly Liberal republic, which was what the majority of her people wanted, would be set up, or whether there would be the most frightful bloodshed with limitless destruction of property and the death of innumerable women and children. Yet they facilitated Lenin's return to Russia. It may well be said that the exigencies of the campaign excused their doing so, and the Allies unquestionably resorted to equally dubious methods of warfare against the Central Powers, but such a state of things showed a moral collapse unparalleled in any previous war.

Trotsky learned of the Revolution from the American

papers when in a Canadian concentration camp, so he was the last of the well-known exiles to reach Petrograd; Stalin had to come from Siberia where he had been in exile since 1913, but he probably owed his life to that as it is said that the intense cold there cured him of tuberculosis. Old Plekhanov was the first to arrive, but Lenin was only three days later. He arrived in Petrograd on April 16th and, to his surprise, was met by a delegation of welcome at the railway station. His faithful disciple Voroshilov was there to greet him and handed him a bouquet of flowers.

The first Prime Minister of Russia's Provisional Government, Prince Lvov, was a highly cultured, refined and sensitive man. His capabilities had been proved as the creator and guiding mind of that Liberal Assembly from which so many of the constitutionalists of the early *Dumas* were drawn, the All Russian Union of *Zemstvos*. He was upright, intelligent, and, moreover, a man who owed allegiance to no party, but he took on the Ministry of Home Affairs as well as the Premiership and these tasks were quite beyond him.

The next most important minister was Miliukov, leader of the old Constitutional Party whom we will henceforth term the Liberals, and Minister of Foreign Affairs. He was a shrewd parliamentarian with a fine understanding of international relations, and his strength lay in his remarkable powers of analysis, but he was not very strong when it came to the practical application of any of his policies. His post was a highly important one as he was responsible to the Allies for Russia's conduct of the war.

A third minister who was afterwards to play a much more important part than any of the others was A. F. Kerensky. In the Provisional Government he only held the portfolio of Justice, but he was already a figure of the first importance. Long before the Revolution he had won great distinction as a young and talented lawyer by defending accused persons prosecuted by the Government, and he had sat as a member for the Labour and Toil group in the early *Dumas*. He was gifted with a very great organising ability and was one of the very few members of the *Duma* who did not lose his wits during the March Revolution.

The Petrograd Soviet had no legal authority whatever, but arrogated to itself the rights of a governing body and, on March 14th, published a manifesto to the 'Peoples of the

Whole World'. This consisted of an appeal to the workers of all nations to ignore their Governments and bring an end to the slaughter, but at the same time the manifesto declared that Revolutionary Russia would defend her freedom from attack from any quarter.

The whole country was rapidly becoming covered with a network of Soviets, and by March 28th an All Russian Assembly of Soviets was summoned which was attended by 497 delegates, representing 138 local Soviets, 7 armies and 39 divisions of troops. From this point onward the Central Soviet became the governing factor in Russian policy and for the moment it was imbued with a patriotic spirit which led it to lay down that the glorious Russian Revolution must not allow itself to be beaten by an Imperialistic Government, and that the troops should continue to resist the invaders of the Republic with as much zeal as they had shown in defending Russia in the past.

On the evening after Lenin's arrival in St. Petersburg he spoke at length to a meeting of the caucus of the Party urging that the Soviet must cease to regard itself as an organisation for exerting pressure on the Government, *it must think of itself as the Government*. 'The art of government,' he said, 'cannot be learned from books. Try, make mistakes, learn how to govern.'

Some items from his programme were: confiscation of all private lands; immediate merger of all banks into one general national bank, and immediate placing of the Soviet of Workers' Deputies in control of all production and distribution of goods. Plekhanov could not swallow such a programme.

Virtually Lenin said to his associates: 'never mind the electors, you are the Government!' So anxious was he to break with all bourgeois traditions of the past that he insisted on the change of his own party's name from Socialist to Communist, so that there should be no confusion of his beliefs with the beliefs of those European Socialists who had entered into Coalitions with their respective Governments for the prosecution of the war. His cry was 'For too long we have kept on the old soiled shirt. It is high time to cast it off and put on clean linen.'

The Mensheviks were in the majority in the Soviet and, while Martov pursued a more or less negative policy, their veteran leader Plekhanov was definitely for continuing the defence of Russia by arms; but Trotsky now came over to Lenin and threw himself completely on to the side of the Bolsheviks.

The country as a whole was prepared to continue defending itself, but it was utterly war-weary and willing to accept any reasonable peace that stipulated the withdrawal of the German troops from Russian soil.

On April 28th, however, Miliukov, the old-school diplomat, Foreign Minister in the Provisional government, issued a note to the Powers which was interpreted as a declaration that Russia was still committed jointly and irrevocably with the Allies, not only to continue the war but to pursue it to the bitter end upon the old lines of an Imperialistic war of conquest; but that was not the intention of the Soviet or of the Russian people.

Early in May the Socialists of the Norse nations, who were neutrals, endeavoured to arrange a World Peace Conference in Stockholm, and there is strong reason to suppose this might have prevented a further eighteen months of massed carnage if certain leading statesmen had not wrecked it.

This matter brought further embarrassment to the Russian Provisional Government as it had assured the Allies that it would not make a separate peace without them, whereas the Soviet agreed to participate in the Conference. On this and Miliukov's manifesto a definite split between the official and unofficial bodies that were jointly running Russia occurred, and it became clear that unless the Government was reconstituted it was bound to fall.

Miliukov was thrown out and a Coalition arranged. There were now three main parties; the old Constitutionalists turned Liberal Republicans, the Mensheviks representing Socialism, and the Bolsheviks who had definitely gone Communist. Only the first two held places in the new Coalition Government. The Bolsheviks stood out and Lenin denounced the Coalition as useless either for bringing peace or furthering the progress of the Revolution.

Germany was heavily occupied in the west and welcomed the virtual cessation of hostilities which had ensued, after the Czar's abdication, on the eastern front. For months past the troops had been fraternising. Only the Russian artillery, which had suffered less from disintegration than the infantry, continued a little sporadic fighting when they received an occa-

sional consignment of ammunition. The German gunners slapped back at them for a few hours; the Russian infantry
laughed when the German shells fell among their own batteries, and the war died down again for another week or so.
Lenin instructed all members of the Party to encourage
fraternisation with the enemy on every possible occasion.

In the Coalition Kerensky was promoted from Minister of
Justice to Minister for War and Marine. He immediately left
for the front to try to restore discipline and a fighting spirit
among the troops.

The activities of the Government were much embarrassed
by the Finns, Letts, Lithuanians, Poles and other minorities,
all of whom had been clamouring ever since the Revolution
for the re-establishment of their ancient national rights. These
problems, which would normally have taken months of care-
ful debate to settle adequately, were rushed through to try and
keep as many people happy as possible. Finland had always
been much in the same relation to Russia as our Dominions
are to us under the Statute of Westminster, the sole link was a
common allegiance to the Crown and the fall of the Monarchy
had liquidated all relations between Finland and Russia. The
Russian Government now recognised Finland's independence
and the Finns re-established their own Constitution. The Government also recognised the independence of Poland, the auto-
nomy of Esthonia and, in principle, that of Latvia, and granted local government to the Caucasus.

In the summer months Lenin had his first opportunity of
contacting the Russian people regularly and in the mass. The
Bolsheviks occupied the palace of Madame Kshesinskaia a
former ballerina, as their headquarters, and it possessed a first
floor balcony from which large audiences in the street below
could be addressed. Every moment he could spare from writing his articles for *Pravda,* receiving deputations, or issuing
instructions to his subordinates, he spent addressing the
workers and army men who continually thronged about the
palace and gathered below immediately he appeared on this
balcony.

In the two months succeeding the Revolution the membership of his party had increased from 23,000 to 80,000 and it
was still growing. The economic situation helped him, since
this continued to go from bad to worse as week succeeded
week. The machinery in the factories had deteriorated to a

shocking degree; the greedy *Kulaks* had dug their toes in and were refusing to grow corn; hordes of deserters were swarming back from the front and idle, unpaid, hungry, were turning themselves into robber bands. Voroshilov was openly recruiting detachments of Red Guards from them in the streets, and Trotsky was hurling his fiery diatribes at the Government.

In spite of these activities the Bolshevik Party still formed a very small minority. The election results in the Provincial *Zemstvos* showed satisfaction with the Coalition and it looked as if the Liberals were going to weather the storm, for the great majority of the people were undoubtedly behind them. Lenin's arrest was ordered, as he employed himself entirely in sabotaging the Government's every move, but he took refuge over the border in Finland and continued to direct the operations of the Party from there. Voroshilov was sent to the Don Basin to strengthen the Bolsheviks in the industrial area he knew so well.

As soon as he arrived at Lougansk he flung himself into the struggle against the Mensheviks. They held a majority in the Soviet there. Clim got himself appointed to his old job in the factory so that he could be elected to the Soviet; the workers were slackening as a consequence of the Revolution and every man now considering himself his own boss, turned up at any hours that suited him, but Voroshilov would have none of this. The work must go on; the factory's output would be needed every bit as much by the Bolsheviks when they came to power as by the old Government, and their hero of pre-Revolution days soon had the men with him.

The Mensheviks were in a big majority at Lougansk and they had a paper of their own called the *Zaria,* which consistently agitated against the Bolsheviks. Voroshilov, well aware of the power of press propaganda, immediately set about the production of an opposition sheet and became editor-in-chief of a Bolshevik organ called the *Donetzki Proletari.*

The Mensheviks did their utmost to suppress it by buying up the owner of the printing press, but Voroshilov and his friends lugged the man out of bed one night and compelled him to turn the handle of the hand-press himself, without stopping until morning, as a lesson; after which they had no more trouble with him. Very soon the tide of opinion was turning in favour of the Bolsheviks and Voroshilov succeeded in gaining a majority in the local Soviet.

Night after night there were meetings when the workers
spurred on the orators with cries of 'Go on, go on, don't stop',
so that the meetings lasted until dawn and the men had to go
straight from them to the early shift. During all these days of
the struggle, Cherviakov tells us 'Voroshilov never fell into the
tone of the professional agitator, using revolutionary phrase-
ology. He always spoke clearly, concisely and to the point, in
explanation of the principles which Lenin had laid down.'

Not content with his activities in Lougansk Voroshilov
established contact with all the villages which formed the railway network of the Don Basin and went as well to the greater
centres of Kharkov and Ekaterinoslav where he initiated the
formation of Party centres. He became by far the most important member of the Party in the whole of that great industrial area of Russia.

Kerensky had put new life into the Government and it is a
great mistake to suppose that because he was afterwards
ousted he was a weak and incapable man. During his tour of
the front he personally addressed hundreds of soldiers' meetings and so strong was his personality that, almost single-
handed, he managed to reanimate the fighting spirit in the
Russian Army. He disbanded many of the regiments that were
disaffected and reformed their better elements into others,
encouraged the officers to take a firm line with the men again
after their having surrendered their authority to committees
of soldiers for many weeks from fear of their lives, and definitely put limits to the rights of these Soldiers' Committees.
It was soon found that if these committees were taken firmly
in hand and their authority limited, but their leaders listened
to, far from their hampering reorganisation, they served an
extremely useful purpose in bridging many points of difference which stood between the officers and men, thus facili-
tating the re-establishment of good-will and understanding all
round. In a very short time Kerensky performed an absolutely herculean labour; fraternisation with the enemy stopped, the 'go-home' movement ceased, and the army became an
effective weapon once again. The Germans were held and, on
June 18th, a great advance was made by the Russians on the
Galician front.

The very next day the sailors arrested their officers at Sevastopol and demanded the resignation of Admiral Koltchak
from the command of the Black Sea Fleet. Lenin's Party-men

scored a success there, and even in Petrograd revolution fever never abated.

There followed another Government crisis in July. The Ukranians wished to set up a separate independent state to be governed from their ancient capital of Kiev. The Liberal Ministers saw that to assent to this meant depriving Russia of her principal source of wealth: the great granary of the Ukraine. They would not commit themselves to such a vital decision until the matter had been placed before the Constituent Assembly. The problem of holding elections in the army during a war presented the very greatest difficulties, yet the troops could not be denied their right to vote. The first Provisional Government had appointed a special commission to frame new electoral laws, but this was still sitting and reported that there was no hope of being able to summon a Constituent Assembly before the end of the year.

The Bolsheviks seized upon this split in the Ministry as a pretext for an armed uprising. The revolt was crushed, but order was only restored by Prince Lvov and most of the other Liberal ministers resigning. A new Government was formed with Kerensky as Premier and representatives of all parties in it except the extreme Right, which for the first time was beginning to manifest itself in the old nobility and officer class, and the extreme Left, being the Bolsheviks under Lenin. The Socialist Mensheviks at last had the power for which they had been striving all their lives, but they were still committed to the war and were saturated with all sorts of humanitarian doctrines which were utterly impossible to put into practice now that the whole country was verging on ruin. They had plenty of idealistic theories, but no concrete policy to offer.

The July revolt taught the Bolsheviks that, although their own numbers were small, they could find plenty of support among the war-weary, also among the hooligans and run-away soldiers who thronged the streets of Petrograd. Against the wishes of his colleagues Lenin opened the ranks of the Party to those dangerous elements and every sort of criminal and ruffian was allowed to join, providing he was prepared to give absolute and unquestioning obedience to the orders of the Party. Lenin now had the bit between his teeth. For thirty years he had laboured, plotted and suffered in the hope that he would one day be the leader of a Workers' Government in his country. It was clear now that only the extremists among the proletariat wanted him; the great majority were quite satisfied to accept half-measures from such leaders as Plekhanov or Kerensky, but Lenin was determined that they should have him whether they wanted him or not. If there was no other way to climb to power he would do so on the backs of the criminal scum of the gutters, but power he was determined to have and absolute power at that.

One would have imagined that Germany needed every man she could muster to resist Haig's assaults at Passchendaele, but at Main Headquarters old Hindenburg performed miracles. In a brilliant campaign, planned on his own special lines of massing troops only at vital points on an extended front when facing an enemy with superior numbers Von Falkenhayn and Von Mackensen had overrun Roumania. German troops were stiffening the Bulgarian front in the Salonika theatre and others under Liman von Sanders were operating with the Turks, yet somehow Hindenburg managed to find the men to stem the new Russian onslaught. On July 19th he ordered a counter attack from the south-west of Brody, and Kerensky's offensive collapsed. The troops of the Central Powers advanced on a wide front and by August they had overrun the whole of Galicia and the Bukovina.

The Russians were still game, however, and retiring in good order, but General Kornilov, who had succeeded General Brussilov as Commander-in-Chief, now attempted a *coup d'état* against the Government in the interests of the Constitutional Monarchists.

It was nipped in the bud, but had extremely grave results because, following so soon upon the abortive Bolshevik rising, it demonstrated very clearly that the country was threatened by one of two evils, either a Military or a Bolshevik dictatorship.

Both of these parties still formed only small minorities and both of them were completely outside the Government, but the threat of their presence tended to divide the great mass of the people into two separate camps. Where before they had given their willing allegiance to the Liberal-Socialist leaders in Office, they now tended to take definite sides and support the extremists either of the Right or the Left from fear that the opposing body might gain power.

The utter and criminal failure of the British super massed attacks on the western front at Passchendaele is now fully demonstrated. Quite apart from failing to gain its objective this three months' butchery did not even serve to pin down sufficient divisions to handicap seriously German operations elsewhere. On September 1st, right in the middle of the third battle of Ypres, Hindenburg felt himself strong enough to decide on a fresh advance in the east on a sufficiently large scale to justify the hope of putting Russia bang out of the war.

The German navy was called out to co-operate with the land forces under General Von Mackensen. The attack was well planned and entirely successful; the Russian Northern army crumpled up and the Germans invaded the Baltic provinces. Their fleet took the island of Oesel in the Gulf of Riga and their troops occupied the town.

The Russian army was in full retreat; Petrograd—as St. Petersburg was now called—was thrown into a panic. It looked as though the invaders would soon be hammering on the gates of the capital itself. All that was left of the structure of State began to crack and fall to pieces. The railways came to a standstill, the postal and telegraph services broke down, nobody outside the Bolshevik Party would any longer accept orders from any one else, and on all sides unauthorised groups of people were seizing power locally as 'Committees for Saving the Revolution'.

By encouraging the most disreputable elements of the population to join their ranks, the membership of the Bolshevik Party had been swollen from 80,000 at the end of May to 200,000 early in October. Even this figure was only a tiny percentage of Russia's 180,000,000 inhabitants, and Hindenburg had accounted for as great a number of Russians in a single one of his major victories, but the strength of the Party lay in the fact that it was well organised, intensely active, and every member of it was sworn to unquestioning obedience to his leaders.

The Party now had a majority in the Petrograd Soviet; the Soviet elected a Military Revolutionary Committee, and the troops of the garrison passed a resolution declaring their allegiance to it. Trotsky, now President of the Soviet, took over the Smolny Institute as Soviet Headquarters and began to issue orders from it as though he was already a minister and the place a Government office. Lenin returned from Finland to the outskirts of the city to be close at hand.

A tremendous propaganda campaign was launched in an

endeavour to make the people believe that the Party were the only possible saviours of Russia. In speech and print they screamed from every street corner: 'We stand for immediate peace—for all land being handed over to the peasants—for the homeless being housed in the mansions of the rich—for the factories and the banks becoming the property of the workers.' They sent their detachments of Red Guards out to drill openly in the streets to spread the impression that the Party was much stronger than it actually was.

Before the October Revolution the men of the Don Basin elected Voroshilov to represent them in the Bolshevik councils at Petrograd. When action was decided upon he sent his subordinates a telegram to notify them that a truckload of arms was on its way, but the Menshevik Government representatives were still in power at Lougansk, and his friend Kravtzov tells us what happened:

'The train was seized by the authorities and a strong guard with rifles placed over it, but Clim had sent us the arms and we had to have them. There were eighteen of us armed only with revolvers, yet we decided to attack the station. The truck containing the arms was surrounded by a triple cordon of Menshevik guards. When we appeared their leader cried: 'If you try anything we'll shoot you down,' but we shouted back: "Shoot away, we mean to take it."

'They began to pull the truck down towards the shops, but one of our fellows managed to get in among them unseen. When we attacked the guards turned their rifles on us and we were beaten back. But our man succeeded in getting the truck open while they were occupied, lugged out a machine-gun and turned it on them. We attacked again and the truck was ours. That was how we got proper arms for our fighting squad.'

On October 25th the All-Russia Assembly of Soviets was due to meet in Petrograd. Lenin knew that the Bolsheviks stood no chance of having a majority in it and that it would carry more weight than the Petrograd Soviet which the Party controlled. He decided to act before the All-Russia Assembly could meet and demonstrate that the bulk of the workers were Mensheviks. At an inner council of the Party he made his intention clear. Practically all the leaders were against him. They said the time was not yet ripe; their last armed rising had been a failure, another so soon was too big a risk, the Party was much too small to dominate the country and retain power

even if they could get it temporarily. Trotsky was nervous;
Zinoviev and Kamenev definitely opposed to the attempt.
Stalin and Voroshilov said little; they were not windbags, but
they were both determined, proved and trusted men, old comrades upon whom Lenin knew he could rely. They stood there
with their hands upon their automatics ready to support their
leader. Lenin's iron will prevailed.

On the night of October 24th the Party issued a proclamation: 'The Provisional Government is deposed. The Powers of
the State have passed into the hands of the Petrograd Soviet of
Workers and Soldiers' Deputies, and the Military Revolutionary Committee.' On the 25th there was a little street fighting, but the mob were on the side of the Bolsheviks and
Liberal-Socialist resistance was soon overcome. By night all
the principal Government institutions and offices were in Bolshevik hands, and on October 26th a new Government was
proclaimed, 'The Soviet of the People's Commissars.' The
numerically small 'Party' had achieved power on their programme of 'Peace, bread, freedom and equality for all'. At the
head of the new Government stood Lenin, who later was to
become as 'absolute' as any Czar.

# 10

# The Peace that was no Peace

The Bolshevik Party now contained many undesirable elements, mainly among its more recent recruits, but its leaders,
Lenin, Trotsky, Stalin, Zinoviev, Bukharin and the rest, must
not be regarded as a bunch of ex-gaol-birds, which, in fact,
they were, or even as just one more group of politicians who
had seized power in a country where the people were dissatis-
fied with existing conditions.

They were very much more than that, because their outlook
was not national but international. They hardly thought of
themselves as Russians at all, but as citizens of the world into
whose hands it had been given, after many years of struggle,
to voice the feelings and ambitions of the great mass of the
people of every race and colour on the face of the earth.

There is a difference of thirteen days between the old Russian calendar and ours. This accounts for references to the
February and October Revolutions when according to our
dates these took place in March and November. The first act
of the Bolsheviks on coming to power on November 8th, 1917
(our date), was to call for immediate peace negotiations, based
on no annexations and no indemnities, among all belligerent
nations.

That the Bolshevik leaders were utterly sincere is beyond
question. Stalin was appointed to the post of Commissar of
Nationalities for the especial purpose of releasing minorities
such as the Ukrainians, Finns, Caucasians, etc., from their ties
with the Mother Country and enabling them to set up their
own separate self-governed states. In pursuance of their ideal
the Bolsheviks were willing that 'Great' Russia should sever
herself from all the conquests of the Czars; they were prepared to give away the accumulated riches of centuries, the
coal mines of the Don Basin, the granary of the Ukraine and
the mineral wealth of Siberia.

They spoke every bit as much for the Chinese coolie, the

Welsh miner, the Indian dock labourer and the German mechanic as for their own people, when they said: 'What have you, whose wish is for a settled life with regular work at a fair wage on which you can support your wives and families, to gain by war? How can it benefit you that your country annexes another great slab of territory, that your war lords present each other with fresh titles and decorations, or that your merchant masters pile up more millions by securing fresh markets for the disposal of their goods?'

Had they been listened to, countless lives might have been saved, but the Allies were convinced that they could beat the Central Powers, and the Central Powers still believed that they could smash the Allies. Moreover the appeal was issued by a group of professional agitators and revolutionaries; men who for years had been associated with bomb throwing and a policy which threatened to wreck all existing institutions. Their call for a World Peace Conference was ignored.

Russia was still one of the Allies, but her partners did not behave well towards the new régime. In the case of the Provisional Government, which followed the abdication of the Czar, their attitude had been very different. Russia was the sick man among them, 'Doctor' Kerensky and his friends looked capable of pulling the country round, so their Government was recognised immediately and every facility of the Allies placed at its disposal to strengthen it in the eyes of its own people. To the statesmen of the Allies the Bolsheviks did not appear at all a similar proposition, but just a cranky, down-at-heel crowd who had taken advantage of Russia's internal troubles to jump on the engine of the train without any authority from the railway company or the passengers.

The statesmen concerned can hardly be blamed for their view seeing that, during their exile, the Bolshevik leaders had given them constant trouble by their pacifist agitations and endeavours to sabotage the war. Chicherin and several of the London group were at that time actually in Brixton Prison. On the Bolsheviks appointing him their representative there arose, for the first time since the reign of Queen Anne, the curious phenomenon of an ambassador of a 'friendly' power sitting in a British gaol. Even so the Government refused to release him and only did so when Trotsky, who had been appointed Commissar for Foreign Affairs, took a strong stand

and would not issue further visas for British subjects to leave Russia until his colleagues were freed.

The French proved equally antagonistic, refusing to use the word 'People's' in addressing the Soviet Government until the Bolsheviks began to return, unopened, all correspondence which did not bear the word. The Americans, Japanese and, in fact, all the Allied ambassadors in Petrograd declined to have any official dealings with the members of the new Government; instead they transacted such business as could not be avoided through semi-official deputies. In this capacity Mr. Bruce Lockhart became the principal agent for the British, Colonel Raymond Robins for the United States, and Captain Sadoul for the French.

The fact that the Allied Governments would not recognise the new Russian 'People's' Government militated tremendously against its general acceptance by the Russian people themselves. Practically every hand was against the Bolsheviks, with the exception of their own numerically small Party, together with considerable numbers of disbanded soldiers and casual workers who could be of little assistance in establishing the new régime as a working and recognised entity throughout Russia and the world.

They were, however, a group of extremely determined men and suffered none of the inhibitions common to the old ruling caste or average politician who had served a long apprenticeship before reaching office. They quite bluntly called a spade a spade and acted with considerable resolution. Moreover they had one really strong card: *the majority of the Russian people were behind them in their insistence on making peace*.

Their disappointment that the workers of other nations did not follow the Russian example and revolt against their war lords was considerable; in fact, it hardly seemed possible to the Bolsheviks themselves that they would be able to continue in power without some outside support of this nature; but they hoped this might eventuate at any moment and in the meantime they set about bringing their own war to an official conclusion.

On December 5th *pourparlers* were begun at Brest-Litovsk. In the subsequent negotiations all the Central Powers were represented; their principal spokesmen being Chancellor von Kuhlmann for Germany and Count Czernin for Austria-Hungary, but their policy was entirely dominated by General

Max von Hoffman. The leading representatives of the Bolsheviks were Trotsky, Kamenev and Radek.

The Bolsheviks wanted to open up on political questions immediately, but the Germans said that they were only prepared to talk upon purely military matters. At Trotsky's suggestion the renewal of discussion was postponed for a further week in order to give the Allies another chance to send representatives so that, even if they came with the greatest antagonism in their hearts towards the Central Powers, there might at least be some chance of their getting together and finding grounds for calling off the general massacre.

He begged them, even if they refused to participate in the negotiations, at least to 'state openly before the world, clearly, definitely, and correctly, in the name of what purpose must the people of Europe bleed during a fourth year of the war.' The Allies continued to ignore him and on December 13th Armistice consultations were entered into by Russia alone with the Central Powers.

Finding they could not save the world from its insanity the Bolsheviks still determined to do what they could to lessen its effects; their first stipulation was that the Central Powers should not remove any of their troops from the eastern front for the purpose of killing more French, English, American and Italians in other sectors. The Germans agreed to accept this provision for one month.

In Petrograd the Government was far from having the situation properly in hand. Mobs of hooligans were looting the drink shops and houses of the rich. On December 19th the city was declared to be in a 'state of siege'. The Mensheviks had a majority in most of the local Government bodies in the provinces and refused to accept the orders of the Central Soviet. In the south General Kornilov was already actively engaged in organising trained troops for a counter-revolution, and General Denikin was equally busy in the Kuban recruiting White Cossacks for a similar purpose.

Yet on December 22nd when peace discussions at Brest-Litovsk were actually opened Trotsky talked more like a victor than the emissary of a tottering Government in a defeated nation. His first demand was that the sessions should be open to the public; he refused absolutely to participate in one of the old hole-and-corner conferences by which the peoples represented were not allowed to know of the decisions by their rulers which might have the result of placing lives in jeopardy at some future date. The Germans greatly disliked this idea of the new diplomacy but gave way. Trotsky then insisted on yet another week's delay to give the Allies a last chance to attend the Conference even if they came with their swords in their hands still dripping blood.

Once more they refused to listen to his appeal and he declared in disgust: 'If the war was ever waged for self defence, it has long ago ceased to be that for both sides. When Great Britain conquers African colonies, Baghdad and Jerusalem it cannot be a war of defence. When Germany occupies Serbia, Belgium, Poland, Lithuania, Roumania and the Moon Islands it cannot be war of defence. This is a war for the division of the world. Now it is clear; clearer than ever.' It must, however, be borne in mind that although Trotsky's first demands for time were completely ingenuous he was now beginning to welcome postponement on account of himself and his colleagues. Their situation was going from bad to worse. It seemed that only another revolution outside Russia could save them. Lenin was overjoyed when they passed their seventy-first day in power as, by so doing, they beat the record of the French Communist Government established in Paris after the 1870 war.

General Von Ludendorff, from having been Hindenburg's Chief of Staff in the early days of the war, had remained with him after his transfer to Main Headquarters, and was now, perhaps, the strongest influence in the councils of the Central Powers. He was undoubtedly a very brilliant soldier and it has recently been the tendency to give him the credit for Hindenburg's victories. This is by no means just, as the great battles which destroyed the main Russian armies were undoubtedly directed by Von Hindenburg; but Ludendorff, besides being an extremely capable general, was also a strong, hard, arrogant man. It was he who flogged the weakening Allies of Germany again and again to fresh assaults and he who was very largely responsible for maintaining the 'Will to Victory' among the German people. Although he treated statesmen and politicians with open contempt, the exigencies of the campaign enabled him to bring enormous pressure to bear upon those of the Central Powers and, in actual fact, he played an even more important rôle as a statesman himself in the latter years of the war than he did as a general.

At this date Von Ludendorff believed that the war might still be won by the Central Powers, so he evinced no more desires for a general peace than the Allies. As it was now quite clear that they had no intention of appearing at Brest-Litovsk, Ludendorff instructed his mouthpiece, General Von Hoffman, that the whole basis of the peace with Russia must be one which would give the greatest advantages to Germany for carrying on the struggle against the Allies if need be, for another two or three years.

The Bolsheviks recognised the independence of the Finnish Republic on January 4th, 1918, and freely surrendered the Ukraine into the keeping of its own governing body, the 'Rada'. They had been half-promised by the Germans, who were in occupation, that Poland, Lithuania, Latvia and Esthonia should also become self-governing states. The Germans might have been willing to barter on that basis at a World Peace Conference, but now the war was going on they declared quite frankly that they had no intention of evacuating these territories.

Trotsky was furious and put up a remarkably good show, but Von Hoffmann proved adamant. The Central Powers were not even bothering to stick to the terms of the truce. In Finland the Germans landed a considerable force under General von der Goltz to support the Finnish anti-Bolsheviks, then busy suppressing the Finnish Reds with the utmost brutality. German troops were still filtering through into the Ukraine and using terrorist tactics to subdue the population. Roumania, still nominally Russia's 'Friend and Ally', had taken the opportunity to seize Bessarabia; and the Turks were overrunning the Caucasus.

However, the Bolsheviks were not altogether idle. Immediately hostilities ceased they had instructed all their troops to fraternise with the enemy, and by printing hundreds of thousands of pamphlets in German, Austrian and Hungarian for distribution among them they were endeavouring to bring about revolutions in the enemy countries.

The Peace Conference at Brest-Litovsk did not seem to be getting anywhere, so Trotsky retired in considerable anxiety to Petrograd. At a session of the Central Committee of the Party three alternatives were put forward: (1) to sign a separate peace with the Central Powers agreeing to their annexations of territory, (2) to raise the country in a revolutionary war against them, (3) to adopt an entirely new line of policy, which was to declare the war ended and demobilise the army but to refuse to sign any treaty at all.

Lenin was in favour of peace at any price, because he could not see the young Revolution having any chance of survival unless it could turn its attention immediately to home affairs. Bukharian and the majority were for rallying the proletariat to fight a holy war with the object of freeing their comrades in the invaded territories from the German yoke. Trotsky was in favour of the last alternative. Eventually a compromise was decided upon and a policy agreed of dragging out the peace negotiations as long as possible.

The Germans countered this by opening separate negotiations with the Ukrainian 'Rada', as the Ukraine was the territory they really wanted and the 'Rada' was willing to invite them in to save itself from the Bolsheviks in the Ukraine who were rising against it.

The Ukrainian Reds got the best of the business and drove the 'Rada' out of Kiev, so when Trotsky appeared at the resumed session of the peace conference on January 30th he was able to bring representatives of the new Red Ukrainian Government with him and thus present a solid front to the Germans.

The delegates of the Central Powers gave a full-dress reception and invited the Bolsheviks. Trotsky was most terribly perturbed; his proletarian conscience boggled horribly at the thought of having to put on a dress suit. He telegraphed Lenin for advice. The Big Shot wired back: 'Go in a petticoat if you can only get us peace.'

The Germans spiked Trotsky's guns by ignoring recent events in the Ukraine and concluding a paper peace on February 9th with the representatives of the now defunct 'Rada'. It was the Ukraine they wanted for its food supplies and access to Baku for oil; they were not interested in a peace with Russia unless they could dictate it.

Trotsky's only recourse was to adopt his own policy and, on February 10th, he declared: 'We are out of the war, but we refuse to sign this Peace Treaty which Germany and Austro-Hungary are writing with the sword on the bodies of living nations.' On February the 18th the Central Powers ordered a resumption of the invasion of Russia upon all fronts.

There were further critical meetings of the Central Communist Committee and stormy scenes among its members. Lenin was still for peace, Bukharin for a holy war, Trotsky wanted to call in the Allies to their assistance. At one meeting which Lenin could not attend a scribbled note arrived from him: 'Please add my vote in favour of the receipt of support and arms from the Anglo-French Imperialist Brigands.' But even while the appeals to the Allies were being made a telegram was despatched to Berlin protesting against the new offensive and declaring the Bolshevik readiness, under constraint, to sign a dictated peace.

The Allies shilly-shallied, and on the 23rd there arrived from Berlin new and much harsher terms than had been offered in the first place. The Council voted upon them, fifteen members being present. Lenin got his way with seven votes against four cast by Bukharin and his friends who wished to continue the war; four members, including Trotsky and Dzerzhinski, abstained from voting.

Bukharin resigned from the Committeee in a rage and now had all the Menshevik elements behind him. On March 11th the Government moved to Moscow. A congress of Soviets was held on the 14th–16th and the question of peace or war put to it. Lenin triumphed by securing 784 votes against Bukharin's 261. Russia accepted 'Peace on the end of the Sword' and was now technically out of the war.

That, however, was very far from being the actual case. Germany had annexed 400,000 square miles of Russian territory which contained sixty millions of her people, just about one-third of her entire population, and these were by no means willing to submit to the invader. Groups of disbanded sailors and soldiers were forming themselves into Red Guard units, and the workers in the factory areas were arming to protect their homes. Voroshilov and other members of the Party, who like him, were not on the Central Committee, hurried to various districts for the purpose of leading the Holy War of the Revolution which Bukharin had advocated in the first place. As ever 'Clim' was completely loyal to Lenin, but he had such immense influence in the Don Basin that his post in this time of crisis was obviously there, and in any case Red forces had to be organised to resist the Whites.

The Germans came to an understanding with the White General, Krasnov, to suppress these risings in the Ukraine, and the Allies, who had tended to grow colder and colder towards the Bolshevik régime, now began to associate themselves definitely with the White General, Denikin.

In spite of the fact that he was still maintaining an army of half a million men in Russia, Hindenburg commenced his great drive for Paris on March 21st. The first attack was launched against the junction of the British and French armies opposite St. Quentin. It was planned with considerable skill as, instead of the old practice of sending over long lines of infantry on a wide front, which could be dealt with as they advanced, the German troops were launched in mass at various points, each body being a considerable distance from its neighbours.

They opened the attack with the biggest artillery bombardment which had ever been known in the history of the world and then launched their columns, being materially helped by the fog, which made it extremely difficult for the British to find out exactly what was happening. The German columns, having penetrated at certain points without the necessity of fighting their way across considerable lengths of the British front line at all, then joined up about two miles behind it and thus were able to take the major portion of the British infantry in the rear. It was the old game of encirclement instead of direct assault, but carried out on this occasion in a large number of local operations instead of by one great outflanking movement. By midday the front of the British Vth Army was completely shattered, and by evening it was in full retreat.

Much controversy has taken place as to where the responsibility lay. General Gough, who commanded the Vth Army, was superseded in his command a few days later, but he maintained that the fault was with the British G.H.Q., which persistently refused him adequate reserves and denied him sufficient troops or material to build an adequate second line of defence, upon which it had been agreed the real battle, that everybody knew was coming, should be fought.

Two facts are beyond question. *G.H.Q. knew the attack was coming and knew where it was coming.* It was expected daily for the best part of three weeks before it actually arrived. Every German prisoner taken had been instructed to give information that it was going to happen to-morrow, or the day after, and in consequence of this the British infantry were made to stand-to at an exceptionally early hour morning after morning, which greatly contributed to the undermining of their morale and their resistance to the attack when it eventually developed. The whole front was in a state of jitters, resulting from the Germans' deliberate policy to make it so.

Further, there was no second line of defence in the real meaning of the term. Innumerable people who were actually present at this battle definitely state that to be a fact, whatever marking Sir Douglas Haig and General Gough may have had upon their maps. Once the advance front was broken through the British Vth Army was powerless to defend itself, and no reserves were forthcoming until the French came to its assistance some days later.

It is true that in spite of their colossal losses at Passchendaele in the previous autumn the British had taken over a further sector of the line from the French just after Christmas, but even so, fresh levies were constantly arriving, and Haig's carefully nursed cavalry army was still grooming its horses somewhere miles behind the front, so the responsibility for the Germans breaking through to so great a depth lies entirely with the British G.H.Q.

The Germans penetrated the western front to the depth of about thirty miles during their first attack, but immediately Hindenburg found that his troops were being held by the Allied reserves he adopted his old policy of breaking off the battle, digging in, and concentrating his masses elsewhere.

A second big break-through was made in the early part of April south of Ypres and so serious was the situation that the British now made preparations to evacuate that blood-soaked ruin, although they had held it, purely on political grounds as the last city of Belgium remaining to the Allies, against all sound military principle, and against the advice of that fine soldier General Sir Horace Smith-Dorrien, who was brought home early in the war.

Owing to this critical situation on the western front it became more imperative than ever that German forces should be detained in the east, and in the Allied countries there arose two schools of thought as to how this should be done.

Mr. Bruce Lockhart, Captain Sadoul and Colonel Robins, who were in actual touch with the Bolshevik leaders, were in favour of formally acknowledging the Bolshevik Government and giving them such support as would enable them to conduct a war against the Germans and Austrians for the liberation of the many Russian provinces and great numbers of Russian people who were now under the heel of the invader. The British, French and American ambassadors, who were not in personal touch with the Bolsheviks, pursued a more or less neutral policy, while their Governments at home were tending more and more to take a definitely anti-Bolshevik attitude.

The other school of thought was strongly sponsored by Marshal Foch and the French, only regarded lukewarmly by the Americans, who expressed a democratic sympathy with the Russian 'People's' Government, but received much backing from the English. It was that the Bolsheviks were not to be relied upon; whereas the White generals who had risen against them were far more malleable and would undoubtedly continue a war against the Germans if they could be backed sufficiently strongly to establish them as the rulers of Russia. Mr. Winston Churchill was the British champion of the White generals' cause, and there is little doubt that, as usual, he was using large maps.

Mr. Churchill was, perhaps, the most persistent, determined and dangerous antagonist, not excepting Monsieur Clemenceau and Mr. Lloyd George, that the Central Powers were faced with in the war.

For three years before the war even started Mr. Churchill, as First Lord of the Admiralty, had been preparing for 'Der Tag' with a thoroughness which left most German generals right out of the running.

In this century British naval reviews have only been held, on average, once in seven years and one had been held in 1911; but on the excuse that His Majesty King George V might like to see his fleet, Mr. Churchill mobilised the most powerful navy the world has ever seen, for a review in home waters ten days before the war started. From that moment he had the Germans cold as far as three-fifths of the earth's surface was concerned. Except for scattered cruisers and submarines the German Navy was never able to put its nose out of doors for more than twenty-four hours without being driven back again. The ports of the seven seas were open to the Allies, but closed to the Central Powers, and, in a mild way, the blockade which finally won the war began.

Directly he knew of the German wheel through Belgium which threatened Paris and the Channel ports, Mr. Churchill, having already dealt with his own province, the sea, took to the land. With a vision doubtless inherited from his famous ancestor, the great Duke of Marlborough, he saw that if a strong striking force could be thrown into Antwerp the German flank could be turned; their whole army rolled up and thrown into confusion.

The British Expeditionary Force was sent to France because Kitchener, who was a great viceroy, but does not appear to have studied Clausewitz, thought it should offer itself to the German frontal attack. It was left unsupported by the French and would have been annihilated but for General Sir Horace Smith-Dorrien's magnificent stand against terrific odds at Le Cateau. Mr. Churchill pleaded that instead of reinforcements being used in a similar manner they should be sent to Antwerp. The War Office of that day had a one-track mind and disagreed.

As First Lord of the Admiralty Mr. Churchill could not control soldiers, but so strongly did he feel that he was right that he decided to employ the Royal Naval Volunteer Reserve. This consisted largely of newly joined, untrained recruits; but men with rifles in their hands were better than nothing and Mr. Churchill flung them into Antwerp, accompanying them himself.

It was not to be expected that such a force could put up an indefinite resistance to the trained troops and heavy guns of the enemy, so they were evacuated again a little later but their presence, while there, served as a most serious threat to the German Army *because they were in its rear,* and the German High Command could not possibly know that the War Office might not, after all, send further divisions of its regulars to Mr. Churchill's support.

Had that occurred it is quite possible that the Germans would have been forced to evacuate Belgium in the early days of the war. As it was they were compelled to detach several corps from their all-important right wing in order to deal with Mr. Churchill. The occupation of those troops at Antwerp, and the time gained, saved us the Channel ports.

It was Mr. Churchill who brought Admiral Beatty, our greatest fighting sailor in the 1914–1918 war, to the front, Mr. Churchill backed him through thick and thin and those who were at Jutland with the Admiral said of him: 'It is as though Nelson were come again.'

Mr. Churchill's receptivity to new ideas and great plans was again demonstrated by his enthusiastic support of tanks from the very first moment this new arm, which possessed such enormous possibilities, was brought to his notice. He wanted great fleets of them constructed and launched in one big surprise attack; but the soldiers fought him tooth and nail. When tanks were forced upon them they only used them in driblets, thereby allowing the enemy to accustom themselves and adapt their defences to these land-ships. Haig's mind was still so far away in the mist of old-fashioned cavalry operations that he would not even permit the transfer of 9000 men to this God-given new arm in the summer of 1917 when on one day alone, by his frontal attacks, he lost 60,000 men in the mire of Passchendaele.

When a deadlock had arisen upon the western front Mr. Churchill saw that Turkey was the weak spot in the Central Powers, and planned the forcing of the Dardanelles. At the date when the fleet commenced their operations the Gallipoli Peninsula was almost unoccupied. With proper military co-operation the peninsula could have been seized and Constantinople directly threatened. As it was Kitchener bungled; his transports arrived a month late, and by the time they turned up Turkish forces were occupying the peninsula. In the end, however, Churchill's genius for planning on an enormous scale, instead of battering his head, as the soldiers did so persistently, against places like Hill 60, brought the war to an end. He had always sought a decision in the eastern theatres against Germany's weaker allies and it was Bulgaria's collapse which led to the break-up of the Central Powers.

As can be imagined, when he was faced with the Russian situation he took the very broadest view. It was obvious that if the Central Powers were allowed to overrun the country they were quite capable of penetrating to Siberia. This would give them domination over nearly one fifth of the world's land surface. With German thoroughness they would undoubtedly exploit Russia's enormous undeveloped wealth of raw materials, and the produce of the Russian lands would bring new life to the half-starved populations of the enemy cities, thereby nullifying the Allies' blockade. The Central Powers would be in a position to fight on almost indefinitely and with shrewd vitality resist even the masses of American troops which were now appearing in the field. Intervention had to be undertaken and intervention on a big scale.

Further, if a new eastern front could be established it would not only hold many German divisions in the Baltic provinces and the north, but the line was so long that it would also offer new prospects to able generals for making a break-through in the south which would enable the Allies to overrun the Balkans and put Germany's associates out of the war.

Mr. Churchill, however, saw even further than that. From the first day of their régime the Bolsheviks had endeavoured to disrupt the Central Powers by intensive revolutionary propaganda and their efforts were only confined to the Central Powers because they had access to them through the fraternising troops. They made it quite clear that they intended to take the same steps against the capitalist Governments of the Allies at the first opportunity.

They did not disguise their intention of confiscating the property of the rich and utterly uprooting the capitalist system throughout the whole world and, although their Central Government cannot be held entirely responsible, having regard to the hopelessly demoralised state of the country, bands of soldiers and mobs with Bolshevik sympathies were already looting, killing and performing the most horrible atrocities upon members of the upper classes in every part of the new Soviet State.

The French particularly, and many English statesmen well acquainted with the facts of history, could not disregard the Red Terror which had gripped France after the Revolution of 1789. Russia appeared to be a parallel case; the same weak Monarch who had granted half a Constitution when it was too late, dismissed his Assembly after he had agreed that it should be called, and endeavoured to suppress it when it met again without his authority. The same Assembly taking power into its hands and deposing the autocrat. The same period of uncertainty while a Liberal Government under Kerensky tried to stabilise Russia just as the Girondins and Mirabeau had tried to stabilise France; the same little clique of professional agitators eventually upsetting the moderates and climbing to power upon the scum of the gutters. In Lenin, Trotsky and the rest, the French and Mr. Churchill saw another Robespierre-Marat group of terrorists. There was very considerable justification for their decision that the world must be protected from such men at all costs. That the Bolsheviks have since come out on top does not affect the matter. If the Allied armies had consorted with them in 1918 or 1919 they might well have returned to their own nations in such a state as to precipitate a general revolution.

Between the two theories of intervention; that of Mr. Bruce Lockhart and his associates who wished to help the Bolsheviks against the Germans, and that of Mr. Churchill and his associates who wished to crush the Bolsheviks in order to re-establish the Whites, who in turn could be brought against the Germans, the responsible leaders of the Allies got themselves into a hopeless tangle. M. Litvinov was officially recognised in London as the Soviet ambassador, but the French flatly refused to acknowledge Kamenev as Soviet ambassador to France.

The Czar, Czarina, and five of their unfortunate children were first exiled to Tobolsk and a few months later taken to Ekaterinburg where they were shot by order of the local Soviet; the Kremlin Government disclaiming all responsibility. The evidence makes it impossible to regard Nicolas II as a competent sovereign, but anti-Monarchist propaganda was responsible for much of the baseless calumny which has blackened his and his wife's names. He was a model of the domestic virtues and she is spoken of as a kindly and charming woman by those who knew her. The news of their murder strengthened anti-Bolshevik feeling abroad and the Czarist Embassies continued to exercise much influence although they represented a Government which was no longer in existence. Few people seemed to think that the Bolshevik régime could possibly last.

In March, Trotsky left the Foreign Office to become Commissar for War, and Chicherin took his place. The Bolsheviks then agreed to accept the Allies's assistance in clearing out the Germans and Trotsky busied himself organising the new Red Army. The Turks were in the Caucasus and the local Mensheviks invited the Germans in to take over the oil wells at Baku. The Allied Military Attachés were called in to organise the Red forces and an Allied mission arrived at Murmansk in the north to arrange for operations through Finland against Von der Goltz's German forces there.

On the other hand, Japan went ahead on her own by landing a large force in Siberia and, under the auspices of the British, an anti-Bolshevik Far Eastern Government was established in Pekin with the Czarist Admiral, Koltchak, at its head. An anti-Bolshevik British mission, under General Dunsterville, set out from Persia, working up to the Caspian Sea in order to assist the Czarist General, Denikin, and the French promised their support to the White Cossack commanders. It seemed that the Allies intended to have a private war on their own, and even to pit troops of the same nations against each other.

That, in fact, is more or less what happened. British, French and American officers trained and assisted Red troops which went out to shoot down other British, French and American officers who were doing their best to organise and help the Whites.

A similarly fantastic situation arose in Arabia. With the idea of harassing the Turks, Colonel T. E. Lawrence went on a mission to Husein, the Sherif of Mecca, while his friend, Captain Harold Armstrong, went on a mission under the direction of St. John Philby to the Emir Ibn'Saud. Lawrence was backed by the Foreign Office and Armstrong by the India Office. Neither of the two had any idea of the plans of the other, nor had the offices concerned. Both Lawrence and Philby were successful in their missions and performed the most amazing exploits. Colonel Lawrence's part is well known, but Philby and Armstrong (the author of those brilliant biographies of Mustapha Kemal and General Smuts, *Grey Wolf* and *Grey Steel*) deserve more recognition for war services than they received since history has proved that they backed the best man, Ibn'Saud, who became king of a united Arabia. Both Arab chieftains served the Allied cause in some measure, but their principal concern was to cut each other's throat. This muddle resulted in a long and bloody war being fought later, which was financed with great sums of money and great stores of munitions, all supplied by two buildings a few hundred yards apart in Whitehall, London.

The perpetrators of such grim farces must not be judged too harshly, however, as the conditions under which these missions to Arabia and Russia were conceived and had to act should be remembered. Secrecy in such matters was of the first importance, so it was out of the question to circularise the whole of Whitehall and all the Government Offices of the United States, France, Italy, Japan and the innumerable other Allies with particulars of each new sideshow devised to prick the enemy in an unexpected place. Further, the major fronts of the war occupied the attention of most of the principal executives and, in such a war, involving the greater part of the world, communications with distant areas could generally only be made with extreme difficulty. Moreover, with regard to Russia particularly, the situation changed from day to day. Literally thousands of the Allies' statesmen, officers and representatives all over the world were doing their utmost to help win the war along any line which offered prospects of embarrassing the enemy. They could not always wait to parley, but had to rely largely on their own initiative, often at considerable risk to their own careers, and trust to luck that their actions would be approved by some higher authority later on.

The Russian situation was further complicated by the presence there of a great body of Czecho-Slovakian soldiers. Many of these had marched over the frontier at the outbreak of war and fought against their hated masters, the Austrians, in the Russian ranks; others had been taken prisoner. In the early summer of 1918 there was a body of 55,000 well-armed and well-disciplined Czechs, under their own officers and commanded by the Czechish General Gaida, right in the middle of Russia.

After the Bolshevik Revolution the Russians wanted to get rid of them and the Czechs wished to enter the war again on the side of the Allies. A mad scheme was inaugurated by which the Czechish Legion was to march across 5,000 miles of Russia from the Urals to the Siberian Pacific Coast and be transported from Vladivostok by the Allies, another 12,000 miles by sea, back to fight on the western front in France.

The British gave them £80,000 and the French 11,000,000 roubles to pay their troops and finance their journey. The Bolsheviks wished to disarm them before they set out and were certainly entitled to their Russian weapons but the country was in such an unsettled state that they refused to surrender their arms. That was just as well for them as the whole of Siberia was now completely lawless, and from the moment they set out they were attacked by Reds, Whites, Greens, Tartar Chiefs and bands of robbers both European and Asiatic, all intent on pillaging their wagons or securing their clothes, boots and munitions. The Czechs, however, were a brave and determined set of men. They performed the amazing feat of fighting their way along the Trans-Siberian railway without support or supplies right across to the Pacific Coast.

By the time they got there the Allies had come over definitely to the Foch-Churchill view that the Bolsheviks were mad dogs who must be shot out of hand. In consequence, instead of bringing the Czechs back to Europe, as they had promised, the Allies told them that they would recognise Czecho-Slovakia as an independent state if the Czechs would remain in Russia and fight against the Reds. That was the one thing nearest to every Czechish heart, and without a murmur, this gallant band turned round and fought its way back again, this time against the Bolsheviks, another 5,000 miles and crossed the Urals into European Russia.

The United States were only persuaded with difficulty to adopt the Allies' policy of intervention and endeavoured to limit the Japanese operations, which were distasteful to them, by an agreement in which both nations limited themselves to a force of 7,000 men each, to protect Allied interests on the Russian Pacific coast. Through an error, however, the Americans sent 8,500 men, so the Japanese felt themselves released from their agreement, landed 50,000, which was soon increased to 100,000, and began to overrun half Siberia. In June the Allies landed a strong force at Murmansk in the north, and instead of advancing into Finland, as had been the original plan, their troops now started to move against Moscow. Another Allied force was on its way to Archangel for the same purpose, all these great troop movements having been undertaken originally on the excuse that the new Bolshevik Government must be protected from its German enemies.

A detailed history of Russia for these few months would run to a dozen bulky volumes and another dozen could be filled with the frantic telegrams of the Allies and Central Powers who were negotiating among themselves, or with the Kremlin, about Russian affairs. Events moved with incredible swiftness and the whole country was in an indescribable state of chaos. The entire male population of Russia, from youngsters in their teens to greybeards, with the exception of a very small percentage in some of the cities, had taken up arms. Foreign troops of almost every nationality were in the country by the legion. Literally scores of armies were fighting on fronts that criss-crossed in every direction. At a moderate estimate the colossal figure of some forty million people must have been attacking each other on the main principle of kill or be killed. Out of this ghastly imbroglio which resulted from the Russian Revolution only one fact emerges clearly.

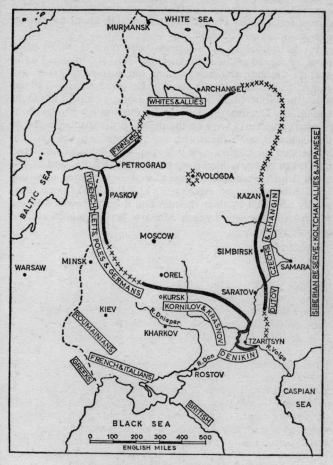

**BOLSHEVIKS' DESPERATE SITUATION, SPRING–SUMMER, 1918**

More or less permanent fronts, marked ▬▬▬▬▬▬ Sporadic fighting, marked xxxxxxxxxxxxx Note the 'salient of death' at Tzaritsyn.

In the early summer of 1918 the territory controlled by the Kremlin, and only very dubiously controlled at that, had shrunk from a vast Empire to a little chunk about the size of France, Spain and Portugal.

To the north-east the Germans were only about 80 miles from Petrograd on both sides of the Gulf of Finland. To the west the German and Austrian line ran in front of Pskov and Minsk; to the south-east in front of Kiev and Kharkov. In the south the White Cossacks, under Krasnov, occupied the Don, and under Denikin the Kuban. In the south-west the Roumanians and Turks were on the shores of the Black Sea and in the Caucasus, while the British were advancing to the Caspian. In the west the Czechs, now linked up with Admiral Koltchak, had taken Samara, Simbirsk, Kazan and Viatka, and in the north British, French and Americans were preparing to attack from Murmansk and Archangel. The Bolsheviks were completely encircled by their enemies and it only remained to see which of them would reach Moscow first to administer the *coup de grâce*.

# 11

# The Epic Retreat from the Ukraine

After the October Revolution Voroshilov was given a post in
the *Cheka*. The Bolshevik secret police had, as its chief,
Dzerzhinski, a Pole of noble descent, who was a sadist and
extremist. Perhaps the most infamous of all the Terrorists, he
was determined to maintain the Revolution against every opposition, whatever it might cost in blood, and delighted in his
work.

Voroshilov developed a great admiration for Dzerzhinski
on account of his efficiency, and has often been heard to declare: 'Now he was a real organiser. Damn it all, that's a man
I envied. If I had half his qualities I could tackle my responsibilities without the least trouble at all.' Fortunately for humanity Voroshilov had not got half Dzerzhinski's *qualities*; he
lacked the subtle mind of a born spy and he loathed the frightful daily shootings of whole batches of people whose only
crime was that the Party wanted them out of the way.

In consequence, he resigned from the *Cheka* and was made
the first Bolshevik police prefect of Petrograd and chairman
of the committee for the defence of the city, but trouble was
brewing for the new Soviet Republic.

Voroshilov's fire and enthusiasm were wasted in an office.
He was sent to his own country, the Don Basin, to raise the
workers there in defence of the Revolution.

When he arrived he found everything in confusion. The
officials of the old Government had fled; the natural leaders of
the people had gone into hiding from fear of the armed mobs.
It was no longer a question of scrapping with the forces of law
and order but being overrun by a foreign foe; an uprush of
patriotic feeling caused the workers to determine to resist the
invader, yet there was no one to guide them and they had no
idea how to set about it.

Voroshilov formed the Lougansk Red Guard and soon had
the best part of 2,000 men under arms, in batches, scattered up

and down the Don Basin, many of them being old comrades who had served in the fighting squads he had organised twelve years before at the beginning of the first revolution.

The out-at-elbows bands of factory workers held a great mass meeting at Lougansk. Voroshilov, with other speakers, urged them to leave their homes and take the field against the torrent of steel-helmeted Germans which was pouring into the blazing Ukraine. The speeches were received with acclamation, but it was a great armed mob without any military organisation, and they had to decide who should be their leader. It was here, amidst the din and shouting, that Voroshilov's future career was settled for him.

'Clim!' shouted the workers, 'Clim, you command us! Take command, Clim!'

'But I'm no soldier,' he protested loudly, 'we must have a military man.' He tried to wave them away but they still yelled their insistence. A young army officer named Nikolia Roudinev, who had long been a secret adherent of the Bolsheviks, jumped upon the platform and slapped Voroshilov on the shoulder, shouting:

'Don't be afraid, Clim. Don't play the fool. Don't wriggle. Take over the command and we'll help you. I'll be your chief of staff.'

A great roar of cheering rose up from the multitude. Voroshilov gave a despairing shake of his head but agreed. 'All right, comrades,' he cried. 'What the hell's the good of wasting time. Since you force me to it I'll take command. Only, bear this in mind. With me shrift is short. This thing is going to be handled in a disciplined manner. You must obey me as though I were a proper general. If you're afraid to die—you can go to hell. If you're not—come with me.'

Thus, all against his will, the ex-pit boy received his first command direct from the hands of his fellow workers.

Most of his Red Guards were scattered in townships and villages up and down the country-side; many of these groups were going off to the front on their own, or with other units, so his detachment numbered only about four to five hundred men. There were plenty of cartridges in the munition factories of Lougansk, so they helped themselves to a good supply and set off for Kharkov. On the way Roudinev and a few other ex-soldiers among Voroshilov's followers gave the men all the training they ever got.

At Kharkov he made contact with Antonov and other Party men who had come from Petrograd to organise the resistance to the Germans. Isolated groups of the Red Guard were already in contact with the enemy, but they were ill-trained, ill-equipped and in many cases ill-led, so they were falling back, often without fighting at all, upon Kharkov. Poplavski tells us:

'I was Assistant Front Commissar and I first met Voroshilov at the station in Kharkov, after we had retired to the Alexandrovsk line. None of us knew what to do and we were up against the well-organised Germans directed by a single mind. We told Voroshilov the situation and asked his advice, suggesting that we should dig in and make a stand.

' "Not worth it until we're better organised," he replied unhesitatingly. "We shall only lose men and gain no advantage. Continue the retreat."

'It was a hot time. We had been badly knocked about and there had been a lot of rain. We were coated with mud and looked like devils.'

To visualise the fighting, think of our own Black Country, or any great industrial area, where open rolling downlands are dotted with grimy, depressing little villages containing rows of small houses all alike; here and there a factory town with its tall chimneys pointing to leaden spring skies. It was open warfare, in which the combatants were fairly safe as long as they could keep the crest of a rise between themselves and the enemy, but that enemy was liable to appear at any moment, or on any side, and machine-guns might open, mowing down a score of men, without the least warning. There was little cover and no connected line; each unit had to fight its own rearguard action and retire when things got too hot for it, without reference to the others. A network of railways linked up the factory towns; there were plenty of derelict trains and plenty of skilled drivers from the engine shops of Lougansk in Voroshilov's detachment, so, as far as he could, he stuck to the railways and rallied his men at each wayside halt or village station.

Zveriaka carries on the story: 'We fell back until we reached Douvoviazodo and there Voroshilov determined on a stand, so we fought our first engagement. We deployed, but the enemy outflanked us. Reports came in that other bodies of the Red Guard were falling back and the men got into a panic, but

Voroshilov galloped up and down on horseback from point to point shouting: "I'll shoot the first man who runs away."

'He jumped off his horse near me, carbine in hand, and the men immediately took up their positions again, but it was soon apparent that all was not well with the units on either side of us. The Germans were well-trained and courageous. They broke through upon our flanks and started to shoot at us from the rear. Voroshilov and his lieutenants consulted as to what was to be done. One of the men knew the district and with him as guide we attempted an outflanking movement. Antonov arrived on the scene with an armoured train and we fell back upon it as a rallying point, but an enemy shell crashed into a truck of ammunition which began to blow up with loud explosions. Many of our men fled in terror. Voroshilov only succeeded in getting the remainder clear from the Germans with the greatest difficulty and we had to abandon the armoured train.

'That evening Voroshilov called us together and asked for volunteers to go with him and get back the train. About fifteen men stepped forward and clambered on to a derelict locomotive. The others waited and Clim said quietly: "You can let us go alone if you like but we're not coming back without that train."

'The rest were shamed into clambering on board. It was dark when we started out and when we arrived we found that the Germans had retired some distance to dig in for the night; so we were able to save the armoured train without fighting, except for the stray shots they sent at us.'

The armoured train proved invaluable and they took it with them down the railway line as they continued their retreat towards the south-east.

General Krasnov had now risen against the Bolshevik régime at the head of a large force of Cossacks. His troops having cleared the Don country behind Voroshilov's men and other Red Guard units which were being driven back by the Germans, then took up their positions astride the main railway line, cutting off the Ukraine from Great Russia.

After the Germans had taken Kharkov, the hastily-gathered Bolshevik army went to pieces entirely. Antonov and the other commanders were killed, captured, or took to flight; their staffs disappeared with them. The army that before had only had the flimsiest cohesion was now in utter confusion; it was composed solely of bands of terrified men numbering a few score, or at most a few hundred, all trying to get away from the enemy but not knowing in which direction to retreat. They were caught between the Cossacks and the Germans; the two enemy armies had them in a vice.

Voroshilov's original detachment from Lougansk was mixed up with this semi-anarchical rabble. At Rodokovo, twenty kilometres north of Lougansk, he held a council of all the prominent men in each group he could get together. He was the principal speaker at the meeting, and explained that the official commanders having let them down they would all be killed unless they acted together. He proposed that they should form the whole mass of stragglers into one unit under a single command and with one headquarters' organisation. His plan was accepted immediately and, as the only leader of any prominence in the old fighting squad days who remained to them, they unanimously elected him as Commander of all the Red forces in their area. Overnight he was pushed up, owing to force of circumstances and his own popularity, in one jump, from leader of a half battalion to General Commanding the Fifth Ukrainian Army.

That army had yet to be formed and a plan made to save it from immediate annihilation. The plan must come first and the details later. He conceived the idea that, if only they could make a break through to the east, they might reach the city of Tzaritsyn on the Volga, which was still in the hands of the Bolsheviks. It seemed sheer madness; the Germans were fiercely assaulting their front, the whole of the Don country behind them swarmed with Cossacks, and half-a-dozen rivers lay between them and Tzaritsyn. Everyone declared that his scheme was impossible.

'What's the good of remaining here,' he shouted, 'the Germans will attack again to-morrow, and they'll slaughter every one of us. We *must* break through.'

Roudinev shrugged his shoulders: 'But Clim,' he protested, 'you don't understand. The retreat you're suggesting is over a thousand *versts*. The Germans and the Cossacks will squeeze us to death long before we get to Tzaritsyn.'

'Well, where the hell are we to go then? You're my chief of staff and I tell you to draft a plan for a breakthrough to Tzaritsyn. Those are my imperative orders.'

To the accompaniment of violent swearing from the turbulent ex-mechanic, Roudinev worked out a scheme for this insane enterprise; a forlorn attempt to cross the Don steppes and reach the Volga by following the twisting track of the railway line.

The council ended about midnight and next morning a large engagement was expected, as the Germans were preparing to advance all along the front. The mob leaders worked like demons all night; by morning Voroshilov had formed his staff, merged the tiny bands of workmen into larger army units and issued field orders for the defence of Lougansk. About midday the army, now reorganised, took up its positions. Some units, anarchistic in mood and not submitting at first to the new measures, had to be re-formed in the rear, and only an insignificant part of the new army was able to be brought into operation.

Voroshilov galloped from group to group on horseback, assuring the waverers that the Revolution was not perishing as they supposed. He told them that their own participation in the recent fighting was only an episode, and that whatever the difficulties and the dangers they must hold together even if they were all destroyed; because the longer they could hold out and the more Germans and reactionary Whites they could occupy, the more time they would be giving Lenin in Moscow to consolidate the centre of the Revolution, which would ensure him the possibility of leading the whole Working Class Movement of the World.

The battle began at about two o'clock in the afternoon. The Germans flung a whole Corps against Rodokovo. The battle went on with varying success; about six o'clock Voroshilov ordered the right wing to make a counter-attack, and routed the enemy. Two batteries, twenty machine-guns and two aeroplanes were taken. The enemy fled, leaving behind a large number of dead and wounded; Voroshilov had won his first battle. The Bolshevik success was only temporary, however, and a far-flung outflanking movement by the German Cavalry compelled him to fall back again. He retired on Lougansk and established temporary headquarters there.

An officer named Sokolov tells us: 'I had under me some men from Lisichan. When we were retreating from before the Germans, I managed to collect a crowd from some of the broken units numbering altogether 450 bayonets and 75 sabres. I reported to M. L. Roukhimovich, the Commissar for War at

Lougansk. In the hotel apartment he occupied, I found a
stranger of medium height with chestnut hair, a stern face and
keen penetrating glance. As I entered the room the stranger
immediately broke off his conversation with Roukhimovich
and deliberately looked me up and down from head to foot.
Roukhimovich introduced us saying: "This is Comrade Voroshilov who has just been appointed as commander of the
newly created Fifth Ukrainian Army. Your unit is to be included in it."

'Voroshilov looked me up and down again attentively and
said: "You're a former officer, aren't you?"

' "I am."

' "Rank?"

' "Reserve cornet—rose to staff captain."

' "Party member?"

' "Former Left Social Democrat."

' "Your unit?"

'I gave him detailed information on the make-up and condition of my unit, and added that I expected to be ready in
about a week. Voroshilov said: "I know the Lisichan boys,
the Menshevik influence among them is strong, but we'll see.
Perhaps the Bolshevik thread you speak of will prove itself;
then something good may be made of your unit!"

'Two days later I was ready to meet the commander's train
at the rendezvous he had given me. About four o'clock it
arrived, but nobody got out. I went to the staff coach and
found Voroshilov discussing forthcoming operations with his
chief of staff, Roudinev. When he saw me he said in a tone that
permitted no discussion: "Comrade Sokolov, I expect you at
Kavanye in two days from now." Then he turned to Roudinev
and the rest of his staff with the words: "Come on, what are we
waiting for!"

'That abrupt termination of the conversation threw us all
into confusion, as not only myself but all the others naturally
expected that he would want to inspect this new unit which
had just come under his command. Roudinev and I suggested
that, but he replied: "I'm not used to parades. I'll get to know
your men in battle." Then turning to his staff, he added:
"Come along, get a move on. We're late as it is." '

In Lougansk, Voroshilov and his staff worked like furies.
Among them was a local tailor, a cross-eyed fellow named
Shchadenko, an old friend of Voroshilov's and destined to

become, with him, another of the great fighting leaders. The
Cossacks were eating up the country through which the newly-
formed Fifth Ukrainian Army must pass to reach Tzaritsyn.
They would be starved into surrender unless they took adequate supplies with them. Derelict trains were filled with all
the food they could lay their hands on. Others were loaded
with cases of cartridges, hand grenades, shells, from the now
silent munition factories, others again with the goods of the
wretched people of the district. Thousands of refugees were
flooding in; old men, women and children, many of them
dependents of the Workers' Army. The Germans were coming. These non-combatants could not be left behind. Every
engine in the Lougansk shops was put into use, and a huge
convoy of trains organised, occupying both lines of the double
track. Under the intrepid leadership of the completely inex-
perienced but courageous civilian soldier the terrible retreat
began.

The difficulties were immense. Day after day, night after
night, they were attacked by the Germans or the Cossacks.
Rearguard actions were fought every day. The pace of the
retreat was the pace of the last in the long double string of
trains, and there were frequent breakdowns. Many rivers had
to be crossed and often bridges needed repair, having been
partially destroyed by the enemy. The line did not run direct,
but north to Likhaia before they could head due east towards
their goal. Sokolov takes up the story: 'When he arrived at
Kavanye with his army, Voroshilov ordered the armoured
train to guard Svatovo station, and deployed his left flank
along the shore of the River Krasnaia. There was a heavy
engagement at Mostki, and our men were forced to retire on
Kavanye under cover of armoured cars. Information came
in that the Germans were outflanking us, and so Voroshilov
issued orders to fall back and we entrained at Kavanye.

'Just before sunrise, a train on the right-hand track overtook
a train on the left-hand track, and through faulty loading
caught the other; as a result of which an open wagon of each
train and an armoured car were derailed. The line was completely blocked, so, one by one, the trains were brought to a
standstill. The sun was already colouring the eastern sky, and
on all faces there was anxiety and alarm, as we knew that the
Germans were in hot pursuit of us. Timorous words of advice
from one to another could be heard, and these gradually pas-

sed to threatening demands to tip the blocking wagons down the embankment together with the armoured car. Suddenly the commanding voice of Voroshilov cut in:

' "What's the matter, what are we waiting for?"

' "An accident."

' "Get that car out of the way. Get that wagon back on the track. Not a nail is to be left for those German bandits. What are you standing like dummies for? Get jacks, crowbars, ropes, pulleys! Look alive!"

'In a second the men were hunting everywhere for tools. Timbers to raise up the wheels were found and the men set to work casting sidelong glances at the army commander who was here, there and everywhere, getting a jack under an axle, risking the car slipping off the track on to him, or gathering stones to put under a lever. He was so enthusiastic and confident of success in shifting the weighty truck that the crowd submitted to his will, and within two hours the trains were running again, one after another, towards Kremennoie. The last train to pass through the town was the staff train, in which Voroshilov and his companions were discussing further operations.

'When the train came to the bridge over the Donetz, there was a loud report and shrapnel whined overhead. A second shell followed and then a third, which struck the bridge just as the last coach of the staff train crossed it. The armoured train which was now the last in the string rapidly came into action and silenced the enemy battery.

'When the trains were under a ridge of country which stretched for some two and a half miles along the track, with buildings overlooking it from the heights, there suddenly came a rattle of machine-gun and rifle fire. Our first impression was that the Germans had surrounded us, but it turned out that a Menshevik organisation of the Sodovoy factory were aware that the Germans were drawing near, and thinking that we Bolsheviks were in full retreat had decided to attack.

'Voroshilov ordered the trains to be stopped and the men formed up for an assault. The shooting ceased immediately and a deputation, including women, came hurrying down the hill to beg Voroshilov not to send a punitive expedition, as they were agreeable to hand over the culprits who had fired upon us. Although they had wounded men and killed one in the armoured train, Voroshilov agreed, and gave the order to move on.

'A few minutes later we heard three gun reports and learned that the men in the armoured train had sent three shells smashing into the factory to revenge their dead comrade. Alyabaiev, who commanded the armoured train, was immediately summoned.

' "Did you order that reprisal?" demanded Voroshilov.

' "I did," Alyabaiev confessed.

' "Then take note I will not allow these terrorist tricks," Voroshilov said severely. "We may be retiring now, but that is only temporary, and in order to ensure a friendly return we mustn't leave enemies in the places we pass through. Make it clear to your men that your shells may have killed or crippled innocent people, and that we Bolsheviks do not make war upon a peaceful population." '

The railway line was only the thin thread which guided the retreating army; their detachments were spread out for several miles on either side of it, but Voroshilov soon grasped the management of this large military concentration. He found that the old method of doing everything in an office from a map and reports was quite useless. Each night he made his dispositions in the staff car of the train and issued his orders, but at daybreak he mounted his horse and, with a few of his staff, rode out to visit his principal units, and see for himself what progress they were making.

When the Germans advanced on Likhaia the whole army was threatened, as there were still eighty trains to come through the junction. Voroshilov was compelled to make a stand and fought a desperate battle. On the old principle that attack is the best form of defence, he flung his best units against the town of Goundorovskaia and here, for the first time, his men came into conflict with General Krasnov's White Cossacks.

The Bolsheviks stormed the town and drove out the Cossacks. Spurred on by victory they felt no fatigue, and chased the retreating enemy for a couple of miles. Beside themselves with delight, they took up a position on a rise of ground, and began to paint pictures of further victories which would enable them to clear the Ukraine, but they had little experience of warfare, and did not realise that this was only a single skirmish on a fair sized front.

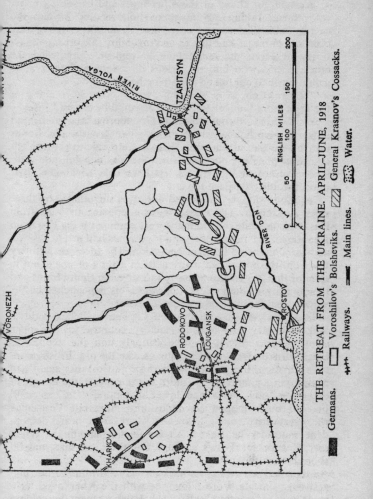

THE RETREAT FROM THE UKRAINE. APRIL–JUNE, 1918

▓ Germans.　▢ Voroshilov's Bolsheviks.　▨ General Krasnov's Cossacks.　▨▨ Water.

✛✛✛ Railways.　▬▬ Main lines.

RIVER VOLGA

TZARITSYN

RIVER DON

ROSTOV

RODOKOVO

LOUGANSK

VORONEZH

KHARKOV

ENGLISH MILES

0　50　100　150　200

The worker Mikhail Ovski recounts the engagement:

'We had got ahead of the other units and had lost contact with them. Taking advantage of hollows and ravines the enemy outflanked us and our whole detachment would have been cut to pieces had not Clim Voroshilov saved us.

'He observed the outflanking movement; despatched the other officers with him in various directions and then came galloping up to our hill on a foaming horse.

' "Retire at once," he shouted; "you're being surrounded on the right from the Donetz. Hurry or you'll be cut off."

'We filed back through burning Goundorovskaia and behind it was a deep hollow which made a dangerous defile. It was only by the skin of our teeth that we were able to get through it in time and save ourselves from the machine-gun and artillery cross-fire of the Whites. Had we delayed another half hour it would have been too late.

'The following day we found ourselves surrounded on three sides at Likhaia. The Cossacks were pressing us hard from Kamenskaia while the Germans were coming up the line from Rodokovo. A large number of our columns had met at Likhaia and the units were in great confusion. The incessant artillery fire from the enemy put many units in a state of panic, but in spite of that Voroshilov managed to save the eighty trains and the majority of the capable units after his first pitched battle, which raged for three days without ceasing.'

The trains crawled on through Likhaia to Belaia Kalitva, and now they had left the factory country for the open steppes. For spring it was suffocatingly hot; the steppe was like a furnace. Drawn up in squares, like the old British infantry formation, they fought off Krasnov's Cossacks again and again. As they marched, in short, uneven spurts, the morale of the troops sank lower and lower, the hope of a successful break-through seemed an impossible thing, but Voroshilov was everywhere among them and wherever he heard despondent murmurs he waved his automatic, shouting: 'Who's spreading panic! Who's leaving? Show me the man and I'll shoot him on the spot.'

Mikhail Ovski relates another incident: 'In one of our biggest engagements, Voroshilov was with the Kharkov detachment and Mamontov's cavalry bore down upon the column with cries that froze the blood.

'A sharp order came from Clim: "Don't shoot. Let them

draw near." The order was caught by the junior officers and passed down the line. The Cossacks came thundering across the grass waving their sabres. There was another sharp order: "Fire!"

'Our men opened a hellish fire from rifles and machine-guns. The front ranks of the charging cavalry seemed to stagger; men and horses rolled to the ground.

' "Comrades," yelled Voroshilov, "follow me to the attack." There was a tremendous answering "Hurrah!" from the men and the Red infantry poured down the hill like a flood of lava on to the disorganised cavalry. We had used all our ammunition and had no cartridges left, so we went at them with the bayonet.

'A Cossack colonel was immediately in front of us. Ivan Lakatosh, the Commander of the Kharkov detachment, did not shout but shrieked in an unnatural sort of falsetto: "Clim, Clim, shoot!"... An oath followed.... Voroshilov aimed. His automatic cracked.... The colonel seemed to jump in his saddle, his fur cap flew up and he rolled off his horse. Our men leapt at him, tore off his silver-mounted sabre and handed it to Clim.'

Again and again Voroshilov's men were driven in, but again and again they rallied round the long lines of halted trains, crawling beneath them and using the wheels and wagons for protection. At last they reached the great railway bridge over the Don at Nizhniy-Cherskaia. It had been blown to smithereens and there seemed no possible way to get the trains over the broad river. Many of Voroshilov's lieutenants wanted to abandon them and, taking only a minimum of stores with horse wagons, continue on down the banks of the river; but he knew that without the armoured trains to give them some protection they would all be massacred.

He refused to listen and dug himself in on a semicircle round the edge of the broken bridge with both flanks of this horse-shoe resting on the river, and for a month he sustained a siege in this position.

He had no materials to make a bridge, no instruments, no engineers, but the immense labour was undertaken of damming the whole river with earth so that it flooded over its banks, but railway lines could be laid across the embankment that dammed it.

One day while this work was in progress an armoured car

was going out scouting in the direction of Pyati Izbyausk, so he took a seat in it. The car was driven into the heart of the White Cossack's territory and the chauffeur, being lost, pulled up at a farm. They had run straight into an ambush; the place was occupied by the enemy and suddenly there was a terrific burst of rifle fire from the farm buildings. The chauffeur panicked in trying to back out of the yard and got stuck, but Voroshilov reassured him that the steel plating was bullet-proof. After fifty minutes of a hellish tattoo they succeeded in getting the car out; two hours later Voroshilov had issued the appropriate orders and the Cossacks were driven out of the farm.

Men, women and children worked on damming the Don. Everybody worked, officers did not cease to be officers, but they were worker-officers; the bridge had to be made so that the armoured trains which were their base and only strength might pass over the river. The saying of a Tartar who was fighting in the partisan ranks ran through the worker-army: 'The land-owner builds an iron bridge which can be blown up, but the worker builds a bridge of sand and the worker's bridge is stronger.' Krasnov made the most desperate efforts to drive the Red army into the river, but at the end of thirty days and thirty nights of incessant fighting Voroshilov had his trains and baggage safely over the Don and recommenced his retreat towards Tzaritsyn.

Progress was slow as the Whites had torn up the railway lines for miles in advance of them and these could not be re-laid at a quicker rate than three-quarters of a mile to a mile a day; so the speed of the retreat was reduced to this tortoise pace.

News now reached Voroshilov that Tzaritsyn itself was in danger. Its main railway cut; isolated from Moscow and the other centres of Revolution, it was almost surrounded by the Whites. The leaders in Tzaritsyn sent Voroshilov an urgent appeal to hurry, and now he was faced with a dual task; not only to save his own forces from destruction but to fling them into Tzaritsyn and so relieve the city.

Near the village of Morozovskaya a long and severe battle took place. Voroshilov's force was completely surrounded and Krasnov flung great masses of his cavalry at the almost exhausted workmen; but finally Voroshilov broke through the ring and staggered on towards his goal. He reached it in the month of June—still fighting.

For three solid months, Voroshilov, the untrained leader with his ragged bands, had out-manœuvred and out-fought both the German Army and the great Russian Cavalryman, General Krasnov. When history comes to be written the story of the retreat will rank with that of the immortal Ney, who saved the remnant of the Grande Armeé in the terrible retreat from Moscow. By sheer will power and indomitable courage Voroshilov, the ex-pit-boy, succeeded in conveying 35,000 non-combatant refugees across a thousand *versts* of enemy territory and bringing 500 trains with a great store of munitions and 15,000 fighting men to the relief of Tzaritsyn.

# 12

# The Great Sabres

It seems quite inevitable that comparisons between the French and Russian Revolutions should be made. After the fall of the Monarchy and the moderate Government in France the new régime was attacked on all sides. The crowned heads of Europe were not only horrified but very severely frightened by the fact that the French people had guillotined Louis XVI and Marie Antoinette. The revolutionaries in France were, as far as means permitted in those days, carrying on a propaganda campaign with a view to stirring up revolution in other countries and, in order to put this dangerous new Republican Government out of the way, a number of Monarchies formed a coalition and invaded France. At the same time the nobility brought about White risings among the peasants of the Vendée, who were deeply religious and strongly Monarchist in sympathy, and a most bloody civil war was waged there.

It seemed impossible that the French Republic could survive; a good proportion of the old army had gone over to it, but many of the best regiments were disbanded, or in sympathy with the Whites, and the Red units lacked officers, as most of these had been imprisoned, executed or had fled the country; yet the Republican Government showed no signs of giving in under the pressure exerted by the circle of its enemies. Instead the mobs surged out of Paris, armed with the most ill-assorted collection of weapons and proceeded to fight the well-drilled troops of the Monarchist countries and the counter-revolutionary bands for the preservation of their new won liberties. A number of ex-Royalist colonels and generals with Republican sympathies, such as Dumouriez, Kellerman and Serurier collected what they could of the old army. Many of them, like Dumouriez, afterwards went over to the Whites. Yet it was not these who later led the armies of Napoleon. Kellerman and Serurier were only made Marshals of the Em-

pire as a matter of policy because Napoleon wished to consolidate his throne by winning back the old nobility.

The real leaders who defeated the armies of the Monarchies
were the most astonishing assortment of men, few of whom
knew anything about strategy or tactics. They just fought
when and how they could, putting up the most desperate resistance to the enemy's well-planned attacks, and taking the
initiative themselves with irresistible *élan* whenever possible.

The great marshals, Massena, Soult, Ney, Bessières, Murat
and Lannes, were the sons of a tanner, a lawyer, a cooper, a
surgeon, an innkeeper and a peasant. The cold impassive
Davout, who was much the greatest strategist and tactician of
them all, was the son of a marquis, and rough uncultured
Lefèvre was a sergeant of the Dragoons.

Precisely the same thing happened in Bolshevik Russia. During the spring and summer of 1918 Moscow was enclosed in a
ring of steel and the country under its tottering authority was
reduced to about 500 miles in each direction. It seemed quite
obvious that the Revolution was doomed, but deserters joined
up again, sailors from the fleet turned themselves into infantry
and the workers marched out in ragged bands to give battle to
the whole civilised world and the counter-revolution in addition.

Ex-Czarist colonels and generals, such as Sytin, Vazetis,
Nossovitch, Muraviev and Yegorov, who had turned Republican, rallied the troops that remained to them. Many of them
later deserted to the enemy; only one, Yegorov, ever became
a Marshal of the Soviet Union.

The real leaders began their military career by their audacious defence of townships or villages which were holding out
against the Whites, or by desperate assaults with little bands
of partisans upon the troops of the invaders.

From this people's army arose such men as Voroshilov,
Blucher, Khvessin, Shchadenko, Gaai and Kotovsky, a mechanic, a mystery man, a barber, a tailor, an actor and a gaol bird.
The misanthropic Tukachevsky, much the greatest strategist
and tactician of them all, was the son of a nobleman, and
tough blunt Budenny was a sergeant of Dragoons.

The fighting was quite unlike anything which had taken
place in the European war. Except for the addition of the
machine-gun and the motor vehicle or armoured train it was
much more like the early Republican wars of the French be-

fore Napoleon came into power. Communications had almost entirely broken down and groups of whites and groups of Reds were isolated from their associates. In the early days it was quite impossible for them to organise supplies and both parties had to live upon the land. Neither of them knew from day to day upon which front they would be fighting next, as during the night another detachment of the enemy might have arrived directly in their rear or have outflanked them. Strategy played practically no part in the operations of either side because few of the guerilla leaders had anything but the vaguest idea of what their brother commanders in other areas were doing; all that they could do themselves was to deal with each fresh situation to the best of their ability as it arose from day to day. In consequence there was little trench fighting except outside beleaguered towns, and cavalry became the all-important factor.

It was, indeed, a war of sabres rather than artillery, and practically every one of the Red generals led their troops into battle personally, not once but on innumerable occasions, just as the practice was in early Napoleonic times. This greatest of all civil wars was fought out for three years over one-sixth of the earth's total land surface.

From guerilla warfare the fighting gradually passed to established fronts. Within a few years the extraordinary assortment of men who commanded the Bolshevik armies were to carry their Red banners to the gates of Pekin and threaten Europe itself by thundering down out of Russia to within ten miles of Warsaw.

In time to come nearly as much may be written about them as about Napoleon's marshals, but practically nothing has so far appeared in the English language concerning the exploits of these audacious Russians, whose careers were often brief but always spectacular, so it is proposed to give some particulars here.

One of the most picturesque was a young man named Kotovsky. He was a Bessarabian of noble birth but poor, and began life as assistant steward on the estate of Prince Cantakuzen. An extremely handsome youth, he was seen by the Princess who immediately fell in love with him and he with her.

They were surprised one day in the forest by the Prince who, furious with rage, raised his whip to strike his wife's seducer. Kotovsky, however, struck first, upon which his master had him trussed up, taken out into the steppes that night, and abandoned there.

It was doubtless during those hours when he was so near death that he came to the decision which was to alter his entire future. At last he managed to free himself from his bonds, returned to the estate, murdered the Prince and set fire to the buildings.

He then collected a dozen lawless ruffians as wild as himself, mainly desperate characters among the local peasantry and escaped convicts, and took to the forest with them.

Under his leadership the band became famous for the audacity of their robberies over all Bessarabia, and he even extended his operations as far as Odessa. All his raids were conceived with the idea of revenge upon the rich, whom he hated and, as during his boyhood he had steeped himself in books of adventure, he imagined himself to be one of the heroes he had read about.

He lost no opportunity of giving a Claude Duval-like glamour to his criminal career, and he soon became known in Odessa as the 'Noble Bandit'. Every sort of fantastic legend became attached to his name. His good looks, courage, audacity and politeness earned for him a number of women adorers, and while the men pressed the local authorites that swifter measures should be taken to capture him, their wives and daughters did everything possible to help the handsome rogue.

He was captured and imprisoned several times, but on each occasion he succeeded in escaping and added further to his extraordinary reputation by making each escape spectacular as well as successful.

At last he was sent to Siberia, but after working as a convict for two years he killed two of his guards, stole a passport and succeeded in getting back to Bessarabia. For a year after his return he lived there quite unsuspected, while working as a steward on an estate but, being a born adventurer, he could not resist entering into his illegal activities again.

During the winter of 1914 he had a band of deserters acting under his orders who carried out an extraordinary series of robberies and depredations, while openly acknowledging him as their chief. For another year the police hunted him in vain, never suspecting for one moment that he was the law-abiding steward, but eventually, unable to resist a spectacular gesture, he gave himself away, was captured, tried and condemned to death.

For many months he lay in prison, only saved from death by a series of postponements of his sentence, which were the outcome of the unceasing attempts by women of influence, who adored him, to get his sentence annulled or mitigated.

Their efforts were in vain and a definite day was at last fixed for his execution, but, with fantastic luck, that proved to be the day when the first Russian Revolution of February, 1917 broke out and with scores of other criminals he was pardoned.

Prison had not chastened him of his spectacular love of posing. On the very evening of his release he appeared at the Opera in Odessa with his manacles in his hand, and later, in the foyer sold them to the highest bidder, handing the proceeds, 10,000 roubles, to an organisation for the maintenance of the new-found freedom of Russia.

He then went to the war and we hear of him as a dashing cavalry leader, operating against the Germans; but Order No. 1, by which the Socialist Minister of War had undermined all discipline, was already doing its work. Desertions from the front became even more numerous, all opposition to the Germans ceased, and the Russian Army fell into a state of complete disintegration. When the October Revolution came, Kotovsky gathered about him the boldest of his men, formed them into his own cavalry detachments, and placed himself at the disposal of the Bolsheviks.

In their service he proved invaluable, particularly in the early days before their power was consolidated. With a false passport he penetrated into Odessa and disorganised the opposition of the Whites. Later, like Budenny, he became famous as a leader of ragged and savage, yet well-mounted, hordes, but, unlike Budenny, he set his face very firmly against *pogroms* of the Jews. His cavalry played an important part in defending Petrograd against the White General Yudenitch.

Doumenko was another spectacular figure, a drunken swash-buckling Cossack, with a curly black beard that came right down to his waist. He openly despised Communists and politicians; his only interests being war and plunder. He was adored by his troops, who would follow him, screaming their war-cries, into the hell of any battle, providing there was the prospect of women and loot after the victory.

Michael Frunze was a man of very different calibre; cold, stern, brilliantly clever, he emerged out of the Revolution to found the Soviet Military Academy. Voroshilov was a great admirer of his, and has often said, as he did also of Dzerzhinski: 'Had I the qualities of Frunze, I should easily fulfil the task which is my great responsibility.'

Blucher, the Man in the Black Mask, is the mystery man of the Red Army. His official biography gives the following particulars. 'Vassily Constantinovitch, was born in 1889, the son of peasants living in the province of Yaroslav. He had only six weeks' schooling, and was then sent to work in a St. Petersburg warehouse. Later he became a locksmith. He took no part in the 1905 Revolution, but in 1910 organised a strike in Moscow, for which he was sentenced to two years and eight months' imprisonment. In 1914 he was mobilised, went to the front as a private, showed great personal bravery and was promoted to N.C.O. In 1915 he was severely wounded and invalided out of the service. In 1916 he was working again as a locksmith and organised a strike for the Bolsheviks in Kazan. After the Revolution he went to Samara and joined the Communist Party.'

Curiously enough this official account omits to mention the name of the village in which Marshal Blucher was born, the place where he served his prison sentence, or the regiment in which he fought during the war. It is also strangely reticent about the strikes he is supposed to have organised, and gives no details at all of the acts of bravery he is credited with having performed. The marshal was never known by any Russian name and Blucher is certainly not that of a *muzhik*. In consequence, nobody believes this story.

A second version of his origin is that he is Major Titz, an exceptionally able officer of the Austro-Hungarian General Staff, who disappeared in the Great War. Major Titz was believed to have been taken prisoner by the Russians, but all trace of him after that is entirely lost. Most prisoners of war endeavoured to lighten the dreary routine of their captivity by learning a foreign language and Major Titz may well have done so. When, owing to lack of supplies, it was no longer possible to feed the prisoners and they were turned loose or broke out of their compounds, it is suggested that Major Titz passed himself off as a Russian, sided with the Bolsheviks and

finding himself rapidly promoted, decided to carve out a
career for himself in Russia under a new identity.

A third theory is that Marshal Blucher was a German officer
attached to the staff of Colonel Bauer, who was in charge of
the Russian section of the German Intelligence Department.
One thing is certain, Colonel Bauer sent an officer, who
strongly resembled Marshal Blucher, into Russia, shortly after
the February Revolution, when Lenin and his comrades were
given facilities to travel across Germany. Colonel Bauer was
an extremely able man, and he foresaw that the abdication of
the Czar would by no means finish the Revolution. In Central
Russia there were many thousands of German prisoners of
war, and Bauer's idea was that his officer should proceed to
organise these against the day when the Kerensky Government showed signs of breaking up, and the whole country fell
into a state of chaos. With determined leadership it was considered possible that the German prisoners might secure arms,
be formed into proper units, and constitute a very severe
threat to the rear of any Russian army then remaining. If this
theory is correct, Marshal Blucher must, once again, have
decided that Russia in turmoil offered better prospects of a
career to an ambitious soldier than Germany and, in consequence, have remained there ever since.

The fourth theory is that Blucher was an ordinary private
serving in a Czecho-Slovakian battalion of the Austrian Army
up to the date of the war. He may have been among those who
decided to cross the frontier and fight with Russia, or a Czech
prisoner taken captive in one of the Grand Duke Nicolas's
operations. Here again, in either case, he would have had
ample opportunity to learn Russian and perhaps, having Bolshevik sympathies, may have decided to carve out a career for
himself when the Revolution broke out, rather than attempt to
get home.

There is a fifth theory, that he is a true Russian, but a criminal who committed some heinous crime before the war and
broke out of prison, like so many other convicts, during the
chaos that reigned from 1917 onward. This suggestion has no
foundation whatsoever. It is based solely on the assumption
that having later become such a prominent commander in the
Soviet Army, Blucher's Government would naturally not like
it to be revealed that in his youth he had committed some
appalling and entirely anti-social crime, which could not be

associated in any way with work for the Party; and, in consequence they have deliberately blacked out all records of his youth.

The probability is that he is either Major Titz, or the German Intelligence officer sent by Colonel Bauer, or, at all events, an officer of some description who passed through a proper military college and regimental training in his youth. His campaigns are so entirely different from Voroshilov's untutored but heroic victories, and show such a high degree of military knowledge, that it is impossible not to believe that he was a fully qualified officer before the Bolshevik Revolution began.

The fact that he always wore a black mask during his early campaigns supports this contention. Every criminal in Russia was loose, so if he had been an escaped convict that would have been no reason for him to do so. There does not seem any particular reason why a peasant or private soldier should so disguise himself, but a well-known officer of an enemy General Staff may well have wished to keep his identity secret from captives and others who would have recognised him. His first command was a band of partisans, and he once actually fought under a Red banner decorated with the Skull and Crossbones.

In the October Revolution of 1917 the majority of the troops of the Samara garrison went over to the Bolsheviks. The city and the surrounding country were in a state of great disturbance, and news from Moscow was uncertain, so the Reds called a meeting of leaders in the 'Triumph' theatre to decide what should be done. It was here that Blucher's authenticated career as a revolutionary began, as he was appointed Assistant War Commissar to the garrison commander.

When he spoke it was in short abrupt phrases, but he talked little and impressed people more by his calm deliberate manner and great self-assurance. He was short, thickset, well dressed, had cold pale eyes and the muscles of a boxer. At this time he wore his hair close cropped. Within a couple of days of receiving his appointment, he had disarmed a Cossack regiment and restored order in the city.

Blucher's first success was against General Dutov, the Ataman of the Orenberg Cossacks. With three brigades of Red sailors he chased Dutov south-east from Samara and captured Orenberg, the capital of the province. Dutov escaped to Uralsk, where he raised fresh forces and moved northwards to attack Chelyabinsk on the Trans-Siberian; his plan being to cut Siberia away from Bolshevik Russia. Blucher, in turn, collected a force, mainly composed of German and Hungarian prisoners of war, which he trained with great thoroughness. During the early summer of 1918 the two generals clashed in many bloody battles, but just as Blucher was gaining the upper hand, the Czech Legion declared for the Whites, seized Chelyabinsk and Samara, and cut Blucher's forces off by hundreds of miles from any other Red units.

He attempted to break through the Urals to Ekaterinburg, and failing there tried to get back to European Russia by Birsk. Again he failed, but all through the long blazing summer he fought his way backwards and forwards through the waterless steppes in the rear of the main White lines, and neither Dutov nor the Czechs could finally defeat and finish him.

Of Blucher and Kotovsky we shall hear more. Budenny's story is tied up with the rise of Voroshilov, and an account of the brilliant Tukachevsky's beginnings, which also includes some particulars of the butcher, Muraviev, and the dashing Gaai, will enable us to continue with the current of events.

About Marshal Tukachevsky's antecedents there is no doubt at all. He was born at Tchembar in the Government of Panza in 1893, the son of poor but noble parents. Koutou-zouv, his schoolmaster, later became Commissar for the Government of Penza, and so Michael Tukachevsky may well have imbibed revolutionary ideas from him when quite young. At school Tukachevsky took first place in arts and sciences, but he was proud, cold, indifferent, a bad mixer and had no friends. To his intense annoyance he was not admitted to the crack Military Academy of Paul I in St. Petersburg, but had to go to the Alexandra School in Moscow. He was there from 1912 to 1914, studied Clausewitz like a Bible and dreamt only of Napoleon.

He was very poor, as the little property of his parents was crippled with mortgages, but he succeeded in getting into the famous Semenov regiment of the Imperial Guard, was gazetted sub-lieutenant in August, 1914, and went straight into the war. He managed to escape from the Russian débâcle after Hindenburg defeated Rennenkampf, and performed a feat of great gallantry by taking a bridge that was in flames. He and his captain were both mentioned in despatches; the captain received the Cross of St. George, and Tukachevsky only got the Order of Vladimir, fourth class. He was livid with jealousy and rage about this, as the captain had taken little part in the operation.

He was a moody, difficult young man, heartily disliked by his brother officers, owing to his hatred of parties and women. One of them was complaining one day about the mud and filth in which they had to live, and their lack of civilised amusements. Tukachevsky replied: 'This war means everything to me. In a year or two, or three at most, I shall have obtained what I want out of it or be dead.' In spite of his harshness, the men admired him because of his courage and called him 'Lion Cub'.

In the winter of 1914 he was captured by the Germans near Suvalkie. This temporarily put an end to his prospects of carving out for himself a career, and the frustration nearly drove him mad with fury. He attempted to escape four times, but was caught on each occasion and eventually, towards the end of 1916, put in the Fortress of Ingolstadt, which was reserved for recalcitrant prisoners. He shared a cell there with a French officer named Fervaque.

One day the Frenchman asked him: 'Do you believe in God?'

'God!' exclaimed Tukachevsky, with an astonished air. 'I have never had time to think about it. All educated Russians are atheists. Don't forget that our idiot of a Czar wears the Tiara of a Pope as well as a Crown,' and he laughed cynically.

His further views as expressed to the Frenchman were: 'I am not a Christian and, in fact, I hold it against our Saint Vladimir to have baptised Russia and delivered her into the bondage of Western civilisation. We ought to have conserved our paganism and our natural barbarity. But wait, they will return—both of them. Saint Vladimir has only put us back several centuries.

'If the Revolution does break out, God knows where it will end. We drank to the health of our Emperor before we left for the front. It was perhaps a funeral ceremony. Plenty of people have had enough of the old régime. They were talking of it at the front before I was captured. A long time ago one felt a wind of treason passing over the Court. The artillery are said to want a Constitutional Monarchy, but I think the infantry wish for something much more than that.

'Personally I think a Constitution would mean the end of Russia. We are real barbarians and we need a despot. Imagine our peasants with universal suffrage—what a farce! As for the Jews, they introduced Christianity into the world, and that is quite good enough to justify the hatred that is their portion; wherever they move they spread a pox and force us to inoculate ourselves with the virus of civilisation substituting for all others the standard of gold—the capitalist standard—just money, which I despise.

'Socialism and Christianism are the same. It does not concern me as to how the land is divided among the peasants or what happens to the workers. My ancestors lived in a communal state, but under their overlord. Jews, Socialists, Christians!—I hate them all with an equal hatred.

'The Revolution may begin with the Jews and Socialists, but I doubt if they will be able to resist the pressure of the true barbarous Russians. They will be swept away by a wave of Russian national feeling.'

As a prisoner, Tukachevsky endeavoured to learn to play the violin, but he played it very badly. He preferred futuristic literature, and said that he would like to see a large factory planted where the Neptune fountain is in the Gardens of Versailles. When the February Revolution of 1917 took place he positively devoured every newspaper that he could lay his hands on, and escape became an obsession with him. He railed against Kerensky and declared that it was necessary to initiate a Reign of Terror.

'When one rolls towards the abyss,' he declared, 'it is much better to go over and touch bottom. Perhaps, if one has not already broken one's neck, one may find a path in some part which leads upwards. We should blow everything up from the bottom to bring Russia back to a state of primitive barbarity, open the doors of the East and slam those of the West in the face of England.'

The officer prisoners in Fort Ingolstadt were allowed some degree of liberty for exercise if they gave their parole. Tukachevsky gave his, but showed a cynical disregard of it by slipping away one day in the late autumn of 1917. His last remark to his French room-mate was: 'Your victory will cost you as much as your defeat, and the Red Flag will triumph everywhere.'

He made his way back to Petrograd which was already in

the hands of the Bolsheviks. In the street he met one of his very few friends, a man named Konliabko, and saw that he wore the Red scarf and brassard of the Central Committee of the Soviets. Konliabko introduced him to Krilenko, a private whom Lenin, in cynical jest, had made the supreme commander of all the Russian Armies; also to Antonov who, with Red Guards and workmen, had assaulted the Winter Palace in October. Tukachevsky left with them when the Government moved to Moscow, and in April, 1918, he was made an Inspector of the Red Army which was then being formed. Trotsky soon picked him out as an officer of exceptional ability and, a few months later, appointed him to the important military post of Commissar for the Defence of Moscow.

By that time Krilenko had been superseded in the Supreme Command of the Bolshevik forces by General Muraviev; another of these fantastic characters who had arisen out of the maelstrom of the Revolution.

In the old days, Muraviev had been a colonel of the Imperial Guard. He was a great lover of wine and women who had endeared himself to his troops, solely on account of his courage and the fact that he allowed them uncontrolled licence. Having brought over a number of the old Czarist regiments to the Bolsheviks, he assisted at the temporary defeat of the White General Krasnov, and Kerensky, who had fled to him, in the first battles of the civil war. Muraviev had then chased the Ukrainian 'Rada' out of Kiev and put the town to sack.

He adored fantastic uniforms which he designed for himself, covering them with silver braid and fur; habitually he wore the dolman of a Hungarian Hussar and dangled a jewel-hilted Magyar scimitar at his side. In Kiev he turned the palace, where he lived, into a brothel, and joined persecution mania to drunken orgies. He shot over two thousand ex-officers who had surrendered peacefully and ordered the ghastly glove and stocking torture to be applied to people who refused to give up their hidden wealth or displeased him over trifles. This consisted of dipping the hands and feet of the prisoner into boiling oil, so that the blistered skin could be drawn off whole from the raw flesh.

After his infamous exploits at Kiev, the Moscow Government made him their general in-chief, and sent him against the Roumanians. His horde of ill-disciplined looters, drunk with alcohol and blood, were assisted by Chinese mercenaries under

Captain Sen-Fou-Yan in the commission of the most terrible atrocities. They drove the Roumanians and the Germans back, and butchered all their prisoners.

In view of these facts, which were filtering through to the Allied Governments, it is hardly surprising that, having held their hand for a few months, they now determined to adopt Churchill's policy and stamp out Bolshevism as a menace to humanity.

Muraviev was then sent to the Russian Eastern front against the Czechs, but here he did not have the same success, and they occupied Kazan and Viatka. By the early summer, as we have seen, the situation of the Bolsheviks was becoming desperate and, on June 6th, a determined attempt was made to unseat the Kremlin Government.

The Social Democrat, Savinkov, had been planning a counter-revolution in Moscow for some months, and he staged a revolt at Vologda about 200 miles north of the capital. Savinkov had arranged for support from the Allied forces which were then landing at Murmansk and on their way to Archangel. If he could have held out, the new northern front would certainly have proved the end of the Kremlin, but the Allies were late in getting their men to Archangel, so, after twelve days of desperate street fighting, the Reds managed to regain possession of Vologda.

On the day that Savinkov's rebellion opened, an event of the utmost seriousness for the Bolsheviks took place in Moscow. Two Russians, Blumkin and Andreiev, presented *Cheka* passes at the German Embassy and demanded to see the German Ambassador, Count Mirbach. Upon being shown in they immediately drew their revolvers and shot the ambassador dead, afterwards escaping out of the window.

Their *Cheka* passes were forgeries, and Dzerzhinski immediately started out to arrest them; but the whole thing appears to have been part of Savinkov's Social Democratic Plot, as Dzerzhinski in turn was arrested by the conspirators and remained a prisoner for some hours. In the meantime an armed revolt took place in which the Social Democrats attempted to seize the Kremlin. The Bolsheviks were only saved by a regiment of Letts. The Letts were by no means fond of the Russians, and would have liked to return to their own country, but it was occupied by the Germans. In consequence, the Kremlin employed them as police troops to put down any trouble in the capital, and they were faithful to their masters. Colonel Peterson and his Letts saved the Central Committee in the Kremlin, released Dzerzhinski and suppressed the abortive rising.

Lenin and his colleagues feared at first that Count Mirbach's assassination would bring serious reprisals from the Germans; but the latter were too occupied with their western front, upon which the Allies were opening their great final offensive, to be able to undertake an advance against Petrograd. An armistice of sorts was agreed between the Bolsheviks and the Central Powers, but great bodies of their troops still continued to occupy all conquered territories, and were now in such a state of disorder that many of them continued to fight on their own account in order to maintain themselves against lawless bands and obtain provisions.

Muraviev was defeated again by the Czechs, who occupied Samara. He turned round and in his retreat took Simbirsk from the counter-revolutionaries, but the Czechs advanced upon him again there, and Simbirsk was on the Volga. Between it and Moscow there now lay only the two inconsiderable towns of Arsamas and Muron; moreover, if Simbirsk fell, Tzaritsyn, in the south, already cut off by rail, would also be cut off by river, and it was up the Volga that the grain barges which fed half-starving Moscow and its armies were coming. In this crisis of the first magnitude, War Minister Trotsky sent his best man, Tukachevsky, to the assistance of Muraviev.

When Tukachevsky joined him the two took an immediate dislike to each other. Muraviev was lording it in Simbirsk where he had allowed his ferocious troops to loot the town and strike terror into the population. The mobs proclaimed him the 'Saviour of the Volga country', and he openly declared that he did not care a fig for the Kremlin Government. His fingers were covered with priceless rings that he had looted; the hotel where he lived was swimming with drink and crowded with women—the sort of thing that Tukachevsky detested. Although a general, he retained his proletarian leather jacket and lived unostentatiously in his railway carriage at the station.

At the news of Mirbach's assassination, Muraviev thought the Bolshevik Government would be finished, so decided to proclaim himself as an independent ruler. Tukachevsky was arrested in his railway train by sailors and taken, with other officers whom Muraviev suspected of being loyal Bolsheviks, to the prison. The rebel general then mustered his cadets at the Hotel de la Trinité, declared an end of the war with the Czechs, and announced that he intended to march south against the Germans.

Under the menace of a revolver a Communist telegraphist was forced to transmit orders to Muraviev's forces in Bougoulma, Syzague and Melekess, that all troops must join hands with their late enemies, the Czechs, and prepare to march south-west into the Ukraine. The Communist telegraphist, however, managed afterwards to get through to Moscow, upon which Lenin sent telegrams in all directions that the Red Army commander-in-chief, Muraviev, was a traitor and that his orders were no longer to be obeyed.

In his prison cell Tukachevsky heard the tramp of soldiers' feet coming down the passage, and quite made up his mind that a squad had been sent to take him out and shoot him; but it was a company of the Letts who were loyal to the Kremlin and, instead, came to release him with the other Bolsheviks whom Muraviev had arrested.

Tukachevsky immediately took charge of the situation. Muraviev was with a number of his officers in the military school, so Tukachevsky took possession of the bandit's playground, the Hotel de la Trinité. In Room No. 4 he placed a reliable man with a machine-gun behind a curtain. In Rooms 3 and 5 he crammed a hundred of the Lettish soldiers; after which he sent a message asking Muraviev to come to the hotel.

The rebel army commander had no lack of courage and came swaggering in, thinking that Tukachevsky and the few men who were with him were alone, and knowing nothing of the Lettish soldiers in the adjoining rooms. Muraviev made a bombastic speech, then drew his pistol to shoot; but Tukachevsky instantly gave a signal. The machine-gun behind the curtain came into action and riddled the gorgeously-clad sadist with bullets.

Tukachevsky now took command of the Russian Eastern Army, which was known as the First Army of the Republic. Owing to lack of discipline the late General Muraviev's forces were in a hopeless state of disorder. The Czechs took Simbirsk and advanced from there on Nizhniy-Novgorod.

In the Kremlin the Central Committee were desperately anxious. They held their sessions in one of the magnificent salons of the ancient Palace, where crystal lustres dangled from the ceiling, priceless tapestries decorated the walls and beautiful antique furniture now bore the threadbare wraps, dirty mackintoshes and beer glasses of the People's Commissars. Between two magnificent mantelpieces, ornamented with cupids, there was pasted up a large placard: 'IT IS FORBIDDEN TO SMOKE.'

Lenin could not bear the smell of tobacco smoke, and one is reminded of the long dead Czar who had once occupied those same splendid apartments and, having a similar dislike, decreed that any one of his subjects found smoking a pipe of tobacco should have his nose cut off. Lenin at least confined his dislike to inconveniencing his colleagues.

Trotsky was there—emaciated, suffering from a chronic stomach malady, yellow, bilious, sickly-looking and quite unlike his published portraits; Stalin, the Georgian, who was once described by an ex-ambassador as '*Un sale type aux yeux jaunes*'; Rykov, a slimy intellectual; Dzerzhinski, the Pole, fanatical President of the *Cheka*; Grishka Zinoviev, President of the Petrograd Soviet, with the face of a dirty old woman and the shrill voice of a shrew; and crafty Kestinsky, the son of a priest.

The committee was in perpetual session, a few members retiring to snatch an hour or so's sleep while the others carried on. When Lenin was in the chair, which was twenty hours out of the twenty-four, he would not allow any member of the committee more than two minutes to express an opinion upon any one question. His continual cry was: 'The country waits! The country waits!'

In August 1918 the policy of the Allies to crush Bolshevism without mercy now being abundantly clear, Lenin and his colleagues turned to Germany for assistance; but the Germans were now in difficulties themselves. Their attacks on the western front had exhausted their armies there and they had counted, after the Armistice with Russia and the Ukraine, on transferring fifty-seven divisions of troops which were occupying Russian territory; but this was no longer possible. To their own cost, in this case, the Bolsheviks were beginning to get their own back on the Germans for the brutal Peace of Brest-Litovsk. The Red propaganda, which never ceased to be pumped out at all hours of the day and night, was beginning to do its work in the homelands of the Central Powers, and it had already utterly demoralised the fifty-seven divisions which were stationed in Russia itself. By constant contact with Bolsheviks and disorder the spirit of revolution had spread among the German troops. In many cases they imprisoned their officers and in all they refused to do anything except live on the conquered land. The Germans dared not bring them home or to the west for fear that they would infect other divisions, neither could they use them to assist the Bolsheviks against the new enemy the Allies.

Now that Moscow was in vital peril from the east, at Lenin's suggestion, Trotsky, the War Minister, went off in person to the Volga. When he arrived he found Tukachevsky endeavouring to cope with a most frightful state of affairs. Muraviev's brigands were looting right and left; many of the officers were deserting and carrying their men over to the Whites, but much larger numbers, consisting of peasants who had joined Muraviev's army for the sake of plunder, were now taking to the woods. They termed themselves 'The Green Army', and preyed upon Reds and Whites alike. Trotsky got into communication with the Kremlin and a 'State of Terror' was officially proclaimed.

The Bolsheviks were now determined to kill and rule, or be killed in the attempt. Dzerzhinski and his *Chekists* began to round up everybody who was suspect of counter-revolutionary sympathies, solely on the account of the fact that they had money or were well-bred. This policy was not the outcome of hatred against the old ruling caste so much as a deliberate attempt to paralyse all anti-Bolshevik activities by fear. For this reason the *Chekists* always arrested their prisoners in the dead of night and spirited them away to unknown destinations. The Red Terror descended like a nightmare over Russia.

In August the Fourth Lettish Regiment refused to go into battle. Trotsky decreed that the Soldiers' Committees should be shot in the presence of the other men. Every officer of the First Army who had gone over to the Whites was listed, the addresses of their families were ferreted out by Dzerzhinski and the whole lot, old men, women and children, butchered without trial. At the Volga front Trotsky bathed himself up to the neck in blood. He even decreed that, to impress the troops, two old Bolsheviks, Zaloutzky and Bakaiev, both Commissars of Divisions, should be shot because they had participated in the retreat. Lenin heard of this in time and stopped their execution by a direct order, but Trotsky was mad with a blood lust which surpasses anything that even Marat could have imagined. He released the two Commissars because he dared not disobey Lenin, but he shot one out of ten of all their men, who were merely wretched conscripted peasants. The Tartars of Kazan, who were tired of the war and wished to go home, he surrounded with Red Guards and machine-gunned the whole regiment so that their corpses lay tangled waist high over an entire field. Tukachevsky appears to have enjoyed and ably assisted at this appalling blood bath, and as the days went on there seemed to be no sign of an end to their ferocious activities. It cannot be wondered that the Allied Governments had determined to stamp out the Bolsheviks.

On August 30th Dora Kaplan attempted the assassination of Lenin. It was thought at first that he would die, as he lost a great deal of blood from his wounds. His oldest friend, Bouch-Brouevitch, said of him as he stood beside the leader's couch: 'Lenin's forehead and face were a waxy yellow, his eyes flickered open and the first words he said were: "Why should they have made me suffer so? It would have been much better if they had finished me off." ' But even during his convalescence he continued to attend to the most urgent business of the harassed State.

As a reprisal for the attempt the *Cheka* spread terror through the entire country. Never in the history of the world had there been seen such fury; even in the villages property owners or ex-officials of small standing were butchered, their women violated and their children carried away spiked on the tops of the *Chekists'* bayonets.

Blucher now reappeared again, breaking through the Urals at last by way of Perm, after having been cut off for nearly ten months. Up to that date the Kremlin had rewarded its warriors with gold watches, but Blucher's feat of maintaining his force for so long entirely unsupported in enemy territory was considered so outstanding that the order of the Red Banner was instituted and he was the first Bolshevik general to be decorated with it.

Trotsky had destroyed two-thirds of the eastern armies, but this terrible purge had left it free of all counter-revolutionary elements. Slavin, a lieutenant of Lettish Fusiliers, was sent north to attack Kazan, while Tukachevsky, now the Big Shot of the whole front, commenced operations against Simbirsk.

Before his first great engagement Napoleon Bonaparte sent an express to the Directory in Paris. 'We shall dine in Toulon the day after tomorrow.' Tukachevsky followed his idol's example and wired the Kremlin: 'Simbirsk will be taken on September 12th.'

The attack began on the 9th; on the morning of the 12th Tukachevsky was at the gates of Simbirsk and at midday he was in possession of the city. His first act was to go to the telegraph office and wire to Trotsky: 'Objective attained. Simbirsk taken.' The Volga was again free for supplies to come up it on the way to Moscow.

One of Tukachevsky's principal lieutenants was an Armenian named Gaai, who commanded the so-called 'Division of Iron.' He was another queer character; an excellent actor and great *poseur*. He swaggered about, winter or summer, wearing his fur *papenka,* and aping the manner of the traditional cavaliers of the Caucasus.

When Simbirsk was taken Gaai raced about the town in a motor-car commandeering every tailor he could find and ordering complete suits of Uhlan uniforms for the men of his entire division. He wired to Lenin: 'The taking of your natal town revenges your first wound. That of Samara will revenge your second.'

Tukachevsky permitted rape and other relaxations to his men in celebration of the victory, but addressed an order to them on the following day: 'Murderers and vagabonds are to be shot at sight. The town must now return to perfect order.' He then put Simbirsk in a state of siege and the following three days shot a further hundred of his own men as an example to the rest.

Trotsky was overjoyed at the victory and, always delighted at any opportunity to write or speak publicly, lauded Tukachevsky as the 'glorious Chief of our First Army who by his conduct gives an example to all others.'

Gaai enjoyed a series of banquets, but the morose Tukachevsky concerned himself entirely with preparations for a new advance. Upon October 8th a great battle with the Czechs and Whites was fought and Tukachevsky retook Samara at the head of his victorious troops.

That battle was known as the 'Soviet Marne'. By it the Russian eastern front was saved and the enemy advance there definitely checked; but the Kremlin had other fronts which were equally seriously threatened. The most critical sector of all was the extreme point of the salient where the Red eastern and southern fronts met at a sharp angle. The city of Tzaritsyn lay at the very apex of the salient. If it fell Moscow and the armies could no longer be fed. All eyes were on Tzaritsyn.

# 13

# 'The Red Verdun'

When Tzaritsyn was first attacked by the Whites the town was held by a defence committee headed by the Bolsheviks, Minin, Yerman and Toumak. The Bolsheviks were in a state of panic. Many of their detachments had to be disarmed on account of disaffection and others hung about in the streets refusing to obey orders.

Information came in that two large Red concentrations were moving down on Tzaritsyn from the Donetz Basin, one under the command of Sievers and the other of Voroshilov. The Bolshevik, Serditch, tells us: 'I remember as if it were yesterday a meeting at the French factory. The Chairman of the Tzaritsyn Soviet, Comrade Yerman, was asked: "What are these units? And who are Voroshilov and Sievers?" He replied: "Sievers is an officer, but according to our information he's on our side. As for Voroshilov he is an old secret Bolshevik worker of Lougansk and absolutely trustworthy." Messengers were sent off at once asking both groups to hurry to our assistance.

'Shortly afterwards Voroshilov arrived with his battered army. The Cossacks were close behind him and pressing us on three sides. Our men were just resisting them as best they could, but there was hardly any central control of the defence at all. We all lived from hour to hour, each unit in the defence helping its neighbour as best it could, but hundreds of the men were loafing in the town, occupying the station as though it were a camp and living in the trains so that these could not be used for getting supplies in from the outer districts.

'Voroshilov showed such vigour and determination upon his arrival that the Revolutionary Committee immediately appointed him to the command of all our forces for the defence of Tzaritsyn.'

Many of the men in his own army were so war-weary that they wished to call a halt. They felt that the city was virtually certain to fall to the Whites, upon which they would all be slaughtered, and that therefore the sensible thing was to get the best terms they could from Krasnov by surrendering right away. They thought that Tzaritsyn was only one among many towns that were being held throughout the country by the Red forces, so that its surrender would not materially affect the safety of the Revolution.

Voroshilov, however, insisted that Tzaritsyn was the decisive point in the whole civil war. Under threats from the Allies, the pressure of the German invaders, and with anti-Bolsheviks flocking to the Whites' standards in every direction, the power of the Kremlin was rapidly slipping away. A bloody fight was being waged upon the steppes outside the new capital by Tukachevsky, but even if he succeeded in holding out, Tzaritsyn meant life or death to Moscow. Not only was the town the key to the granary, but it was also the last hope of preventing a junction between the White forces of Admiral Koltchak and General Denikin. Tzaritsyn was the only Red wedge driven into the White armies and Voroshilov insisted to his comrades that they must hold it at all costs.

He immediately set about organising the scattered units, with his own tried fighters as the nucleus, into the Tenth Army of the Republic, gave orders for the strengthening of the defences at critical points and began preparations for a prolonged siege.

Tzaritsyn lies on the west bank of the Volga, but the mighty river bends sharply away from it on both sides, forming an angle; one arm of which runs north-east towards Saratov, Simbirsk and the Urals, and the other south-east to the Caspian Sea. General Krasnov's army occupied the west bank of the Volga encircling the town on three sides. The railway to Moscow was cut, but the pointed east bank of the river remained open to the Bolsheviks and the river itself was still free although under fire. As long as the town held out they were able, by running the gauntlet of machine-guns and artillery each time, to send long strings of barges loaded with grain up to Saratov, and from there the cargoes could be railed to the starving centres of the Revolution.

Only a short time before there had been music in the gay town park and plays had been given on the open-air stage, but now the place resembled a military camp. Government buildings, theatres, cinemas and big private houses were turned into hospitals. The prisons were filled to overflowing with Mensheviks and Whites. In the streets and at every crossroad were patrols stopping all passers-by and examining their documents. Two cruisers, a destroyer and an armoured steamer lay in the Volga. Round the town itself, which formed a 'U' in the great salient of the southern revolutionary front, proper trenches were dug and barbed wire defences put up. Communications were established with the Red partisans who were fighting on an irregular front along both the far-flung wings which stretched for several hundred miles. Soon Voroshilov was directing not only the defence of Tzaritsyn but the operations of the Red forces as far north as Archeda and as far south as Astrakhan. Even the North Caucasus and, for some time, the Red front at Baku came under his control. The total length of the line he was holding exceeded 375 miles.

When Voroshilov took over the defence of Tzaritsyn he not only became the fighting general responsible for this important point, but took a hundred other matters into his capable hands as well. As a metal worker of many years' experience he understood munition plants, and as one who had slaved like themselves, the factory workers responded to his appeals for co-operation in a way they would never have done for a regular soldier. He soon had the idle machine shops running again and staffed by willing workers, who plugged at it night and day turning out every sort of munition.

He organised his command into six divisions and certain additional brigades of specialists as army troops. Their number was nothing like sufficient to hold so wide a front, so he had to devise a way to keep his main bodies perpetually on the move from one threatened sector to another. This was in 1918, when the great armies of Western Europe were still drearily foot-slogging from place to place. 'Waste of energy,' declared Voroshilov, 'and loss of what may be vital time.' In consequence *this civilian soldier was the first man to mechanise an entire army*. He commandeered every working vehicle in Tzaritsyn and repaired all the old ones so that they could rush his infantry to each danger point in turn, built dozens of armoured cars to support them, converted 39 ordinary trains into armoured trains and made 11 more brand new ones. It was, perhaps, because he had spent his early life in the machine shops instead of exercising horses that he was able to visualise war from a new angle. The following passages are from the memoirs of Tarassov-Rodionov who was present at the siege.

'The Soviet Government was not then a year old. Trains hardly crept from one station to another in twenty-four hours. All over Russia rusting factories stood in cold grim silence. The worker families pounded potato peelings and greedily waited for any word from their vanished bread-winners, who were scattered over the innumerable and endless fronts of war. At that time from the walls of houses greyish tatters of newspaper placards frenziedly shrieked the grim news.

'LOCKHART AND NOLAN'S PLOT AGAINST SOVIET GOVERNMENT. . . . DORA KAPLAN SERIOUSLY WOUNDS LENIN. . . . GERMANS PLUNDER UKRAINE. . . . FRENCH LAND ARMY AT MURMANSK. . . . ENGLISH TAKE ARCHANGEL. . . . CZECHO-SLOVAK WHITE GUARDS EXECUTE KAZAN WORKERS. . . . JAPANESE MOVE ON CHITA. . . . GENERAL KRASNOV CONCENTRATES ALL FORCES ON RED TZARITSYN.

'Had you entered the Central Recruiting Depot in Moscow and pushed your way down the dark narrow corridors of that stuffy house through crowds of torn leather jackets, with volunteers awaiting travelling papers for all parts of the country and had you, at last, asked any of the secretaries, "Comrade, which of all these fronts is at present the most dangerous?" you would unquestionably have received this answer: "Tzaritsyn, Comrade. At present it is the sole key to our food supply; without grain we cannot keep on. Tzaritsyn too is the only Red wedge we have thrust into the United Counter Revolution by which our enemies are hemming us in."

'In Tzaritsyn the factories were working at full blast turning out the thousand-and-one necessities needed by the army. Middle-class folk huddled in their little homes peering through their windows, constantly saw the newly-formed units of Red Guards marching off from the barracks to the front, repaired armoured cars issuing from the factory gates, wagons taking mountains of bread, bundles of uniform coats, ammunition and cases of water-melon sugar to the Army supply centres.

'Voroshilov was everywhere. Something went wrong with the dockers who were loading the grain barges; he went down to the docks and settled it. The Mensheviks tried to sabotage our motions in the Soviets; he threw them out. The downhearted elements at the factories talked of throwing up their jobs; he put new life into them.

'The troops of Krasnov lay like an iron horse-shoe round the town; their flanks resting on the banks of the flooded Volga. The whites knew that the fall of Tzaritsyn meant an open road to Moscow and victory. They dared not leave it untaken in their rear.

'In August, Krasnov's attacks became positively ferocious. He sent his bearded Don Cossacks under Mamontov hurtling against us and his White Officer infantry battalions sometimes came to the assault with the bayonet as often as three times in one day. They pressed us right back on to the Volga and at some points they penetrated to within five miles of the town. Our units, badly armed, half equipped, bleeding, ragged, fought rearguard action after rearguard action. They became so desperate that one night a number of the Commanders met to arrange for a retirement across the river the following morning.

'That evening an order came from Voroshilov: "Not a step back. We counter-attack at dawn." He had roused the whole town, equipped a worker regiment to reinforce us, and was forming still further battalions all that night in the French factory, which reached us during the course of the morning. After fierce fighting at Beketovka and Vorotonov the Whites were thrown back and retired with heavy losses.

' "Food, food," came the perpetual cry from the divisions. "Why so little sugar issued? We must have a little meat. Not enough boots—we must have boots!" Somehow, Voroshilov found time to see to everything and yet was always present whenever a sector was seriously threatened at the front. Here are two typical incidents. Riding out to the south of Krivaia-Mouzda one day he saw that the so-called "steel division" commanded by Zhlova, which numbered some 5,000 bayonets, 2,000 sabres and 25 guns, had been badly shaken by a cavalry attack and that the Cossacks had succeeded in turning the division's left flank. Voroshilov rode straight at the enemy. The men who were fleeing before the Cossacks rallied immediately upon seeing his well-loved figure. The encircling movement was checked and the White cavalry driven off.

'On another occasion, the Whites were making a separate attack on Goumrak. The day was silvery with a pale sun. Voroshilov had gone himself to the front to see that his orders given during the night had been carried out. He entered a staff coach on a train at Voroponovo station, a few miles outside

Tzaritsyn, for a conference. He took his seat in a corner and bent over the map. Next to him sat black-bearded Koulik, the commander of the Army artillery; on the other side Alya-baiev, commander of the armoured trains, his pale young face propped in his hands from weariness. Khoudiakov, commanding the First Communist Division, which was holding a distant sector, came in unshaven and hoarse from shouting; he dragged a wounded foot, wrapped in a sock and soft slipper.

'Through the window we could see the trains loaded with goods and refugees from the Don, standing peacefully on the sidings; and other trains with the wounded, some of which were from the previous night's battle. There were not sufficient engines at this time, and the station was hopelessly choked. As the army commander and his assistants were intently studying the situation there came a sudden wild cry from somewhere near the trucks: "Cossacks!"

'In an instant the half-naked children and women and old men refugees poured shrieking from the wagons, on to the track, under the wheels, out on to the level grey steppes; and the wounded soldiers creeping round the door jambs tumbled out on to the ground, their bandaged stumps bleeding, groaning and gasping. Some of them tried to grip their rifles under their elbows and load them with their teeth, though all that hopeless heroism was useless among the helpless mass of fleeing refugees.

'Voroshilov, Koulik, Alyabiev, and the rest leapt out of their coach in a second, and stood staring towards the south. The wounded Khoudiakov was already running down the station platform; one foot in a boot and the other in a sock only as his slipper had fallen off. He was cursing terribly, waving his revolver in the air, and trying to turn out a dozen Red Army men who had hidden beneath a truck.

'Voroshilov calmly unslung the carbine he always carried. Against the background of the village orchards to the south could be seen a cavalry column of the enemy making for us across a hollow. Perhaps it was only a few squadrons, perhaps it was a whole regiment, which had broken through. None of us knew, but one thing was clear, there was no force at the station which could put up a defence. In about five minutes the enemy would be on us and cut every man down. Someone beside Voroshilov whispered swiftly: "Your horse is good. Get off at once. Escape! Escape!"

'The speaker had voiced the thoughts of us all. Our one reaction had been—how can we save our irreplaceable and beloved army commander. Voroshilov turned and looked the man who had spoken up and down with a scornful glance. Next second his eye fell on a machine-gun just by the station building, evidently mounted for defence, but now abandoned in the panic.

'He rushed at it, tumbled it into a ditch behind the building, trained it on the enemy, pushed a ribbon of bullets into it, and suddenly the angry tattoo of the gun echoed hollowly among the abandoned trains. We all rushed to help him, but the squadron of enemy cavalry, deploying as it came out of the hollow, was already plunging about in disorder as the bullets found their mark. The rearward ranks hastily turned about and galloped off into the distance.

'Voroshilov left some of the Red Army men posted by the gun and, pulling his map out of his pocket, went back to the train. He took up the conversation exactly where it had been broken off, as though those recent moments, when we were all in imminent danger of our lives, had never happened.

'He used to say: "We must always be ready to fight in an unexpected position. It is better to perish in an attack than to be killed or wounded while falling back," and he grafted that idea on the army.

'Even such chance Allies of the Red Army as Doumenko, the Cossack chief, whom Voroshilov restrained from excesses and showing their brigand natures, who recognised neither party nor the decencies of humanity, who stayed with us only from love of fighting; even these, who would not accept orders from the Revolutionary Council, obeyed Voroshilov with respect—but only Voroshilov.

'He was always at the front among his lads. Some he would teach quietly, others lecture, and others again give a thorough blowing up, but he would always do it without any fuss. To those who had behaved stupidly he would give a sharp, fixed glance, then smile and say something so simple, but at the same time so much to the point, that the culprit would immediately wish that the earth would open and swallow him up.

' "Of course," he would say later, "we are all partisans. We have had no military schooling, and for lack of that we are paying dearly now. One cannot expect too much, but all will be well as long as the men continue to show such splendid courage.'

'Sometimes those civilian soldiers were under the fiercest pressure from the trained troops of the enemy, and the bands of gold-epauletted officers nearly broke their way into the outskirts of the city. Then the sirens shrieked the alarm. The workers streamed out of the munition factories and made for the hillocks or a roof-top nearby, with the very rifles which they had been repairing still in their hands. The troops of the Czarist Army could not break them.

'In the middle of the town the three-storied mansion of a rich mustard manufacturer had been taken over as the headquarters of the Tenth Army.

'The ground floor held the general offices, where typewriters rattled without cessation, and the telephone exchange. There were lines to all the principal units and a direct one to Moscow. Roukhimovich hung on it night and day without a sign of weariness, except for blinking his eyes which were red from want of sleep. Tall Marochkin also worked there; he could constantly be seen with his Guban fur *papenka* on the back of his head running between the office and the factories. Koulik, the ex-sergeant artillery commander, too; he was known as "Grand-dad" in the army on account of his thick black beard.

'Voroshilov, wearing a felt cloak, a leather jacket girt round with a strap, and a Mauser pistol at his side, would come storming in from one of his daily tours of the battle front.

' "Marochkin!" he would shout. "Are we never to have the girths and traces promised us? Koulik, where are the panoramic gun sights short on the last order? Roukhimovich, get on the telephone to Moscow and hurry them up with the heavy shells. You're all asleep, damn you!" and he would curse loud and long.

'The first floor of the great house contained the ballroom, where sessions of the Army Council were held, and other rooms for the Operations Staff; Efim Shchadenko, an ex-tailor, Maguidov, an ex-watchmaker, and Minin, the son of a priest; all key men in the defence of the beleaguered city. Here also was a big room in which the fluctuations of the battle front were marked off on a large wall map with scrupulous care in coloured wools. Not a single non-Party man was ever allowed inside that Holy of Holies of the War. Young Roudinev guarded it with the jealousy of a tiger, until he was killed on one of his trips to the front; then his place was taken by the new chief of staff, dour, thin Matziletski, whose sunken eyes glinted darkly from beneath the crumpled forage cap he always wore.

'On the top floor were the living quarters. In a spacious, well-lit dining-room five or six of the Revolutionary Council always fed, and any divisional commanders who had come in from the front. The food was simple and good, but during this time of critical operations, Voroshilov would never allow any spirits on the table. Outside was a sort of cupboard where Voroshilov's faithful follower, Shchadenko, the Political Commissar of the Tenth Army and special emissary of the Central Military Council of the Revolution, dossed down on a tumbled heap of coats and top-boots. Across the landing was Voroshilov's room, where his young wife, that stylish elegant woman, Caterina Davydovna, the ballet dancer, spent a good part of her time lounging on a wide mahogany bed, smoking cigarette after cigarette, while the cursing, stamping din went on below.

'When she was bored she would amuse herself dashing up and down the town in a military motor car, wearing a wide-skirted Persian lamb coat and a rakish Cossack *papenka,* cocked at an angle on her handsome head. She seemed much too much of an aristocrat for the wife of a workers' leader; they resented the sight of her beautiful clothes and carefully tended person in that war-scarred city, but Voroshilov had never been a hypocrite. He had never held that because the workers led drab and ugly lives they should always remain drab and ugly. He wanted plenty and culture and beautiful things for all. For many years he had given eleven out of every twelve waking hours to his work for the Revolution, but he reserved his right in the twelfth hour to enjoy himself as he saw fit; and he was a great enjoyer. No man living could accuse him of ever having sold the cause for special benefits. Clim Voroshilov was above reproach and even the revolutionaries who believed that one could not be a true proletarian without dirty hands, suffered the presence of the beautiful Caterina Davydovna without a murmur.'

All through the summer, Lenin and the Council of People's Commissars, in Moscow, had been tensely watching Tzaritsyn. They had no troops with which to reinforce it, but among them was one man who was worth an army corps; a round-shouldered, unimpressive-looking individual with a long drooping moustache and a face pitted by smallpox—'Koba' Stalin.

In the autumn, Lenin asked him to go to the 'Red Verdun', as the Bolsheviks so proudly called Tzaritsyn, and by his presence support Voroshilov. Before his departure, Stalin said in a tired voice to the council: 'For a long time now I seem to have become a *specialist* in cleaning up the Augean stables of the Ministry of War.'

That was a sly dig at his irreconcilable enemy, the journalist Trotsky, who was President of the Revolutionary Army Soviet and War Lord of the new Republic. Every general was under him, and all supplies and munitions and army reserves were in his hands. His was supposed to be the final word in all army matters, but wherever his arrangements broke down or a Bolshevik army looked like being smashed—in fact, at every danger point in turn—Stalin, the incorruptible, would suddenly make his appearance, secure the dismissal of incompetent leaders, weed out the untrustworthy element among the officers, and support the most dependable through his immense power of personal touch with Lenin, and his privilege of going over Trotsky's head.

Trotsky, as we know, was also now appearing in person on the most important fronts at critical times, and the methods of both these men for strengthening the resistance of the Red troops were the same—merciless cruelty and wholesale executions. Trotsky would also address meetings of the worker masses before the shootings, making speeches of hysterical denunciation against the men who were to be shot, and lengthy exhortations to fighting troops which were meant to go down to history. Stalin, on the other hand, could neither speak nor write well, but he had the nose of a ferret for disaffection and carried out his work in ruthless, sinister silence. The two men hated each other; Trotsky because of Stalin's interference, and Stalin because he considered Trotsky an incompetent windbag.

Before Stalin left the Kremlin, Lenin expressed anxiety regarding a revolt of the Mensheviks in the south, but Stalin reassured him in his melancholy voice.

'You can rest quiet about those hysterical creatures, Vladimir Ilyich. I'll have no scruples whatever. Enemies must be treated as enemies,' and pressing Lenin's hand he departed.

In dusty Tzaritsyn on the Volga, the dried leaves were fluttering down from the trees and the wind was whistling through the streets with the penetrating cold of the October steppes when Stalin arrived. He knew Voroshilov well, having worked with him as an underground revolutionary at Baku in 1911. They worked together again with complete trust and confidence in each other.

Voroshilov remained the actual army commander responsible for the defence of the town. Stalin was the political agent of the Kremlin; there to stamp out treachery and strengthen Voroshilov's hand by overawing the civil population into a state of terror which should ensure their not striking the army in the back. They were in communication with Moscow by direct wire and it was in use every hour. It was rumoured that the pair never slept at night. Voroshilov planned and organised. Stalin controlled the personnel and broke traitors without mercy.

With them, in the mustard manufacturer's mansion, was Cherviakov, the head of the Tzaritsyn *Cheka* and his executioners. Those arrested on Stalin's orders were taken to the Volga where, in the middle of the silvery water, lay a long black barge. It was there, almost nightly, that executions took place and the bodies were flung overboard into the river. Stalin was doing his work of clearing out the Augean stable and his name was only mentioned with bated breath. The Red Terror gripped the town.

The siege dragged on. Voroshilov was desperately short of men. Trotsky promised him reinforcements and sent the whole Volskia Division down the Volga. The officers were reactionaries and untrustworthy and allowed the men to desert. Only one brigade reached Tzaritsyn and that did not withstand the first enemy attack. Part of it was taken prisoner and part of it ran away; Voroshilov had to rush up his fighting partisans to fill the gap. These worker-soldiers became so devoted to him that they began to call themselves 'Voroshilov Men', but he refused to allow it, saying that they must regard themselves as 'Lenin Men' only.

By this time Voroshilov had developed into an extremely capable fighting general. He knew nothing of strategy and tactics as laid down in military manuals, but he had enormous energy and was prodigiously brave. Even the Whites wrote of him in November: 'One has to give credit where credit is due. Though the former mechanic Voroshilov is no strategist in the generally accepted meaning of the word, it cannot be denied that he has great ability for stubborn resistance and for shock tactics.'

He showed his presence of mind in many a battle. Over and over again he led the attack on the enemy's machine-guns himself or rushed in his car to a point in the line where danger threatened to take a hand personally in driving off the Cossacks.

Nominally he was under the orders of the ex-Czarist General Sytin, and later the ex-Czarist General Vazetis, whom Trotsky had placed in command of the whole south revolutionary front, but he refused to obey orders and went on fighting in his own inimitable way. Stalin supported him, telling him again and again: 'You are the Red general for the men, Clim. They know you're to be trusted and you're worth a hundred of these treacherous ex-White officers.'

Trotsky was not slow to see that an opposition of strong determined men was being forged against him in Tzaritsyn. Stalin, Voroshilov, Shchadenka and the rest were not of the Intelligentsia, neither were they international revolutionaries; they were Russian working men who had determined to build a new Russia from their own knowledge of how the Russian people could better work and live. They were anti-intellectual and anti-Semitic. Tale bearers whispered that in the mustard manufacturer's mansion talkers and theorists were despised, and that a real Russian spirit reigned there, including the enjoyment of drink and women. They would not listen to the advice of the ex-White military experts, but were determined to fight their own war in their own way.

One night when the Tzaritsyn Army Council was in session, in the big ballroom, the Whites were pressing forward and the position was desperate. Instead of sending more shells Trotsky sent an angry telegram from Moscow that the ex-Czarist General Nossovitch was on his way to take over the command.

Voroshilov was furious. 'Of course,' he shouted, 'we are only partisans. We've had no training in military schools and academies, but that fool Trotsky will never learn his lesson and realise that we are more to be relied upon than these ex-

Czarists who don't give a damn for the Revolution and would betray us at the first opportunity.'

The taciturn Stalin, ever sucking at his pipe, sat slouched over one corner of the table. He took the telegram and scribbled across it: 'No notice to be taken."¹ Voroshilov gave an order to Cherviakov of the *Cheka* that General Nossovitch was to be arrested immediately he arrived and confined on the black barge in the river. The Council continued its session.

Autumn drew into winter. Voroshilov had succeeded in straightening one wing of his salient and cleared the railway, opening up communication by train with Moscow. The snow had come, the men were freezing in their trenches, and Mamontov's Cossacks were still attacking doggedly. Urgent appeals were again made to Trotsky for reinforcements. He promised to send the Eleventh 'Iron' Division, but this also failed to arrive. When it reached Novakhopersk, the much praised 'Iron' Division with its two brigades of 35 guns and 100 machine-guns, under the command of officers just released by Trotsky's express orders from the Nizhniy-Novgorod *Cheka*, unfurled its banners and went straight over to the Whites.

'We must send cavalry that we can trust against Mamontov,' said Voroshilov, 'but where the devil are we to get it? Doumenko is a good fighter, but he's cunning and we can't depend upon him. If he were to find Mamontov too hard a nut to crack he might quite well take his men over to the enemy. We know from the *Cheka* report that Krasnov wrote him a letter promising forgiveness if he would. You, Shchadenko, keep a sharp eye on Doumenko. Send him reinforcements, but see that there are plenty of trustworthy politicals among them. There's one fellow called Budenny, a great big chap with an enormous moustache, an ex-sergeant of the dragoons. I noticed him the other day: he's bold and reliable. Send him, and make him responsible for Doumenko's good conduct.'

It was in that way that Budenny, who afterwards became famous as the great cavalry leader and was christened 'The Red Murat', first came to prominence through that eagle-eyed picker of men, Voroshilov.

In spite of the magnificent way in which he was conducting his operations Main Headquarters were constantly sending in complaints of him to Trotsky. 'Voroshilov will not obey orders. Voroshilov does not reply to questions. Voroshilov has

1. This telegram is now in the Soviet War Museum.

arrested General Nossovitch whom you sent to supersede him in his command.' Trotsky sent frantic telegrams to Tzaritsyn but Stalin tore them up.

In the Kremlin, however, Lenin was growing anxious. Could Voroshilov's 'resistance of the people' continue to withstand the strategy of the White generals? Had the ill-favoured 'Koba' Stalin succeeded in giving this 'resistance' a renewed strength?

From the Headquarters of Vazetis Trotsky sent telegram after telegram to the inscrutable Lenin who had not yet pronounced in favour of either party, and ended up with one which read: '*Imperatively insist upon the recall of Stalin. Tzaritsyn is in a bad way although we have a preponderance of man-power there. Voroshilov is capable of commanding a regiment but not a force of 50,000 men. I have ordered him to send me reports of operations and reconnaissances twice daily. If this is not done tomorrow I shall have him court-martialled.*'

It seemed as if Trotsky had won this internal war, for Lenin recalled Stalin to Moscow and Trotsky went down by train himself to Tzaritsyn to tackle Voroshilov.

Trotsky's train drew up in one of the stations beside that of Stalin who was proceeding in the opposite direction, to Moscow. Stalin got out of his train and slouched across to Trotsky's carriage. The War Minister was there surrounded by his staff of commissars and *ci-devant* officers. Stalin stood in the doorway wearing a worn soldier's coat, a dirty cap and unclean top-boots. The splenetic journalist rounded on him, crying: 'I must have a Left Wing to the Southern Front that I can depend on. I must have it. I will have it. I will have it at all costs.'

Stalin leaned against the door jamb; a faintly insolent smile in his lazy oriental eyes. He sucked at his pipe and spat: 'But surely, Comrade Trotsky, you don't intend to get rid of all the leaders at Tzaritsyn, do you? I shouldn't try that if I were you. They're good fellows.'

'These "good" fellows will ruin the Revolution,' raged Trotsky, 'and the Revolution can't wait for them to grow up. I don't know yet who I shall get rid of, but somebody's got to go. There's one thing I insist on, Comrade Stalin, and that is the inclusion of Tzaritsyn in Soviet Russia. Do you understand? Whoever is in command there must take his orders from me.'

Stalin screwed up his yellow eyes, shrugged his sloping shoulders and left the carriage.

When Trotsky's train steamed into besieged Tzaritsyn a few hours later Voroshilov did not come to the station to meet him. He was busy and in his place he sent his reckless adherent the artful, heavy-browed, squint-eyed Political Commissar Shchadenko, the ex-tailor. While Shchadenko was feeling out the lie of the land Voroshilov was raging up and down his room at Headquarters swearing in good Russian at Trotsky; the ex-Menshevik who had only come over to the party eighteen months before. He cursed him for a miserable cosmopolitan *émigré* who had not set eyes on Russia for years yet dared to come there and threaten to sweep out the real Russians who had made the Revolution; for a meddling Jew who had the insolence to talk of replacing them by treacherous Czarist generals.

When Trotsky arrived Voroshilov received him in the room where the Army Council sittings were held. He had with him his chief of staff and Trotsky was accompanied by his secretary. Voroshilov had just returned from a visit to the northern sector of his front; he was clad in his usual leather jacket, girt round with a strap and had a Mauser pistol at his side. He had thrown his felt cloak over the back of a chair.

The two men differed in every way; in culture, in mind, in habit of thought, in temperament as well as in appearance. The one, a typical Jew with a sharp, rather cruel face and oriental head of black wavy hair over a big forehead; the other, a typical broad-nosed, square-jawed Russian workman, with a cleft chin and blue eyes as hard as ice.

When they were seated Trotsky took off his glasses, wiped them carefully and spoke: 'In my quality of President of the Army Soviet, Comrade Voroshilov, I consider it my duty first of all to put one cardinal question to you. Do you consider it necessary for the victory of the Revolution to obey implicitly *all* the orders of the Commander in Chief?'

Voroshilov drew his eyebrows together: 'I consider it necessary to obey *such* orders as I recognise to be right.' He stared with open hostility in front of him and his fingers drummed upon the butt of the automatic in his belt.

This was something very different to the reception Trotsky had been used to from other revolutionary generals. 'Comrade Voroshilov,' he said, 'in my quality of President of the

Army Soviet responsible for all fronts of the Republic, I must bring to your notice that unless, here and now, you undertake in future unconditionally to obey *all* orders and carry out *all* operations as instructed, I shall send you under guard to Moscow to be tried by the revolutionary tribunal.'

'What!' shouted Voroshilov, springing up and kicking away his chair from under him. 'I'm no diplomat, Comrade Trotsky. I go straight to the point. While I'm in command at Tzaritsyn I will obey all orders I consider suitable. I'm in a better position here on the spot to judge than either you or the C. in C. Vazetis at Headquarters. You sent me a White general and where is he now, this Nossovitch? I arrested him on his arrival as a suspect, instead of having him shot as I should have done. At your order I set him free and like the snake he is he has deserted to the Whites with all his staff and all the confidential papers of one of your armies. That's the man you would have liked me to hand over my command to. As for the tribunal— all right. I'm a Bolshevik and a Bolshevik of older standing than you. I've no fear of any tribunal. I've worked in the *Cheka* myself. Let them judge me.'

Trotsky's sickly face went white with rage. 'You fool,' he sneered, 'the time for guerilla warfare is over. If we keep on as we have in the past, the train of the Revolution is going to crash. As for the desertion of Nossovitch, are you sure he didn't go over to the Whites because you put him in the hands of the *Cheka* instead of letting him do the work he was sent here to do? He didn't desert while he was with Sytin. D'you know how many military specialists we've won over to our cause? Thirty thousand! Would you replace them all by untrained worker partisans?'

Voroshilov banged the table with his clenched fist: 'I know how many Don Basin workmen broke through the hornet's nest of Cossack armies with me. I know how much real heroism was shown by these plain people uneducated in military finesse. They'll fight like devils under me, but they won't fight under your ex-Czarist generals and colonels whom they've every reason to distrust.'

'We'll see about that,' sneered Trotsky, and he stamped from the room.

That night Trotsky, stretched on a sofa in his room upstairs, said to his secretary: 'I can see that Stalin has been very clever here in choosing all the people with corns that have been trodden on; but I know how to deal with them.' He laughed, and went on to mention whom he would dismiss and whom he would replace by whom in Tzaritsyn. But Trotsky did not send Voroshilov under guard to Moscow, nor did Voroshilov submit to Trotsky.

In the meantime Stalin had arrived in Moscow and seen Lenin. Next morning a telegram was handed to Trotsky from the master of them all which read, *'Stalin has arrived today, bringing with him the news of three great victories to our arms at Tzaritsyn. He has persuaded Voroshilov and the rest of those whom he considers valuable and even irreplaceable to remain on and in future work with Headquarters. In Stalin's view the sole reason for their dissatisfaction is the extreme delay in your delivery of munitions to them. That is also why the Caucasian army of 20,000 excellently disposed men is being destroyed. In bringing these statements of Stalin's to your notice I ask you to think them over and reply, firstly, whether you are willing to have a heart-to-heart talk with him yourself, for which he is quite prepared to come to you, and secondly, whether you think it possible under certain stated conditions to put aside all former misunderstanding and too arrange to work together, which is what Stalin so much desires. As for me, I am of the opinion that it is absolutely necessary to do all in your power to attain co-operation with Stalin.'*

Trotsky knew that Stalin had beaten him for the moment, but he was not resigned to accept total defeat, and without seeing Voroshilov again he wired to the Kremlin: *'Agree to meet Stalin, but to leave Voroshilov here after the failure of all attempts at compromise is impossible. We must send a new staff and a new commander to Tzaritsyn. Moving Voroshilov to the Ukraine.'*

Party discipline demanded that Voroshilov obey the order. Frowning and cursing, he penned a farewell order in his schoolboy hand to the army of the Red Verdun, calling upon the men to continue stubbornly and mercilessly in the fight to beat the enemy. Gloomily thumping his heavily iron-shod greased boots, he went downstairs to the staff offices and threw the order to a typist to copy. Immediately afterwards he set out for Moscow with his personal entourage and Caterina Davydovna.

In Moscow he found that the representative of the Tzaritsyn army, a sailor named Zhivoder, had already been 'liquidated' by Trotsky. In Moscow, too, on Voroshilov's arrival Trotsky's friend Sosnovsky, the editor of the *Pravda,* published an article under the heading, 'The Small Defects of our Machinery.' It was a detailed account of one of Voroshilov's Tzaritsyn orgies when, after a victorious battle, the commander of the army, accompanied by his friends, had galloped madly about the town in three spanking *troikas* with women and, in one of the villages outside, had danced the *trepak,* made a row and finished up by smacking somebody's face; which performance, so the article ran, brought grave discredit upon the Soviet State.

Voroshilov was furious. 'All right,' he stormed, 'I did smack somebody's face. And drank. And kicked up the devil's own row in the company of women! Well, and what then? Do I cease to be a man just because I command an army?' But on the advice of his friends he wrote a refutation to *Pravda*, saying that nothing of the kind had ever happened, and that all this talk was sheer invention on the part of counter-revolutionaries.

For the moment Trotsky, the scribbler and windbag, had bested him; but only for the moment. Lenin had known him and trusted him for many a year. 'Koba' Stalin, the round-shouldered, shrewd-brained Georgian who was the power behind the throne, had worked and fought, with him for many months and realised his capabilities. The army that he had led out of the death-trap in the Ukraine to the shelter of Tzaritsyn would have died for him to a man. The soldiers who had defended the Red Verdun with him had adored him for his bravery. Even the ex-White officers who had come over to the Reds admired the splendid vigour of his tactics and to the fighting workers he was still one of themselves, yet gifted beyond them all. From June to December, unaided by experienced military commanders, he had held the Red Verdun against the Cossack hordes. Whatever might happen now, Voroshilov would go down to history as the man who had hung out in the 'salient of death' on the southern front, fed Moscow, and saved the Revolution.

# 14

## The 'Little Napoleon' and the 'Organiser of Victories'

Within three weeks of Tukachevsky's capture of Samara, and while Voroshilov was still commanding at Tzaritsyn, events of the first magnitude occurred in the west. At the end of October Bulgaria collapsed; the Dual Monarchy and Turkey followed a few days later and finally, Germany, the colossus who had held the tottering Central Powers together for so long, asked the Allies for an Armistice.

The German Army had performed the stupendous feat of holding 250 miles of western front and an eastern front averaging 500 miles for nearly four and a half years; had overrun Belgium, Poland, part of France, Roumania, the Ukraine and the Russian Baltic provinces; had sent specialists, divisions and often several army corps to the support of its weaker Allies on every front; had assisted the Turks in Palestine, the Bulgarians opposite Salonika and enabled the Austrians to smash the Italians on the Piave, yet it remained unbroken to the end.

The Churchill plan of breaking the iron ring of the Central Powers at its weakest point having matured, it is impossible to say how long the Germans alone could have withstood the entire weight of the Allies. For some months the Americans had been arriving in great numbers on the western front, yet if they had not been used to better purpose than the British in the previous year many months of further carnage might have ensued before they could have forced a decision. One thing is certain, the German Army would have stood again on the line of the Meuse and fought desperately in defence of its homeland along the Rhine if it had not been for the British navy and the Council of People's Commissars in Moscow.

The blockade had reduced the home population of the Central Powers to semi-starvation by the autumn of 1918 but, so strong was the German 'Will to Victory' that even so they would probably have fought on if it had not been for the Peace of Brest-Litovsk. The intensive revolutionary propaganda pumped out by the Bolsheviks from that date not only incapacitated the 57 divisions stationed on Germany's eastern front, as we have seen, but filtered back through soldiers on leave and many underground channels, once the eastern frontier was reopened, to the civilians in German cities. It enormously strengthened the Pacifist activities of the German Socialists and undermined the staying powers of the non-combatants. On November 8th the sailors at Kiel, in the big battleships which had seen very little war service, revolted, arrested their officers and established Soviets. On November 9th risings took place in many German cities and the German Revolution became a *fait accompli*. This instantly affected the army of the west, and while many units continued firm others began to disintegrate; the men deciding to march home without orders. On the 11th the Germans signed the Armistice.

The termination of the war in the west was later to have a great bearing on the Russian situation, but for the time being it did not affect it at all. From his headquarters at Omsk Admiral Koltchak proclaimed himself the 'Supreme Ruler' of all Russia on November 18th. He had made an excellent impression on the representatives of the Allies and they were prepared to back him to the limit. The Japanese had penetrated as far as Irkutsk and with the Ataman Semenov were subduing the country behind him; the Czechs held Chita, the Urals, and beyond.

Tukachevsky had temporarily saved the Russian eastern front, but the Bolsheviks were now threatened on many others. Under the terms of the Armistice the Germans were to evacuate all territories annexed by the treaty of Brest-Litovsk, but the French more or less ordered them to remain in the Ukraine until the White general, Denikin, whom they appointed 'Dictator' in the south, could take over, and landed 12,000 mixed troops on the western shore of the Black Sea to support him. The British, who were established at Murmansk and Archangel in the north, sent a squadron into the Baltic to land arms for the anti-Bolshevik Esthonians and the White General Yudenitch and reinforced the Kuban by landing a division at Batum.

The most pressing danger lay in the south where the old

Hetman of Don Cossacks, Krasnov, was still hammering at Tzaritsyn and Denikin had also crossed the Don, bringing with him the flower of the White Army; General Kornilov's battalions of officers and General Chkouro's 'Division of Wolves', celebrated for their rapid and unexpected advances. Between them they entirely cut to pieces the Bolshevik Second Army.

Vatzetis, the Bolshevik C. in C., wished to deploy Tukachevsky's army towards the threatened area. Tukachevsky was extremely loath to break off his victorious campaign in the east, and the usual battle of telegrams began. Lenin supported Vatzetis and Tukachevsky was compelled to give way, but at his patron Trotsky's insistence, he was now made second in command of the whole front. In his new campaign against Denikin and Krasnov he had to fight against his old companions of the Semenov Regiment, so he was faced with the gibbet or glory, as the Whites gave no quarter.

On December 2nd, 1919, the Bolsheviks broadcast a plea for peace, offering even to settle the defunct Empire's financial obligations if they were given time to pay, and as an earnest of good faith, the granting of gold and mining concessions with immediate shipments of flax and other raw materials. Convinced that a few months would now see the Whites in power, the Allies ignored these overtures.

With Tukachevsky's withdrawal from the Russian eastern front, Admiral Koltchak gained victory after victory. The 'Supreme Ruler' now attempted a gigantic operation. The White leaders on the other fronts acknowledged him as C. in C., and in spite of the enormous difficulty of communication, he arranged a joint effort with them. His southern armies were to cross the Volga on a bridge of boats and retake Simbirsk, whilst those in the north were to combine with the Allied Expeditionary Force under General Ironside, at Archangel and descend on Petrograd. In the meantime General Yudenitch, commanding the White forces in the Baltic Provinces, was to march on Petrograd from the south-west.

Owing to Trotsky's antagonism, Voroshilov was temporarily under a cloud. After kicking his heels in the capital for some time, he was made Minister for Home Affairs in his native Ukraine, and employed himself in endeavouring to put down countless bands of robbers and the sporadic risings which were constantly occurring there. It was police work rather than a soldier's business and consisted of innumerable small affrays without any fixed front or major operations.

On March 4th, 1919, Koltchak launched his great offensive. The Fifth Red Army was outflanked and Birsk taken; the Bolsheviks panicked and the road to Moscow now lay open. At this new crisis the Kremlin ordered everything to the east, and Lenin issued a telegram to all commanders: 'Arrest at all price the advance of Koltchak. If between now and the winter we are not masters of the Urals I shall consider the failure of the Revolution as inevitable.'

Michael Frunze was appointed to direct the operations against Koltchak, and gave the brilliant young Tukachevsky, who was sent to his support, command of the Fifth Red Army. Tukachevsky thus once more assumed the principal rôle in the defence of the Kremlin and immediately laid a new plan before Frunze. This extremely capable soldier said of him: 'He is a cold man, a stranger to all the joys of youth, and his sole passion is war. He is a great gambler, intrepid, but almost too daring.' However, he accepted Tukachevsky's scheme for the new campaign.

Tukachevsky was pitted against the White General Kanghine, and both commanders attempted the same operation of opening the wings of their forces like the pincers of a claw. The clash took place on May 30th, and the whole fate of the campaign hung upon the result of the battle. The Cossacks of Orenberg and Prince Galitzine's division of white Bashkirs fought with magnificent bravery, but Tukachevsky was victorious.

He was following up the retreating enemy with tremendous vigour when, to his intense fury, he was halted by an order from headquarters to abandon the pursuit and move north on Birsk. After heated protests he submitted and earned new glory in a fresh advance, taking Birsk on June the 7th and Oufa on the 9th. This great battle was fought out under a brassy sun and it was considered as the 'Soviet Aisne', after which the war on this front was to turn in the favour of the Bolsheviks.

In the meantime the drive south from Archangel had failed to mature and, after an initial success, Yudenitch's advance from Revel was checked almost at the gates of Petrograd. Vatzetis, at Bolshevik G.H.Q., was nervous, however, and interfered with Tukachevsky again, stopping his pursuit of the enemy on the eastern front and demanding a halt to consolidate the position. Frunze supported Tukachevsky who wished to press on over the Urals, Trotsky backed the ex-Czarist general, but Lenin interfered and agreed that Tukachevsky should be allowed to go forward. Trotsky was so outraged that he resigned, but Lenin refused to accept his resignation.

By this time Tukachevsky was so confident of having Lenin's support that without waiting for Moscow to argue out the matter he had already made his dispositions for the passage of the mountains. He had with him as Political Commissar an extremely able Communist named Smirnov, who proved invaluable. Smirnov's business was to organise the politicals; both among the soldiers and for special work. He sent many of those into the enemy country to stir up disaffection in the towns behind the Whites and to sow discord among their troops.

At the end of June Tukachevsky put into operation a daring plan. Large numbers of his men passed the peaks of the Urals by scaling little-known rocky paths unguarded by the enemy, and concentrated upon the Siberian side of the range. By July the 5th his main forces were well behind the White lines and, taking them entirely by surprise, he massacred the whole of Kanghine's Twelfth Division. The 2nd and 3rd Armies of the Republic were sent to Tukachevsky's assistance and by the end of July he debouched on to the Siberian Plain, having achieved a very great strategic victory.

He always lived on his special train where he had a compartment fitted up as a cabinet-maker's workroom and, in it, employed his leisure making violins. He gave the instruments he made to anyone who would accept them; his own playing was still execrable. His brother and his wife lived on the train with him. The brother was a clever mathematician; he never fought but remained there because, as a nobleman, it was the only place where his life was safe. Tukachevsky had married Maroussia Ijnatiev, an old friend of his school days but a girl of bourgeois parentage.

During the Ural campaign she went on leave to see her family and knowing that her people, like most others in Russia at that time, were desperately short of even the barest necessities, she took some flour and jam from the army stores with her. This was reported to her husband. On the night of her return he charged her with it. Divorce was easy under the

Soviets, but poor Maroussia preferred to shoot herself on their private train.

Life and women were cheaper than flour and jam in Russia in those days, and during the purge of the Army it had become a routine with Tukachevsky to butcher more men in cold blood than he smoked cigarettes, every day. There is no record of his being particularly perturbed by this tragic episode.

It is interesting to compare a happening in Voroshilov's private life. A great lover of gaiety, the theatre and pretty girls he once had an affair with a young actress. After a time he discovered that she was a secret agent of the *Cheka* set to spy on him. He flew into one of his honest, downright rages at the idea of anyone thinking him capable of treachery and taking such steps to trap him; marched straight round to the offices of the dreaded *Cheka,* up to the chief's room, overturned his desk, blacked both his eyes, and gave him a terrific hiding. No one else in Russia would have dared to do such a thing and his audacity might well have cost him his life, but the Kremlin took no action against him, and having the justice to realise that the girl had only been carrying out her orders, he sent her away without a word.

Advancing from the south by forced marches, Tukachevsky rolled up a portion of the White Army, but this rallied at Chelyabinsk and another large White army appeared in his rear. He was now a great way from his bases and his daring looked as though it must prove his undoing. The Kremlin became extremely anxious knowing that their best general had got their Eastern Army into a situation where it seemed extremely probable that it would be annihilated.

On August 5th a great battle was fought, and Tukachevsky would certainly have been defeated if it had not been for the invaluable services of his Political Commissar, Smirnov.

The many secret agents that Smirnov had sent behind the enemy lines were working feverishly and efficiently. A large number of them were in Chelyabinsk; these raised the workers and mobs of the town who sallied out to Tukachevsky's assistance and they turned the tide in favour of the Reds. The Whites sustained a major defeat, and Tukachevsky's armies proceeded to chase them through Siberia.

At the Kremlin telegram after telegram came in announcing the fall of town after town as Tukachevsky's soldiers fought their way eastward. 'Koba' Stalin tossed a pile of the flimsy

messages across the table to Lenin with the cynical remark:
'This little guards officer's a wonder, don't you think, Vladimir
Ilyich? He's got quite the makings of a Napoleon.'

Lenin shrugged: 'Oh, let the boy go on. He serves us well
and if he gets too big for his boots we can always shorten
him a little.'

Stalin nodded: 'Yes, let him go on. We know how to deal
with Napoleons, don't we, Vladimir Ilyich?'

Tukachevsky could not be in two places at once, however,
and it seemed that wherever he was not, acute danger still
threatened the young Republic. In October, Yudenitch made
another attempt to take Petrograd. He failed, largely because
he tactlessly antagonised his Esthonian allies by refusing to
recognise Esthonia's independence, but the defence of the old
capital occasioned the Kremlin grave anxiety, and they were
threatened with an even graver danger from the south where
Denikin's armies were achieving the most striking successes,
Tzaritsyn, no longer animated by the spirit of Voroshilov, fell
to General Wrangel; the whole of the Ukraine was overrun;
the Whites came streaming northward. Tula, only a hundred
miles south of Moscow, was directly threatened from Voronezh and Orel. Kornilov was only eighteen marches from the
capital. The situation was again desperate.

In this, the worst crisis of the whole Civil War, Lenin asked
Stalin to become President of the Military Revolutionary
Committee controlling the Southern front. Stalin and Trotsky
had hated each other since their very first meeting, and this is
the point in Russia's history where Stalin emerges as the more
important of the two. He stipulated that he must be allowed
an entirely free hand with no interference from the War Minister, and that Trotsky was not even to be allowed to set foot
in the territory of the Southern armies. Lenin agreed and
Stalin set about his greatest work in defence of the Revolution.

His first thought was of his old friend who had worked
shoulder to shoulder with him so splendidly at Tzaritsyn in
the previous year. Under Trotsky, Voroshilov had been given
an inferior command; a division of sharpshooters. Stalin at
once recalled him to Headquarters.

So far, Voroshilov's record was that of a brave partisan
worker who had led a force out of the Don Basin under almost
insurmountable difficulties, and, for the best part of eight
months, defended a town of vital importance, but he was now

called on in a completely different capacity; consulted like a Churchill, a Smuts, a Clemenceau or a Geddes, not to devise a strategic plan but to initiate some entirely new policy which might enable the Red generals to stem an invasion. He responded to his task in a most brilliant manner.

He was quick to realise that the success of the Whites lay in their extreme mobility. Mamontov's Cossacks were in one place one day and suddenly appearing thirty miles farther east or west the next. In the enormous areas over which the fighting ranged it was easy for them to outflank the Red armies and take them by surprise. The Bolsheviks had no arm with which they could counter this or any means of defending themselves from these unexpected attacks.

During the siege of Tzaritsyn, as we have seen, Voroshilov had mechanised his army; but it was one thing to mechanise an army based on a central town which had its own workshops and factories, quite another to endeavour to do so when the front consisted of the chain of shifting divisions without fixed bases, and the cities behind them could not be vitalised by the presence of one dominant personality who controlled both troops and workers. Nine-tenths of the factories were either destroyed or broken down ; no new plant had come out of Western Europe to replace deficiencies for over five years; time was an all important factor; the organisation for equipping a mechanised army in such circumstances would have taken months. Even days were precious; the Whites were less than half the distance from Moscow that they had ever been on Tukachevsky's, or any other, front.

Since he could not mechanise a large portion of the Red armies, Voroshilov suggested the next best thing. Each division and even battalion, had a certain number of mounted troops, varying from a few dozen to several hundred, with it. In the chaos of the Revolution there had never been time to create uniform establishments; the men fought on foot, or on horseback if they were capable of riding and could find a mount to carry them. The mounted men must be collected, said Voroshilov, and welded into one terrific striking force.

Stalin agreed immediately and asked Voroshilov to undertake the formation of this new weapon. A Military Revolutionary Council was appointed to command the cavalry. Voroshilov was President; he chose the ex-dragoon sergeant, Semyon Budenny, who he had picked out at Tzaritsyn to take

care of the untrustworthy Doumenko, as actual commander
of the troops and, as the third member of the Council, the
indefatigable ex-tailor, cross-eyed Shchadenko, who had also
served him with such dog-like fidelity at Tzaritsyn.

Early in October the First Cavalry Corps was formed from
scattered bands of horsemen serving with several of the armies.
From the 14th to the 24th it operated against the Whites and
achieved striking successes from its very inception, retaking
Voronezh and Orel. By November 11th other units of cavalry
had been collected, including those of the ex-brigand Kotovsky, the Armenian ex-actor Gaai, the Division of the wild
Cossack free-booter Doumenko, and the whole consolidated
as the First Cavalry Army of the Republic.

Now that he was back in a position of the first importance
Voroshilov worked like a demon. This army of horsemen for
which he was responsible was a very different affair to the
infantry and worker units which had formed the majority of
the fighters in his previous commands; most of them were true
proletarians, whereas the mounted men were nothing of the
kind. Large numbers of them were Red Cossacks, Circassians,
Kalmucks, and Tartars; the rest partisans, peasants who had
risen to seize the land from the White landlords. It was a mob
of reckless disorderly *muzhiks* and semi-Asiatics who believed
neither in God nor the Devil, but thought only of loot and
pillage. They never spoke of Communists except with the utmost contempt, loathed Jews, and did not give a fig for the
Revolution.

Their nominal commander, Budenny, was little better. A
tall, well-set-up man with a coarse peasant face and a moustache like a horse's tail, he had been a cavalry soldier in the
Primorsky Regiment since 1903, served with distinction in the
Russo-Japanese war, and in the World War on the German,
Austrian and Caucasian fronts. A product of the St. Petersburg Riding School, he was the best horseman in his division,
but the quality of his mind is illustrated by a passage from an
article which he wrote a dozen years after he had become
famous and, with the other heroes, was called on frequently to
proclaim his political integrity:

'The iron insistence and bolshevik sturdiness and irrefuta-
bility of marxistically founded argumentation, and, finally,
the party-political authority of Voroshilov helped to over-

come the extreme danger that was hanging over the Red Cavalry.'

One can visualise the poor old chap's great thick fingers, so used to gripping a sabre but so awkward with a pen, laboriously scrawling that sentence in big, straggling characters, then scratching his head as he cursed all politicians, while his good friend 'Clim' laughed kindly at his elbow.

Yet in him, Voroshilov had picked, with unerring judgment, the right man to lead the Cavalry Army. His magnificent figure, his stentorian voice of command and superb horsemanship appealed to the men. He did not understand what fear was and had a born eye for terrain. Within two months of his appointment his name was known in every war office in Europe. They called him 'The Red Murat' after the Marshal Napoleon made King of Naples.

He never read reports unless they concerned the situation of the moment, but carried them for days stuffed in the pockets of his breeches, and he had no more time for Communists than his men.

Once, when he returned to battle headquarters after having been called to Moscow for a special conference, he announced: 'Well boys, there I was in Moscow. I must say I was received quite decently. Drink. Then a motor car was brought round. Fine, powerful car too. Then, just fancy, they gave me this,' he pulled from his breeches pocket a thing that 90 per cent of the proletariat work for years to get and most would give their eyes for—a membership card of the Communist Party—and flung it on the table.

The others roared with laughter. 'Well, shove it back in your pocket,' they said. 'It doesn't require feeding, anyway.'

His troops said openly: 'Communists! Communists are garbage! We're not Communists, and we don't need to be taught how to fight. As for politics, we're not children either. We know what we're fighting for and we're prepared to kill till all's blue for our peasant State.'

In addition to planning innumerable battles with Budenny as they fought their way south, it was Voroshilov's task to bring about the political conversion of these hostile ruffians and try to instil them with the ideals for the betterment of humanity.

Most of them could not even read, so he had the letters of the alphabet painted on large pieces of cardboard and these

hung on the men's backs. As the squadrons rode over the
steppe each trooper had to gallop out in front of the ranks in
turn and the rest had to shout the letter aloud. Then he arranged the men so that the letters on their backs made up
snatches of popular songs and the men in the rear had to sing
them in chorus. Very soon they had all learned to read.

Next began the issue of a Bolshevik paper called *The Red
Cavalryman,* and it became so popular that each copy fell to
rags before it was a day old because so many eager men
handled it. In every regiment men who had some education
were picked out to act as schoolmasters so that lectures and
lessons in a hundred different subjects might be given to the
troops as they sat round their camp fires at night.

His keenness on education is illustrated by one of his cavalry
captains, Gorbachev, who tells us: 'At the height of the fighting
on the Caucasian front Voroshilov called me to headquarters
to entrust me with the formation of a regiment for a special
purpose. Just as I was leaving he said, unexpectedly: "You
speak very badly and that won't do." Then he rose to his feet,
picked up a book and gave it to me. "For a start here is
Turgenev's *Huntsmen's Notes.* Do you know Turgenev?"

'I must admit that my literary attainments at that day were
nil and I confessed as much.

' "Well," he said, "you just read this and then I'll give you
some other books. They'll help you to grow up and help you
to choose your words better. You must study. A Commander
especially needs to study."

'I carried the copy of the *Huntsmen's Notes* in my saddle
bag and took it out at free moments. After a few months I
found that my vocabulary was much bigger and that I expressed myself infinitely better.'

Not content with these immense activities, undertaken during constant fighting, this extraordinary man still found time
to organise hospitals and to think of the civilian population
behind the lines. Having penetrated to the Don he conscripted
the civilian population, got the coal mines working again, sent
the conscripts down the mines, and by their labour was able to
send presents of hundreds of thousands of tons of coal to all
the fireless Bolshevik cities which were suffering from the
desperate cold of the Russian winter.

When he first came among them the men met him with
covert sneers. 'Of course,' they said, 'he's sat in prison and all

that, but sitting in prison's one thing and sitting a horse is another. Can he ride, that's the thing? We know all about these workmen, standing watching their machines all day.'

If he was not a born horseman he soon convinced them that he could manage a horse remarkably well. He challenged that superb horseman Budenny to race him to the next village.

Budenny only flashed his white teeth in a smile and shot forward on his grey stallion like an arrow. The two horses flew like birds over the open plain under the eyes of the joyfully whooping troopers. Budenny's stallion only beat Voroshilov's favourite charger, the English thoroughbred, Mouser, by a neck.

He turned his horse and rode back to the men. 'Now, boys, a song—singers to the front,' and he opened up himself with a resounding chorus:

> 'A cuckoo in the forest
> Counts the years we have to live,
> And a well-aimed leaden bullet
> Cuts short our years of life.'

When quarters were reached in the evening, the staff of the cavalry army pored over their maps in some abandoned country house or cottage by the light of a kerosene lamp. All the benches and stools were littered with cloaks, fur caps, field glasses, swords and revolvers. In addition to the Revolutionary Military Council they had a trained staff; a cavalry general named Klinev, and a Cossack officer named Zotov.

Budenny, always easy-going and jocular, would say: 'Let them talk, Clim. We'll rest. Our business is fighting,' but Voroshilov would listen to their advice and sometimes take it, sometimes reject it, always settling important decisions himself.

In the Don Basin the men began scrounging, piling all sorts of stolen and abandoned gear on their carts and wagons, but Voroshilov would have none of it. He knew that was the reason why the White armies could never make the most of their victories; they could not resist loot. The peasants of the Vendée supported the nobility after the French Revolution because the monarchists stood for their deeply cherished religion, and the majority of the Cossacks fought under the leadership of the White generals for the same reason, but they were such plunderers that they would even rob the churches; saying as they did so: 'Pardon, Holy Mother of God, but if we don't take this the Bolsheviks will.' After a victory they were always weighted down with loot, and their officers could not induce them to leave it behind. That was the one reason the Whites had not been in Moscow long ago. This lust for loot nearly always gave the Reds time to rally. Voroshilov would allow no man to march with anything except his barest necessities. That was why his unceasing blows were so swift and staggering to the enemy.

Southward and ever southward rode the First Cavalry Army of the Republic, fighting all the way. At its head always three horsemen riding together; Voroshilov, in leather coat and breeches, a felt cloak over his shoulders and a tall Cossack cap on one side of his head, in the centre; on his right Budenny, resplendent in a green tunic and bright scarlet breeches; and to his left the hawk-visaged, wily Shchadenko.

Every man in the army delighted to follow all three of these inseparables. Voroshilov, as quick, as gay, and as dauntless as D'Artagnan. Budenny the mighty fighter, like another Porthos, while Shchadenko had just a hint of the sly, clever Aramis in his make-up. These three modern musketeers were worth an army corps.

Athos was somewhere on the other side, a gallant gentleman prepared to sell his life dearly; for his beliefs, all that he held dear, his murdered family; but the odds were against him in the combination that Stalin had sent to drive him out of the country he held dear.

Village after village, town after town, city after city fell before the wild Red cavalry. Nothing could stop them, and, all the while, through the will of one dominant personality they were being brought to heel and educated. It sounds like a two-year campaign, but in reality that amazing ride of 600 miles occupied only three months.

At last they came opposite the Cossack capital, Novocherkassk, and its neighbour, the great city Rostov-on-the-Don. Denikin, with his Cossacks and White officers, came out to meet the Reds. Voroshilov's army was thirsting for another battle.

'Give us Rostov. Give us Rostov,' they yelled at the top of their voices as he rode down their lines inspecting this extraordinary collection of horsemen; some in civilian overcoats and English shoes on bare feet, some in tattered uniforms and

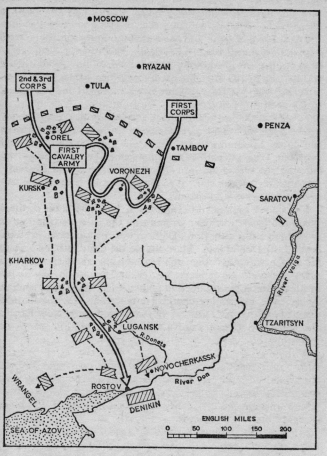

OPERATIONS OF THE FIRST CAVALRY CORPS
(OCTOBER) AND THE FIRST CAVALRY ARMY,
NOVEMBER–DECEMBER, 1919

Forces of Denikin and Wrangel.    Bolsheviks.

Water.    Furthest advance of Whites.

old army gaiters, and some in women's fur coats and expensive
Morocco leather riding-boots taken off the feet of executed
officers.

The frosts had set in and snow already fallen. On the bound-
less white plain the two armies deployed for battle. They stretched for nearly ten *versts* across the snowy steppe. It was a
perfect setting for a great cavalry engagement. Waiting their
turn to attack, the reserve columns sat mounted, ready to dash
forward instantly in the rear of the front lines. The winter sun
glinted on 40,000 sabres. In shock after shock Red cavalry met
White. Like the waves of an agitated sea great masses of men
and horses careered over the plain. The battle swayed this way
and that. The staccato rattle of machine-guns, the crash of
bursting shells and the screaming war-cries of the Cossacks
rent the air. It was a combat to the death, and in it the counter-
revolutionaries were broken.

Voroshilov succeeded beyond the Kremlin's wildest dreams.
When the battle was over he had split the enemy's front clean
in half from top to bottom. Denikin was flung back south-west
beyond the Don and the Manych into the Caucasus and Wrangel driven south-east over the Dnieper into the Crimea.

On the night of January 8th, 1920, with the joyous howls
of his men and the thundering hooves of 17,000 horses ringing
in his ears, Voroshilov charged into Rostov where he could
gaze upon the sea. Can it be wondered that Red Russia
acclaimed him 'Organiser of Victories'?

# 15

# Frontal Attack

This last great victory drove Budenny's scallywags mad with excitement. On the very heels of the fleeing Whites they came streaming into Rostov; but no farther. For the time being they had had enough of fighting; why follow the retreating enemy when in the city there were an abundance of drink and women? They broke their ranks, dashed into the cafés, and smashed in the doors of the mansions. Rostov groaned; given over to a night of unheard of pillage and destruction.

Voroshilov and his staff had gone straight to the great house of Paramanov, a wealthy merchant, which, until a few hours before had been the headquarters of the White generals.

In vain he stormed up and down the ballroom cursing and threatening his corps, and divisional commanders. To the echo of their war-cries his Sythian horsemen were committing incredible acts of murder and violence; the glare of the fires flickered through the tall windows on the high ceilings and reddened the night sky; the screams of the wretched bourgeois, being put to the torture to make them disclose the hiding places of their jewels, and the hysterical shrieks of young girls, dragged away to be raped by a dozen brutal ruffians, came up like the cries of the damned in hell from the streets below.

'Budenny! Zotov! Apanasenko!' yelled Voroshilov. 'Put a stop to this pillaging. The bloody swine! They're disgracing our army. Send Communists to all the squadrons. Get out of here and bring the men to order.'

The ruffianly corps commander, Doumenko, only roared with laughter in his face, and Budenny shrugged his Herculean shoulders. 'What's the use, Clim? Let the boys stretch themselves and rob the bourgeois a bit. Don't be so stingy; what d'you think they've been shedding their blood for? As for sending Communists to them, why, we haven't got any Communists in our army and never did have. They'd hang Karl

Marx himself upside down over a bonfire if he tried to lecture
them on his funny ideas to-night.'

Doumenko, of the great black beard that curled right down
to his waist, the legendary swordsman beloved by all the
troopers, spat contemptuously and swaggered from the room.

Later that night, during an orgy with his friends and some of
the prettiest girls his men had dragged from their homes and
stripped naked for his amusement, Mikalazd, his Political
Commissar, protested. In a drunken fury Doumenko shot him
dead and threatened to lay open the front to the enemy if the
army was to be run 'by Jews and Communists'.

Trotsky, the arch-murderer, seized the opportunity to send
a telegram to his old enemy Voroshilov. *'Complaints of abuse
of power do not cease. I consider it absolutely necessary that
an end should be put to the violence of undisciplined troops. I
am informed that there is not enough force to put a stop to the
marauders. The guilty must be punished on the spot. No single
case of violence should be left undealt with, the Central Military Committee holds you responsible.'*

It was the second time that Voroshilov had been threatened
by Trotsky with the Revolutionary Tribunal and it was Voroshilov's own riotous child that swamped Rostov in vodka, in
blood and in the chaos of banditry.

Doumenko was arrested by Voroshilov's orders and he had
all the drunken soldiery of the army formed up outside the
town. As he cantered up surrounded by his staff, on magnificently caparisoned charges captured from the Whites, the
army gave him a terrific ovation; but when he began to read
an army order conveying the gratitude of the Republic to its
heroes which went on to chide them for their robberies and
depredations the men howled him down.

'Enough! Enough!' they cried, 'give us Budenny.' Budenny
clapped spurs to his mount; making it curvet before the lines
of troopers.

'Go on, speak to them,' cried Voroshilov furiously.

In his stentorian voice the ex-Sergeant bawled: 'Comrades!
Lousy bloodsuckers that you are. We come here as liberators.
The Rostov proletariat has not had the benefit of Soviet rule.
It is our task in this den of bourgeois corruption to set an
example by keeping our weaker brothers from drunkenness,
robbery and violence.'

'Not a drop more alcohol,' he suddenly yelled with all the

power of his lungs. 'We were met by the proletariat of Rostov with open arms and we have replied to their welcome by whole-sale drunken pillage. Shame on you! Down with the counter-revolution. Long live the power of the Soviets! Long live our invincible First Cavalry Army!'

'Hurrah,' bellowed the troopers, waving their *papenkas*. 'Long live our leader Budenny.'

The sack of Rostov had given the Whites breathing space to dig themselves in at Bataisk; an immensely strong position on a line of hills with the broad Don running just below them and a great area of marshy ground upon the Bolsheviks' side of the river. Russia was now in the grip of winter and the river was frozen over, but heavy rains made the marsh ground almost impossible for cavalry operations. Fresh pools of water lightly coated with ice covered the marsh and firmer ice beneath. The horses slithered about, breaking their legs and bringing their riders to the ground. It was sheer madness to attempt the taking of such a position by a cavalry charge or any form of frontal attack.

The Eighth and Ninth Red Armies had now come up behind Voroshilov, but on January 17th, 1920, the cavalry alone were ordered to assault and take Bataisk which was held by seven corps of Denikin's Whites with much artillery. The ex-Czarist colonel, Yegorov, was in command of the southern front, and, with him at his headquarters was Shorin, another ex-Czarist officer who, owing to yet one more of Trotsky's almost weekly changes, was now Commander-in-Chief of the Red armies. They seemed to think that Budenny's horsemen need only gallop up the hill to throw the Whites into the sea.

This mania for frontal attack among the officers of the High Command in all European armies during the Great War is a thing that passes all understanding. The third battle of Ypres will live in history as an example of how wars should *not* be fought on that account.

In the spring of 1917 Haig commanded the most powerful army that the British Empire has ever put into the field; in the spring of 1918 it was so exhausted that it was unable to resist the enemy's assault, and we came within an ace of losing the war altogether. Haig squandered a hundred million pounds and the life blood of a generation in the mire of Passchendaele. By that battle he jeopardised the whole campaign yet failed to gain his objective, and failed, to any appreciable extent, to

weaken his opponent. The verdict of posterity can only be that
he was responsible for the most terrible defeat that has ever
been sustained by British arms.

It might be said that since the western front was one long
solid line of concrete and barbed-wire fortifications during
the greater part of the war there was no way to encircle or
outflank it; but this suggestion does not stand examination.
Two methods could have been adopted for the undoing of the
Germans without this enormous sacrifice in troops to no purpose.

Firstly, as Mr. Churchill so frequently pointed out, there
were other fronts. When the stalemate arrived, while still retaining sufficient masses in reserve to meet any emergency,
considerable bodies of troops, in fact those which were slaughtered instead, could have been sent to those other fronts.
Secondly, a retirement of any depth in a well-chosen sector
would not only have straightened the line and thus econo-
mised troops, but would also have almost certainly brought
the Germans out of their strongholds and given an opportunity to meet them on equal conditions. A few French villages, a town or two, might have had to be sacrificed, but what
was that when a world-war was involved and the inhabitants
could easily have been evacuated. Hindenburg tells us in his
*Memoirs* that he hated to have to do it, but in his first campaign he deliberately abandoned a great piece of German territory and allowed the Russians to overrun this portion of his
homeland: yet that withdrawal enabled him to inflict the most
crushing defeat upon the enemy shortly afterwards.

With the exception of the Hindenburg school, the most
brilliant exponents of which were Von Mackensen and Von
Bulow, the majority of the other cavalry-obsessed generals in
the High Commands of the warring nations were as brainless
as the British. The French bled themselves white by their attacks on the Chemin des Dames, the Germans upon Verdun,
and the Russians upon the foothills of the Carpathians, *yet
none of them reaped the least advantage from it*. One would
have thought that an elementary schoolboy would have realised the tremendous superiority of defence over the attack
which has changed war entirely since the introduction of the
machine-gun and quick-firing field artillery. But these pre-war
trained generals, who nearly always lived many miles behind
their fronts and visited them only on very rare occasions,

seemed to have been so soaked in the traditions of the Crimean and Franco-Prussian Wars, where soldiers who had dis-
charged their rifles were compelled to fight hand to hand, that
they had no conception of modern conditions at all. Their
appalling casualties should have made them think a *little*, but
they continued the same old operation for month after month
quite unperturbed. Even up to the very end of the war these
massacres of troops were planned by the hide-bound general
staffs, and when the unfortunate Americans arrived on the
western front they were sent to their deaths by the thousand
in exactly the same way.

Fortunately these battles are now only sad pages of history
and should the youths of today be called upon to face the horrors of another war they will at least have the consolation of
knowing that this generation of generals is dead or in retirement. An extraordinarily high level of intelligence is now demanded of all officers on the General Staffs and as, fifty
years ago, they were only juniors serving in fighting regiments,
they suffered from the stupidity of their seniors just as much
as the private soldier. Frontal attacks in mass at the same
point for weeks on end are hardly likely, therefore, to take
place again in our lifetime. Witness the constant shifting of the
sector of attack on the fronts in the Spanish Civil War. Each
time the defence rushes up supports and a new line is established the battle is broken off and the offensive resumed elsewhere.

The pre-war trained Shorin and Yegorov were tarred with
precisely the same brush as most of the Allied and German
generals during the Great War. In the middle of January, 1920,
they sent Voroshilov's magnificent cavalry eight times in succession against Bataisk. The position was impregnable, the
slaughter of the Reds appalling. In the eighth attack, which
was made at night to the flicker of Very lights and the flash of
bursting shells, Voroshilov's horse pitched into a shell hole in
the ice of the river. He nearly lost his life and was only rescued with the greatest difficulty.

Livid with rage, he called off the insane battle, went straight
back to headquarters in his dripping, half-frozen clothes and
tackled the half-witted generals.

Yegorov agreed with Voroshilov that they should abandon
this senseless and criminal attack, but Shorin would not hear
of it. Voroshilov then rebelled, hammered the table furiously

and shouted at him: 'You tell me not to argue with you, but to go where I'm told and the result is a hideous mess. I flatly refuse to carry out any more frontal attacks.'

Most of the telegraph wires were down, but after hours of cursing Voroshilov managed to get a telegram transmitted from one point to another half-round Russia to Stalin in the Kremlin. '*I must express my indignation with the Commander of the front at the absurd way our glorious cavalry is being used. I beg you to come yourself or to send someone who is your equal in order to convince yourself of the stupidity of what is being done.*'

The wise old 'Koba' came to Voroshilov's rescue once again. Tukachevsky was pressing on with Blucher from victory to victory through Siberia. Koltchak's army was broken; early in February, 1920, a body of the 'Supreme Ruler's' own troops rebelled and shot him. Stalin persuaded the Kremlin to recall Tukachevsky from the east, and give him command of the Russian Southern front.

Tukachevsky arrived to find that Voroshilov, still rebellious, had withdrawn his troops, but that the lunatic Shorin had thrown the whole of the Eighth Red Army away in futile attacks against the heights of Bataisk. The Whites had an enormous superiority in artillery and had blown it to bits in the marshes without it having achieved an advance of a single yard.

Voroshilov, however, had already worked out a plan for the encirclement and destruction of Denikin. Tukachevsky immediately adopted it.

The scheme was that the First Cavalry Army should make a semicircular march to Taganrog, already in Red hands, and attack the heights of Bataisk from the rear. Just about the same time Denikin conceived a similar manœuvre for outflanking the Bolsheviks. He sent his cavalry under General Pavlov to accomplish it.

Pavlov carried out a forced march of forty *versts* across the icy salt plains, but Voroshilov had anticipated him by forty-eight hours and was already in Taganrog. The White general had no time to rest his troops; they were half-frozen and utterly exhausted when they met the Reds. On February 25th Budenny's demons cut them to pieces, taking 7,000 prisoners, 1,700 wagons and 67 guns. Denikin's cavalry was totally wiped out.

The White lines at Bataisk, which had cost the Bolsheviks so many of their men, were taken from the rear. Another desperate battle was fought at Byeoglina in which Tukachevsky finally routed Denikin's main army. The remnants of the White forces scattered and took refuge in the Kuban. Tukachevsky's slaughter of White officer captives was utterly appalling. It is said that for some days the Don literally ran red with blood.

Ekaterinodar, the last stronghold of the Whites north of the Caucasian Mountains, was taken. The refugees streamed down to the Black Sea coast and were taken off by Allied shipping. The British battleships, sitting quietly in the bay, flung a few shells from their great guns into Tukachevsky's vanguard, but his victory was complete. He had driven all that remained of Denikin's army literally into the sea.

The effect of the cessation of the war in the West on the Russian situation had now been apparent for some months. Marshal Foch, Monsieur Clemenceau and Mr. Winston Churchill, very ably backed by Sir Henry Wilson, probably the most talented officer of field-marshal's rank who emerged from the British Army during the war, might be absolutely convinced that Bolshevism must be destroyed for the protection of the world, but now that the major war was over it was one thing to plan the invasion of Russia and quite another thing to carry it out.

All but a very small proportion of the enormous armies that the British Empire had mobilised were civilians who had signed up 'for four years or the duration of the war'. Directly the Armistice was signed, in their view, the war was over. Few of them even realised, at that time, that if they had immediately packed up and gone home there was at least a theoretical possibility of the enemy dishonouring the truce and renewing the offensive with the most disastrous results to the Allies. Their duty was obviously to remain until a proper peace was signed and the enemy armies disbanded. In actual fact, there was little to fear, as the Central Powers were rendered entirely impotent through internal revolutions. But that is by the way. The British 'Tommies' and their companions from overseas considered that they had fulfilled their contract and, having wasted four years of their lives, demanded immediate demobilisation.

They began to sing with more raucous gusto than ever:

'Do we love our Sergeant Major,
He can fetch my ——— tea;
Once I get my civvie clothes on,
No more ——— wars for me.'

A large majority of the officers were in entire sympathy with the men. Many of those who were over twenty-five in 1914 had been carving out careers for themselves by their own ability and had given up safe jobs to volunteer; while the younger ones had curtailed their education or sacrificed good prospects to come and fight. Their view of the intelligence and somewhat restricted charm of most of the regular officers under whom they had had to serve for a number of years was not exactly one of unmixed admiration. They wanted to get from under them with the least possible delay and be done with the whole rotten business.

It was no easy situation for the Government, as such an enormous number of men could not be absorbed into the civilian population overnight without grave risk of trouble, and the General Staff wished to retain as many of the troops as possible for further operations, with Russia and Turkey particularly in mind.

The troops, however, both civilian and regular, showed their extreme antagonism to any suggestion that they should be set off to fight another war in Archangel or on the shores of the Caspian Sea. There were some very ugly scenes in Havre among the men whose demobilisation had been delayed from one cause or another; and the General Staff was compelled to report to the Cabinet that, however much they might wish to crush the Bolsheviks the British Army was certainly not prepared to play.

The Americans took exactly the same line and, in fact, had never showed any keenness to support White Czarist generals against a Democratic People's Government in Russia. They had only agreed to intervene in the first place under pressure from the Allies because it was considered policy that they should participate to some extent in all ventures against the Central Powers.

The conscripted troops of the other Allies proved equally adamant in their determination not to fight any more. After the Armistice the bulk of the French and Belgian armies just demobilised themselves without reference to their superior officers and walked home.

Further, the political situation throughout the whole of Europe was extremely unstable. Bolshevism had spread to Italy, Hungary and Austria, France was threatened with grave labour troubles and in Britain the first big post-war strikes developed in London and Glasgow, causing the Government grave concern.

The French, and many British statesmen, were still convinced that it was their duty to their own people to destroy the Kremlin if they could and, although there was no longer the necessity for maintaining an eastern front against the Central Powers, their previous attempts to intervene had placed them under very definite obligations.

A great many of the White officers and men would never have taken up arms against the Bolsheviks, but preferred to emigrate, or take a chance that by surrendering they would have been allowed to settle down to a normal life in their own country, if it had not been for the categorical pledge given to them that they should have abundant Allied support. Bolshevik generals, such as Tukachevsky, were now murdering every prisoner that they took. Could the Allies, with any honour or decency, leave these unfortunates to be butchered after having deliberately encouraged them to take up arms?

Obviously the best solution lay in a peace by which the Bolshevik Government guaranteed a complete amnesty to all Russian subjects who had taken up arms against it. Within a month after the Armistice, ringed in by her foes, the Kremlin had begged for peace and been denied it. Now, fourteen months later, when the People's armies had proved victorious in the east and in the south, they were no longer so eager to make terms.

The old Czarist embassies which handled the affairs of the White generals still exercised great influence in the Allies' capitals and large numbers of *émigré* Russian aristocrats, with close connections in London and Paris, had arrived to plead in person for futher Monarchist support. There was still the risk that the virus of Bolshevism might spread more quickly to other countries once peace was made, so the French and British statesmen determined on yet another attempt to stamp it out.

For many months it had become increasingly difficult to get

the troops of the Allies to go and fight the Bolsheviks. Field-Marshal Sir Henry Wilson laid it down that Britain should withdraw all her troops except those stationed in the area of Baku and this exception was made entirely with the idea that we should cling on to the Russian oil-fields if possible. Archangel was consequently evacuated in March, 1920, while the French and Italians brought their men home from the shores of the Black Sea in April. On the 6th of that month, the Whites having been suppressed over a large area in Siberia, a republic friendly to the Bolsheviks was established there with its capital at Chita. Denikin and Yudenitch had been finally defeated, as we have seen, and certain British statesmen, including Lloyd George, had come round to the suggestion that trade relations should be opened up with the Kremlin Government.

It looked as if the Bolsheviks were at last going to have a little peace, but the French were as rabid as ever against them and now decided to use Poland as their catspaw.

On the signing of the Armistice the ancient Kingdom of Poland, which had been torn asunder by Catherine the Great of Russia, Frederick the Great of Prussia and Joseph II of Austria, became once more a free and independent state.

Marshal Pilsudski, a great Polish patriot, arose as its dictator. His career had been one long, amazing adventure, and he had known exile in Siberia under the old Czarist régime in his younger days. He was very able, but over-ambitious and, not content that by plebiscites, and other measures, all the territory which contained a predominance of Polish-speaking people should have been incorporated into the new Poland, his avaricious eye was fixed on the Ukraine.

The Polish claim to this rich and fertile territory was based on no more than the fact that the old Polish Kingdom had once included it, way back in the dark ages; but Pilsudski was filled with the old ambitions of territorial conquest and wished to extend the frontiers of Poland by force of arms from the Baltic to the Black Sea.

His army had been organised and equipped by the French with just such an attack upon the Bolsheviks in mind. They had suffered terribly in the wars to exterminate the counter-revolution and it looked as though Russia was prostrate. General Haller, a member of the Foreign Mission, warned Pilsudski with the words: 'Is it not better to leave a wounded beast alone?' but, although Pilsudski hesitated a long time, he would not be dissuaded from his attempt.

Petlura, the Ukrainian patriot, was now General Hetman there and had been fighting Whites one month and Reds the next in order to maintain his independence; but the Bolsheviks had got the upper hand so Pilsudski made a treaty with him to deliver the Ukraine from the Red yoke. In March, 1920, the Poles advanced into Petlura's territory and the war-worn Kremlin was faced with yet one more crisis.

# 16

# The Wings of the Red Eagles are Clipped

As we know, it was part of the Communist programme that the Ukraine and other subject provinces of the old Russian Empire should be allowed self-determination. If they chose to invite the Poles in, that was surely their affair. The Bolsheviks still had Wrangel to attend to in the Crimea and their Far Eastern Dominions to subdue. The Polish members of the Council, Dzerzhinski, Marchlevski and Kon were extremely antagonistic to a war against Poland, and Trotsky supported them, but in Lenin's eyes the self-determination of a people dominated by a determined nucleus (of Communists) was one thing, and self determination of any other kind, quite another.

The revolutions which the Bolsheviks had anticipated in other European countries soon after their own *coup d'état* had not fully matured. Even Germany, Hungary and Austria were more or less pacified; although in the hands of Socialists their governments were Menshevik in character and by no means the sort of thing the Communists desired. Lenin laid it down that if the workers in other countries could not be induced to rise by propaganda they must be assisted with force. As usual, he had the final say, and the Kremlin declared war against Poland. The Poles had tanks, aeroplanes and quick-firing French 75-mm. guns, so they promptly blew the Second Red Army to pieces and occupied Kiev.

A great conference was immediately called, among those present being Trotsky, Kamenev, yet one more commander-in-chief of the Bolshevik armies who had just been appointed; Frunze, Vatzetis, Tukachevsky and Voroshilov. A discussion was held as to who should receive the supreme command of the new front. Tukachevsky was only twenty-seven years of age, yet he was selected on a large majority of votes and Lenin approved the choice. All the best fighting divisions were now to be concentrated in the west, and Gaai, Tukachevsky's dare-devil Armenian lieutenant, was given command of a Second

Cavalry Army which was now being formed owing to Voroshilov's stupendous successes during the past winter with the First. Voroshilov was ordered to bring his collection of brigands from the Caucasus half across Europe to the Polish front.

When Budenny was told he simply shrugged his shoulders. 'It's all one to me what front I go to. My business is to fight. The only pity is,' he went on ruminatively, 'that we've got so few sabres. What can one do with a mere 17,000? During the World War we had forty cavalry divisions. Just think of it— 300,000 horsemen. And what the devil did their Excellencies the Generals do with them? Now if I had 300,000 troopers I'd plough up the whole of Poland with their horses' hooves and we'd be clattering through the squares of Paris before the summer's out.'

Most of the men, however, did not take that view at all. Great numbers of them came from the Don country, which was not so very far away, and in fighting over it they had felt that they were winning the very land for themselves once the Revolution was established. To suggest taking them to Poland was, in view of their low state of education, much the same as telling them that they must go to Siam. They complained that both they and the horses were worn out with fighting and demanded that, if they must go to the end of the world for the sake of the Revolution, they should at least be given railway trains to travel in.

Voroshilov scowled as black as thunder and shouted at Budenny: 'What the devil are you about? It's time to be on the march and those ruffians of yours are mutinous. Railway wagons indeed? Where the hell do they think such things are to come from with every factory in Russia idle or blown up? Tell them they are to march through the Ukraine to clear it of the *Kulak* bands.'

A good few of the cavalry were Ukrainians. They knew that the *Kulaks* had been plundering their homes and to have a cut at the robbers proved a tempting bait; the army was won over and set out on its 1,400-*verst* march.

More trouble was waiting for Voroshilov when they reached Rostov. He spoke of it to Budenny long before they reached the city. 'There's only one thing I'm afraid of—that swine Doumenko should have been shot long ago, but the Tribunal goes on shilly-shallying and he's imprisoned in Rostov still.

I'll bet my boots the men'll start kicking up a fuss about him once we get there.'

He was perfectly right. As soon as the First Cavalry Army entered Rostov the Cossack division remembered their old commander and many of them went to see him in the prison. Doumenko seized upon the chance and addressed his old comrades through his prison bars.

'Thank God you've come, boys! Look what they've done to your poor old friend, these Communist swine! Just think of it—they put me in prison because I knocked off the necks of a few bottles of vodka and had a bit of fun with half a dozen girls. Who's going to try me, eh? I won't stand much chance of a fair deal if it's to be those mean-souled Jews and Commissars. Why not the old law where Cossacks judged each other, eh? You try me, boys; try me yourselves. I don't give a damn what the verdict is if it's given by judges who're my fellow-Cossacks.'

More and more Cossacks rode up and the prison yard became an absolute pandemonium. They swore that he needn't be afraid, they wouldn't let him down, and that they would show the blasted Commissars who were the real masters.

Next morning, at a review which Voroshilov had arranged on the race-track, in response to a welcome of the army by the proletariat of Rostov, he was faced with one of the most difficult situations in his career.

The Cossacks began to shout in unison. 'Give us Doumenko, liberate Doumenko,' and the Fourth Division, breaking its ranks, surged round him seething with angry excitement.

The men shouted him down and would not give him a hearing so, seeing that all discipline would be gone unless the riot was dealt with at once, he turned to Budenny and rapped out: 'Commander, explain the situation to your men.'

Budenny was one of themselves and could always get a hearing. 'Red Eagles,' he bellowed at the top of his voice, 'what have we been shedding our blood for? What have thousands of Cossacks laid down their lives in the steppes for? For the people's right. Whoever is against us—off goes his head. Doumenko is a traitor. We've got the papers which prove he meant to sell us out to the Whites. We don't give a damn about his drunkenness. It's because of his treachery that he's going to be shot. Now, who's it going to be? You can't have both of us —and you've got to choose between Doumenko and me.'

Instantly the wild cries of loyalty to Budenny, the 'Red Murat' of the Revolution, drowned those of Doumenko's supporters, and the mutiny was quelled. That night, as the First Cavalry army took the road north-west again to Poland and fresh fighting, the swashbuckling Cossack Doumenko with the curly black beard was shot by *Chekists* in the prison yard.

On May 30th the army was shipped on a fleet of rafts across the Dnieper, and by early June the Red concentrations were complete.

Tukachevsky now had his great opportunity. The best troops of the Bolsheviks were at his disposal. With the one exception of Blucher, who was left to continue the subjugation of the east, all their great fighting generals, Voroshilov, Frunze, Budenny, Yegorov, Kotovsky, Sologub, Khvessin, Apanasenko, Kork and Gaai were under his orders. The men were no longer deserters and down-at-heel workmen, but tried troops who had sustained nearly three years of almost continuous battle. Yet Tukachevsky looked upon his brother commanders and his soldiers alike, with contempt; echoing the words of his idol, Napoleon: 'Alone this rabble is good for nothing. With me, it is invincible.'

Nevertheless, to secure their personal devotion, he went about among them with extraordinary activity; attending during the few weeks of preparation for the campaign and while they were deploying to their positions, no less than 400 meetings, 144 lectures, 69 concerts, 139 displays and 611 reunions. His old policy of destroying the morale behind the enemy's front was also developed to the maximum. Tracts and brochures by the million were distributed by his agents among the Polish troops and civilian population. In the meantime, he had evolved a plan of battle worthy of the great master of war upon whom he modelled himself.

The Poles held the line of the Berezina, but had their main forces farther south between Kiev and Uman. Tukachevsky engaged them heavily on their central front, sent his 16th Army under Sologub to force the passage of the Berezina and ordered the First Cavalry Army to attack Uman from the south-east.

Pilsudski naturally supposed that the Russians intended an attempt to outflank him in the south; and had no idea at all that his real danger lay in the extreme north. Here, between Polotsk and Vitebsk, nearly 500 miles from Uman, Tukachevsky had concentrated yet another army, the 15th, under Kork. With it he also had the Second Cavalry Army under the audacious Gaai. This great 'secret' force, hidden behind the extreme right flank of Sologub's 16th Army, was intended to strike right down through Lithuania, past Vilna to Warsaw, while Khvessin, and the rest of the infantry army commanders, heavily attacked the Polish centre and Budenny's cavalry created a major diversion in the south.

Voroshilov and Budenny were originally ear-marked for the dash from the north, but Stalin was President of the Military Revolutionary Council controlling the southern front and Voroshilov arranged to be placed under the immediate supervision of his old friend, so Gaai, and the Second Cavalry Army, were sent to the north instead. It is possible that this change of plan jeopardised the issue of the whole campaign as, although Gaai was a dashing leader, he certainly had not Budenny's positive genius for cavalry operations; and with Budenny was the dare-devil ex-brigand Kotovsky as one of his corps commanders, and with him, too, was the 'Organiser of Victories' himself, that great Captain, Voroshilov.

The Poles were good fighters, but ill-led, and Pilsudski bungled badly. The Russians drove him out of Kiev on June 13th and, although he counter-attacked heavily at Zhitomir, they pushed him back again.

Meanwhile, the invincible First Cavalry Army of the Republic was gaining more laurels for itself. Uman was taken in the first days of June and they pressed on north-west to Berdichev. Here they came upon two Polish armies, hacked their way clean through them, and got behind two more that were trying to make a stand at Zhitomir, cutting their communications completely. At Novograd-Volynsk the Red cavalry fought another bloody battle and poured over the frontier into Europe. They had not only done what Tukachevsky had required of them, but torn a gap 50 miles wide in the enemy front and were now swarming through it into Poland, razing and destroying as they went like a flight of locusts. The French general with Pilsudski had to admit that he 'did not believe anyone had ever witnessed such magnificent cavalry work since the days of Napoleon.'

N. Ratikin gives us a good picture of this astounding 400-mile dash through the Polish armies, from Uman to Lublin.

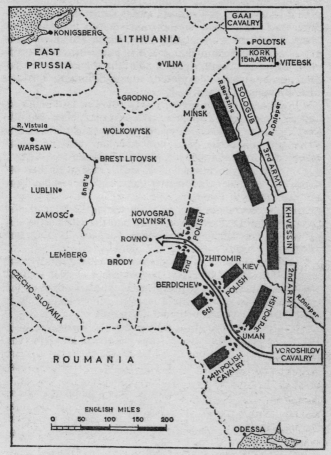

POLISH CAMPAIGN: FIRST PHASE, JUNE, 1920

Poles.  Bolsheviks.  Sea.

'Last night and this morning, battle, thunder, but now there is the sun with its caress, and the scent of the soil stirring one's blood and the horizon wrapped in transparent haze. Divisions of the cavalry army pursue the enemy with cold steel, bullet and shrapnel, and pave paths and roads with blood and death. At the head of the column the Special Regiment reaching in a winding ribbon behind the Military Revolutionary Council.

'From here, will to victory drives waves of lead and steel ahead, ever ahead. The spring air opens one's chest and fills one's muscles with wild strength. A village, scattered half a mile wide on a rise of ground. Laughing with its white-washed houses and waving its windmill sails at us.

' "Well, Semyon Mikhailovich, we'll press on to that village and then see who's master there, eh," Voroshilov says to Budenny with a smile.

'The horses' shoes rang as if on the anvil; hind hooves overtaking fore hooves. We break into the village; the sun laughing, we laughing, Voroshilov laughing, beating Budenny by a head.

'Little white tufts of cloud over the village, neatly cut, against the tender blue sky. The whine of a shell and the sound of a series of sharp explosions. The armoured car of the 6th Division dashes up; a machine-gunner leaps from it and reports "Polish armoured train ahead".

'Half a mile beyond the village was the forest, out of it came the smoke and steam from the armoured train. The smile vanished from our faces. Under the shelter of the last cottages orders were given. The squadron wheeled as it rode, steel blades are flashing.

'The Poles were endeavouring to clear a dump of shells in the forest; a few shots as we come dashing through the trees and we catch them nicely. The armoured train is ours. Half an hour later the regiment is again thundering along the dry road.

'At night in another village. Towards dawn the Poles make a sudden bold attack. Shells crashing into the houses, shrapnel bursting overhead, rifles and machine-guns rattling. Our horses are out on the rising ground behind the village protected by strong pickets. Everything is confusion in the narrow street. Voroshilov dashes out of his billet and collides with another man coming round the corner. It is the

Divisional Commander. Voroshilov's voice rings out: "To horse! Attack at once and smash the enemy."

'The divisional Commander stammered: "But, Comrade Voroshilov. It's dark—and misty. We may run into wire."

' "Never mind that," shouted Voroshilov, "better die attacking in the open than wait here to be shot down in the village street. To horse, I tell you!"

'Ten minutes later a charge was made in the uncertain light of the early summer dawn and the Poles were routed. The remnants of their forces scattered into the forest.

'The Polish infantry took Zopatino. The regiments of our Special Brigade were flat on the ground about half a mile from the village. It was essential to act before reinforcements reached the enemy. The men had to be got on their feet somehow.

'On a dun horse, under a hail of bullets, Voroshilov rode down the lines calling on the men to advance. The men got up. One attack was beaten off. The men took cover again. A second attack; the enemy staggered and fled. Hundreds of prisoners were taken; dozens of machine-guns.

'A whole division of Poles descended on Otrada unexpectedly and surrounded it. Fighting in the village streets; rifles rattling, machine-guns barking, men with lances and sabres fighting hand to hand among the houses.

'A Polish Uhlan with a lance charged Voroshilov; the lance missed him, but pierced his heavy felt cloak; the lance struck again. Voroshilov fired and missed; a Red trooper sprang to his assistance and cut the Pole down. The lance flew into the fence, the horse galloped off, the Uhlan dangling grotesquely from his saddle.

'Another division of Poles came up; our brigade was driven back. Voroshilov was everywhere among the men rallying them. Till morning our one brigade fought two divisions of Poles and next evening we retook Otrada.

'Voroshilov smiled at me as we rode past him. He had a wonderful smile. His upper lip curled up and the corners of his mouth went a little to one side; his nose wrinkled a trifle round the nostrils and caresses looked out of his eyes. Any sense of injury was dissolved instantly in that smile. You recalled it for weeks, months. We rode on again to fresh victories.

'Months of incessant fighting and thousands of miles rid-

den; the men were worn out, the horses weak from sleep-
less nights and lack of fodder. Weariness was getting us
down; but every moment was precious.

'The enemy was retreating, fleeing, had to be finished off,
crushed completely. Voroshilov's eyes were bloodshot from
peering at maps all night and at the country before us all
day. His voice was hoarse; but still it called us on. From
Rostov to Berdichev, Berdichev to Rovno, Rovno to Brody,
Brody to Lemberg and Lemberg to Zamość. There was no
limit to his strength—no limit to his spirit.'

Voroshilov's personal bravery is mentioned by all writers of
memoirs dealing with his campaigns. At Novograd-Volynsk
the Poles attempted a desperate resistance. In the crossing of
the River Sluch, Budenny's troopers were met by a devastating
rifle-fire from the Polish legionaries and were stopped at the
fords in utter confusion. Machine-guns swept the river banks
and shells sent up great columns of water. In his cloak and
Cossack cap Voroshilov galloped up to one of the brigades.
'What the hell are you waiting here for, damn you?' he
yelled. 'Into the ford, clear out those men,' and, waving his
sword, he plunged into the water at the head of the troops.

Having led them across, he yelled: 'Swords to the attack,'
and charged up the opposite bank followed by his horsemen
of the steppes straight on to the Polish rifles.

After the Sluch was cleared the First Cavalry Army proceeded to Rovno, blazing a trail of sack and murder as it went.
From there it swept like a torrent into Europe. The villages
flashed by like some mad cinematograph film, leaving behind
them on the map of the earth only spots of blood. They were
advancing in marches of fifty *versts* a time.

During the attack on Sangorodok, Apanasenko's Sixth Division was thrown back in confusion. Budenny came galloping
up in a cloud of dust and, spurring straight at Apanasenko,
bellowed: 'You're retreating, you swine! Get at them, man,
get at them!'

Voroshilov appeared a moment later and, seizing Apanasenko by the lapel of his coat, shook him in his saddle, muttering through his clenched teeth: 'Commander of the Sixth, you
either take Sangorodok or you die in battle.' The assault was
renewed and the township taken.

Some extracts from Voroshilov's diary are interesting as

showing his estimate of his own army. July 18th, 1920. 'The troopers are beyond all praise. The commanders are brave to the point of madness, but as leaders they are beneath criticism. They do not know the first thing about leading, but to some extent their shortcomings are due to unfamiliar country—forests, marshes, rivers and creeks—so different from the open steppes which form the proper element of our wonderful warriors.'

July 19th. 'The enemy repulsed a cavalry attack by the 14th Division, then counter-attacked and swept our infantry lines aside and occupied the eminence on the south side of Smordv. By concentrated fire from three batteries the enemy unit was literally swept from the face of the earth. But as the result of the same old ramshackle work of our officers, after that brilliant artillery work the enemy was able to reach the forest. ... Our divisional officers are slow, indecisive and bad at finding themselves in a new situation. Divisions working side by side know nothing of each other.'

August 14th. 'Reports come in speaking of huge numbers of prisoners and enemy casualties. Once again we could not trust report. So I suggested to Budenny that we went to check up ourselves, whereupon we were able to count seventeen to twenty dead.... The enemy had been allowed to escape from the mouse-trap.'

No information regarding the enemy meant finding out for himself where the enemy was, so, at considerable risk to his life, Voroshilov went right out in front of his forces almost daily in a car; carrying only a light machine-gun as protection against ambuscades.

Another passage from his diary written during the same campaign gives us a delightful glimpse of this great commander. 'I nearly forgot to record a trifling, though interesting happening. Towards night, on the way back from the positions near Smordv, one of the men noticed a horse's head sticking out of a well in the meadow and thought he saw it move. I suggested to Budenny that we should go and put it out of its pain. Only its head was above water, but it was alive and apparently unwounded. With great difficulty, holding it by the ears and mane, we pulled out a small grey mare, but quite a nice mare. She could not stand so we held her up some time. She had probably been in the water 6–8 hours. Ten minutes later our little horse, literally snatched from the jaws of death, was following us. This might serve as a nominal compensation to the species for its faithful and enormous service to our cause.'

On July 4th Pilsudski launched a terrific attack on Tukachevsky's centre, but the Red armies beat it back and forced the Poles to retire on to their frontier. At the same time Tukachevsky ordered Sologub to cross the Berezina. There was more desperate fighting in the north and the Red 16th Army forced the passage of the river.

With tanks, the latest French guns, poison gas and aeroplanes to help him, Pilsudski made a determined stand on his own frontier, but even with these special armaments the Red infantry could not be checked and beat him back into Poland.

Desperately anxious now, Pilsudski telephoned the General commanding the fortress at Brest-Litovsk. Could it hold out for ten days? The General assured him that the fortress could hold out for double that time and that the Reds would break their teeth on it. That same day three divisions of the main Red Army took its principal bastion by assault. That night the Polish Communists, worked on by the propaganda of Tukachevsky, got into the citadel and strangled the General and his staff. Only the River Bug now lay between Tukachevsky and Warsaw.

In the north Sologub was pushing forward, Minsk fell to him on July 11th and before the Poles could make a stand he was over the Nieman. Just to the rear of his right flank the still secret 15th Army of Kork, and Gaai's cavalry, wheeled down through Lithuania, passing Vilna on the 14th. The great moment was come for them to sweep right round the unprotected Polish flank to Grodno—Wolkowsysk—Warsaw.

Three hundred miles south of them Voroshilov and Budenny had broken right through to Rovno and curving south swept on to Brody. 'Give us Lemberg! Give us Lemberg!' yelled their troopers, once more wild with excitement, and the two generals decided to attack the great capital of Galicia.

Following close on the heels of the main Red Army came Dzerzhinski, Marchlevski and Kon, ready to form the first Polish Soviet Government directly Warsaw had been taken.

In London, Paris and the other European capitals the situation was viewed with the gravest alarm. General Weygand, the chief of staff to Marshal Foch, flew to Warsaw in the hope that he might be able to save the 'Bastion of Europe' which was being smashed in by the Bolsheviks. The English Government hastily offered to act as mediator in order to try and halt the Russian advance by peace; but Lenin was now in a situation very different from that in which he had been two years or even one year before. He in turn ignored the plea for peace and instructed Tukachevsky that his furthest advance for the time being must be the Rhine.

The critical moment of the whole campaign had arrived. The Poles were retreating upon all fronts. Tukachevsky's Central Army was within twelve miles of Warsaw, the spires and crosses of its churches could be seen from the hill-tops glistening before their eyes in the summer sun. It only needed his secret army, which was executing the encircling movement still all unsuspected by Pilsudski, to fall on Warsaw from the north and Poland would be under the Russian heel again. They had passed Grodno and Wolkowsysk and were ready to fling themselves across the Vistula straight at the capital.

But General Weygand had arrived from Paris. One of the few really brilliant soldiers who emerged from the Great War, he was instantly uneasy about that unnaturally quiet area to the north and sent aeroplanes to investigate the situation. On August 14th Tukachevsky's cat was out of the bag; Weygand had divined, and now verified, the enemy's intention. He temporarily took the battle out of Pilsudski's hands and flung the whole of the Polish reserves against Kork and Gaai on the line of the Vistula.

Tukachevsky wired frantic orders to them for the most desperate attempts to be made to break the Poles in this all-important sector; but the Polish troops were good soldiers when they were properly led and they stood their ground.

On August 16th Weygand told the Polish General Staff, 'Now is your Battle of the Marne. If you would save Poland you must take the offensive,' and the entire Polish army rushed to the attack.

On the 19th Tukachevsky wired Budenny to come to his assistance and attack Warsaw from the south. If this order had been executed immediately it is difficult to say what would have happened. The Polish aeroplanes which were attacking the First Cavalry Army would certainly have reported its change of direction and troops might have been diverted to form a front south of Warsaw to meet this new threat, thus weakening the Polish northern and eastern fronts sufficiently to enable Tukachevsky to break through. On the other hand, Budenny was 200 miles from Warsaw and, even by forced marches of 25 miles a day, he could not have come into action effectively in under a week. Weygand was far too able a general to divert troops a moment before he had to when a major battle, which had already been raging for five days, was in progress. It is virtually certain, therefore, that in view of the First cavalry Army's position on August 19th, so far from the main conflict, they could not have affected events on the decisive front until the battle had been decided.

On receipt of Tukachevsky's order to turn north-west, Voroshilov got into touch with his immediate superior, Stalin. He said that he could take the great city of Lemberg, which would be a fine physical and moral victory for the Bolshevik arms; it was absurd to abandon such a prize now it was in his grasp, and further, the movement ordered would lay open the Southern front; surely the other Red armies must be made of poor stuff if they could not manage to take Warsaw between them. Stalin, as usual, agreed with Voroshilov and Tukachevsky's order was ignored.

This flagrant disobedience to the central command appears inexcusable. It can only be palliated by the fact that Stalin and Voroshilov had often acted contrary to the orders of their G.H.Q. before and always justified their decisions by results. Other leaders of genius have also done so, and we recall Nelson putting his telescope to his blind eye so that he could not see his superior's signal at Copenhagen.

A battle of telegrams began. Voroshilov and Budenny continued to carry all before them, but Tukachevsky was held in front of Warsaw. He flung every man into the battle and sent wire after wire demanding that the First Cavalry Army turn north-west to his assistance. On August 22nd Voroshilov was within three miles of Lemberg, but the demands for help in the north had become so imperative that with the utmost reluctance he abandoned his prey. The First Cavalry Army turned in its track and headed for Warsaw; but it was too late, Tukachevsky's front had already broken.

Weygand had performed the 'Miracle of the Vistula', and now dominated the situation; the patriotic Poles were rushing to join reserve regiments which were thrown straight into the fray and the whole army put every ounce of its weight into the

POLISH CAMPAIGN: CRITICAL PHASE, MID-AUGUST,
1920. SHOWING BOLSHEVIKS' DEEPEST PENETRATIONS

▓▓ Poles.　□ Bolsheviks.　░░ Sea.

attack; the Red Armies disintegrated under the shock. Tukachevsky's 4th and 15th Armies were annihilated; of his 3rd and
16th only a few thousand men escaped the débâcle. Thousands of prisoners were taken, hundreds of guns, and the remnants of the Bolshevik forces streamed back in utter confusion
over the Russian frontier.

The two cavalry armies, left unsupported, were cut off. In
the north Gaai fought with desperate valour, but was cornered
up against the German frontier and forced over it, so that he
and his men had to surrender their arms, and spent long
months in a concentration camp outside Berlin before negotiations for their return to Russia were finally settled.

In the south, by one last superb effort, Voroshilov managed
a dash of another hundred miles and nearly reached Lublin,
half-way to Warsaw, but there he was held by infinitely
superior forces and pushed back on Zamość, where he was
completely surrounded.

Overwhelming odds now lay between the First Cavalry
Army and Russia, but, still undaunted, Vorishilov, Budenny,
Kotovsky, Apanasenko and the rest held their men together.
Day after day and night after night they were bombed by aeroplanes and shelled by superior artillery. Masses of cavalry,
masses of infantry, tanks, armoured cars and armoured trains
were sent against them, but nothing could stop them. They
cut their way out of the ring of death to safety. Voroshilov had
led his men further into Europe than any other Red general
and he was the only one to bring back a still unbroken army
into Russia.

When they had escaped, however, the First Cavalry Army
got out of hand just like the others. The semi-educated men
reverted to their former barbarity and took their defeat out of
the wretched civilian population. They ceased to be an army
and became a great band of freebooters. There were no longer
reports of victories, but of *pogroms,* murders and wholesale
drunkenness. Instead of the annihilation of Poland and Europe
there were only the scattered feathers of Jewish mattresses,
the cut throats of old women, smashed cupboards, torn purses,
ripped-up stomachs and devastated dwellings.

Voroshilov stormed and raved in vain; they took no notice.
At a meeting of his officers in Lutsk he shouted: 'Death rather
than such disgrace,' but they could only shrug their shoulders

helplessly; none of them any longer had the least control over their men.

General Weygand and the valour of the Polish troops had saved Europe. Tukachevsky had sustained an utter and irremediable defeat. The wings of the Red Eagles had been clipped.

# 17

# The Aftermath

The Red Marshals still had plenty of fighting to do, but from this time on the Bolshevik diplomats played a large part in consolidating the gains of the Revolution, and in their own sphere the diplomats who came out of it were as able as the Marshals.

Trotsky's record makes the Terrorists of the French Revolution look like small, vicious children, but there is no denying that he put up an extraordinarily fine show against the trained diplomats and hard-headed generals of the Central Powers during the Brest-Litovsk peace negotiations. His sphere very shortly afterwards became War, for which he appears to have had little talent, but Chicherin succeeded him in the Soviet Foreign Office and did remarkable work there for the young Republic. Krassin, as Commissar for Trade, which naturally links up very intimately with foreign relations, seconded his efforts most ably and, in addition, they had the services of Maxim Litvinov, sometimes known as M. Finklestein, who has since proved one of the ablest diplomats of his generation.

For nearly two and a half years Europe had closed the doors of its council chambers against the Bolsheviks. They made repeated and continuous efforts to open negotiations with a dozen different countries, but their Communist propaganda was so feared by the capitalist nations that these set their faces against any conversation with the Kremlin which might lead to general communications being established with Russia through normal channels.

Seeing that Russia, torn to ribbons by six years of war, could not possibly heal her wounds without foreign aid, Lenin determined on another major effort to break down the barriers; he equipped Litvinov with full powers as a special Peace Ambassador and Trade Merchant. Litvinov operated from Copenhagen, and during the spring and summer of 1920 he succeeded in getting a foot wedged into the ministerial doors of numerous Governments.

The Kremlin's first success was a Peace Treaty with Esthonia in February, 1920. Lenin, the greatest statesman of them all, gave the Esthonians most generous terms in order to encourage other Governments to give his representatives at least a hearing. Lithuania followed Esthonia and was also given excellent terms. It was this which enabled Tukachevsky to march his 'secret' army down through Lithuania in the Polish campaign, although the Peace had not then been actually ratified. Latvia was the next country to establish friendly relations with the Soviet.

England was the first of the great capitalist powers to consider burying the hatchet. Lloyd George had endorsed Churchill's policy at the beginning, but he veered backwards and forwards in his attitude to Russia in accordance with the success or failure of the campaigns of the White generals. After Denikin's defeat in the spring of 1920 he tended more and more to the view that, as the Bolsheviks now seemed to have the people really behind them, negotiations should be opened. His attitude, of course, was governed by the factor which has always dominated British policy—the possibility of trade. Russia was a ruin from end to end. She obviously could not reconstruct herself and the sale of British machinery, etc., would help employment and bring money into British pockets. In consequence Krassin was invited to London to negotiate a trade agreement, and arrived in May.

The civil war was not yet ended; there still remained General Baron Wrangel in the Crimea. Geographically the Crimea is somewhat similar to the Isle of Wight, but just about ten times its size, being some 200 miles east to west from point to point and 120 miles north to south from point to point, as against the Isle of Wight's 20 miles by 13. There is, however, the essential difference that whereas the Isle of Wight is separated from Southern England by a strip of water, the Crimea is attached to Southern Russia by a short isthmus only about six miles in breadth at its narrowest part. The shape of the Crimea caused the Russians to compare it with a flagon, or old-fashioned squat bottle, the isthmus being its neck and the fortifications at Perekop, near the mainland, its cork. The great Peninsula represents a natural fortress which can only be attacked from the sea or through its solitary gate, in and out of which General Wrangel could pop at will, pulling the cork back after him, so he became known as 'The Baron in the Bottle'.

Upon Denikin's collapse Wrangel retired into the Crimea with a portion of the White forces and slammed its doors by the creation of a 'Hindenburg line', consisting of the old Turkish rampart strengthened by concrete pill-boxes and six deep belts of barbed-wire, across the isthmus. The Black Sea was virtually a British lake from the moment the Dardanelles were opened after the Armistice was signed with Turkey. The Allies handed over to Wrangel the Ex-Czarist Black Sea Fleet and a great deal of other Russian shipping; they also gave instructions to their own warships there that, while they were not to undertake offensive operations against the Russian cities on the mainland, they were to come into action in the event of the Bolsheviks attempting to drive Wrangel out of the Crimea, and to give his shipping their protection.

Wrangel was thus able, without interference, to transport the remnants of Denikin's forces across from the Kuban to the Crimea and concentrate a new White Army there at his leisure. France, Britain and Italy continued to give him their assistance by way of vast stores of munitions, of which they had abundance from the late war, and considerable sums of money.

As we know, in the spring of 1920, Tukachevsky, Voroshilov, Budenny and the bulk of the Red Armies had to be transferred to the west to meet the Polish threat, so Wrangel, who was much the most energetic and forceful of the White leaders, was able to sally forth from his stronghold. In the early summer he popped out of his bottle with a well-equipped army of 75,000 men, defeated the Red troops left in South Russia, advanced into the Don country and headed direct for Moscow. To create a diversion in his favour a British fleet shelled the Russian Baltic ports even while Krassin and Lloyd George were smoking cigars together in London. By the end of August Wrangel had become a definite threat to the Kremlin.

Fortunately for the Bolsheviks Poland had suffered almost as much during the war as Russia, and the Poles were in no condition to sustain a long campaign. After their victory they were only too willing to negotiate a treaty, so the remnants of Tukachevsky's army were collected together and moved south late in September.

The First Cavalry Army had escaped the débâcle but were in a state of semi-mutiny. The worst offenders were the men of Apanasenko's Sixth Division and when Voroshilov at last got them together he took extremely strong measures. Parad-

ing the division, he stripped them of their colours and demanded they should give up the ringleaders who had incited them
to appalling acts of pillage which had disgraced the army.

The men proved stubborn and difficult, but Voroshilov was
a man of immense courage. Facing the whole mutinous crowd,
practically alone, he produced a machine-gun from his car and
told them that if they did not surrender the ringleaders he
would turn it on them and kill as many of them as he could
before they killed him. They had seen him at work too often
not to know that he meant exactly what he said. Their courage
wilted under his iron determination and they surrendered 150
men, whom he had tried for pillaging, and shot. Having thus
re-established his authority over the First Cavalry Army, he
led his men south-east against Wrangel with other units of the
Red Army that had been reorganised.

Wrangel was a strategist of considerable ability; the Red
generals endeavoured to cut his communications with the
Crimea but failed. On October 14th, a major battle opened
which lasted for seven days. The Bolsheviks were forced to
throw 150,000 men into the fight before they could break the
Whites, 20,000 of whom were killed or taken prisoner, but with
his remaining 55,000, the Baron, still unbroken, managed to
pop back into his bottle. The Red armies then hurled themselves at the isthmus of Perekop, but they were simply battering
their heads against a wall. It was a sheer impossibility for
numbers, however great, to force this well-defended gateway
of the Crimea, which consisted of the old Turkish ramparts
reinforced by every means known to modern military science.

It was at this impasse that Blucher, returning from the East,
came on the scene and performed a most daring operation
with the aid of a most extraordinary and unusual combination
of the elements. Along the isthmus of Perekop the sea and
mouth of the river Siwasch are very shallow and once only, so
it is said, in a hundred years a terrific wind, coming from the
west, blows with such  tremendous strength that it forces
back the shallow water, leaving the sea-bed dry and exposed.
This occurred early in November, 1920. Alone, however, this
rare phenomenon would have been of no assistance to the
Bolsheviks as they could not march their men over the muddy
sea-bottom; but winter had set in early and a frost, once again
of quite abnormal strength, froze the exposed mud.

On the evening of November 8th, Blucher realised the possibilities offered by this sudden and undreamed of manifestation caused by the change in the weather. Without a second's hesitation he acted and, during the night, led three divisions across the frozen land which normally was covered with water. The risk involved was a ghastly one, as a single match struck by one of his men might have been quite enough to give his manœuvre away to the Whites, in which case his army would have been caught in the open without a shred of cover and completely massacred by direct fire from the side of the isthmus. In addition, if the wind had changed the waters would have come rushing back like a flood tide to drown them all.

Those who seek a natural explanation for Moses being able to lead the Israelites through the Red Sea out of Egypt may regard it as a similar phenomenon, and will remember that when Moses had reached dry land the waters surged back to engulf Pharaoh's pursuing chariots.

In the operation at Perekop the wind *did* change, in the small hours of the morning, and the last of Blucher's terrified men had to wade ashore up to their armpits in water; but he had succeeded in out-flanking the steel gates of the isthmus, and when dawn came his three divisions, complete with artillery, were stationed *behind* Baron Wrangel. Blucher was now cut off from the main Red Army by the sea and had to conquer or die. At the sound of his guns the other Red forces attacked the Turkish rampart from the front and Wrangel, caught between two fires, was defeated in the battle that ensued. On November 10th he evacuated the Crimea, transporting the White refugees to Constantinople in 500 vessels and leaving the Bolsheviks, at last, in full possession of the whole of European Russia.

In September, 1920, Lenin, now convinced that there was little hope of Communist revolution in the European countries, turned his attention to the East, and a great conference was arranged at Baku. The delegates, Kalmucks, Persians, Turkomans, Armenians, Chinese, Afghans, Hindus, Bashkirs, etc., numbered 1,891 and it was probably one of the most picturesque gatherings that has ever taken place. Nearly every Near Eastern and Asiatic people was represented there by men who wished to upset the Imperialist Governments that dominated their countries. Zinoviev, Radek and the Hungarian Terrorist, Bela Kun, stirred them up and sent them forth with money and promises of support to aid their attempts in sabotaging the British rule in India and elsewhere, and a terrific war of Bolshevik propaganda was initiated in the East. At the same time the Bolsheviks succeeded in winning over the Afghan and Persian representatives, treaties being signed with both countries in February, 1921.

After his spectacular feat of arms at Perekop and a reception of honour in the Soviet capital, Blucher left hungry Moscow for the East once more. The Far Eastern Soviet Republic, which had its capital at Chita, was separated from Blucher's previous conquests round Krasnoyarsk, west of Lake Baikal, by a great territory now dominated by an independent general named Baron Ungern Von Sternberg. The Japanese were believed to be conspiring to create a buffer state out of Von Sternberg's conquests, and that would not have suited the Bolsheviks at all.

Baron Ungern was, if anything, an even more fantastic figure than the Red Cavalry leader Kotovsky. The Baron was not one of the recognised White leaders, but nevertheless he was fanatically anti-Bolshevik and a very grave danger to the Siberian Soviets. His troops consisted of a horde of Mongols, Tibetans, Chinese, Buriats and Cossacks, mainly Buddhists. He was a deeply religious Buddhist himself and his co-religionists looked upon him as 'the Son of Heaven'. The costume that he favoured was a bright yellow Mongol kaftan with the shoulder straps of a Russian general sewn upon it.

Ungern was extremely superstitious and consulted a sorceress every time he was about to go into battle. He claimed to face death willingly, for his task of awakening the people of Asia and descendants of Jenghis Khan to overrun Europe and bring it the peace of Buddha was about to be accomplished. In spite of his Buddhism he was unbelievably cruel, and his name had become a terror throughout a great portion of Asia. In view of Tukachevsky's philosophy, as stated by him when a prisoner of war in the fortress of Ingolstadt, it seems that he and Baron Ungern would have made a pretty pair of boon companions if they had ever got together. Russia was not spared much, but she was at least spared that horrible and dangerous combination.

Early in 1921, Blucher of the Black Mask arrived in Chita and took over the War Ministry, a seat on the Revolutionary Council, and command of the Siberian 'People's' Army. Baron Ungern's base was the town of Urga, 200 miles on the other side of the Mongolian border, somewhere in the little-known northern wastes of the great Desert of Gobi, that strange romantic country beyond which lie the mountains of James Hilton's *Lost Horizon*.

The Baron was harrying the borders of Russia round about Kiakhta, south of Lake Baikal, and crossing the Ingoda river, Blucher caught him there. Black Mask defeated Yellow Robe —the fantastic Baron was later executed—another great slab of territory came under the Kremlin's rule, and Blucher was temporarily given diplomatic powers to represent the Soviet at a conference with the Japanese in Darien. He was yet to earn fresh fame in two more wars.

After the Crimean campaign Voroshilov's cavalry was ordered to the Ukraine to put down the bands of robbers that were still laying waste the country-side. It was mostly police work again, but quite severe guerilla fighting. The forces of the brigand leaders Karetrikov and Makhno were so strong that he had to bring whole divisions against them.

The state of the country was appalling beyond conception. The great famine of 1921 caused 30 million starving people to leave their homes and rove shelterless in search of food. In spite of the wonderful work done by the American Relief Association, 5 million of them died. Cholera had been ravaging the Russian cities ever since the breakdown of the sanitary services in the anarchy of 1917. Typhus, dysentery, enteric and scurvy were carrying people off by the thousand.

When his police work was accomplished, Voroshilov, ever thinking of the welfare of the masses, almost literally turned his men's sabres into ploughshares. He set his whole army to plough tens of thousands of hectares of poor peasants' land, rebuild their farms and help, in innumerable other ways, in reconstruction.

When the hot, dry summer came the horses began to wilt and die from lack of grass. Voroshilov represented to the Kremlin that his cavalry should be transferred to the steppes of the Kuban where there was abundant fodder and where sporadic risings among the White Cossacks were still to be suppressed.

Trotsky would not hear of it. He said that the First Cavalry Army was not politically trustworthy; once they were in White country they might go over to the enemy. Horses began to die with heart-breaking frequency; Voroshilov's beloved army was falling to pieces under his eyes. He went to the Kremlin and banged another desk with righteous fury. 'All right,' said Trotsky. 'If you insist, but I make you answerable with your head for the good conduct of your army.'

'I'll take full responsibility,' snapped Voroshilov, and he was made Military Commander of the Northern Caucasus. The Cavalry army was saved and he pacified another great area of Russia.

With the collapse of Wrangel the position of the Bolsheviks was enormously strengthened and His Britannic Majesty's Government led the way among the Great Powers to at least a partial recognition of the Kremlin as the established Government of Russia, by entering into an Anglo-Russian Trade Agreement in March, 1921. Many of the other countries soon followed suit and sorely-needed goods began to trickle into Russia at last.

In the early days of the Revolution all the Communist theories had been put into practice. The country and everything in it belonged to the workers; every service, so far as it existed in the tumult, was placed freely at their disposal; money was abolished; everyone was supposed to do his share and hand the surplus products of his labour over to his soviet —the result was chaos.

It was no longer necessary to pay when one went on a tram-car. Thousands of children and idlers rode about in the trams all day purely for their own amusement, and the people who had real jobs to do were compelled to walk. As the telephone service also belonged to the people, and no one had to pay for the use of it, the service became a new toy and the warriors of the proletariat talked to their girl-friends by the hour, once they managed to secure a line, or put through trunk calls to relatives in distant towns. The cities fell into an appalling state. *In Moscow there was no running water for two and a half years*. Lack of proper sanitation bred epidemics of a dozen horrible diseases.

All that had to be changed, but up to 1922 Lenin had had little opportunity to organise the State. During the period of the Civil War the army had been the one imperative consideration; the rest of the people had to be sacrificed to its necessities and, to feed it, they had been reduced to near-starvation. The whole of the Russian people suffered incredible hardships and they decided that if this was Bolshevism they didn't think much of it. As a natural consequence of foreign intervention the people had rallied to the defence of the Kremlin, but now the Civil War was over they felt that the good things they had fought for should be given them at once.

That, of course, was an utter impossibility, but many of the Communists were no less disappointed at the new régime than the bulk of the people. These disgruntled Communists felt that Lenin's Government was not Communist at all; instead he and his colleagues appeared to have formed an autocracy which was just as rigorous as anything they had experienced under the Czars.

This was certainly true in that men were conscripted and forced to fight whether they wished to or not, and were also conscripted for labour purposes; further, no man in Russia could call his soul his own; the dreaded agents of the *Cheka* were ten times more numerous than the old secret police of the Czars and the least word against the Government was liable to cost the speaker his life. In the Czar's day political malcontents had been exiled to Siberia, but now they were arrested and shot out of hand: literally tens of thousands of people were killed in this way by Dzerzhinski's soulless *Chekists*. The 'Liberty' which the Bolsheviks had promised was a myth; the 'Equality' a farce, since their Commissars ruled everywhere with a rod of iron, and took for their own use, generally without payment, the products of the peasants and workers. Now that foreigners had been thrown out of the country, a great wave of anti-Bolshevik feeling swept it.

The peasants, who still formed 80 per cent. of the population, were told that they must hand over their surplus grain to the authorities and in exchange they would be given, instead of money, clothes, agricultural implements, vodka and what you will. They did not think much of the arrangements from the very beginning, but they tried it out and soon found that it did not work. What was the good of receiving a new spade for a bushel of turnips when you had already been given a new spade for a sack of potatoes the month before; and although you simply could not get along without a new pitchfork, they hadn't a pitchfork to give you. Worse still, supplies of manufactured goods were incredibly scarce and the Government had not got enough to operate this system of barter.

The result was that the peasant adopted his age-old policy of digging his toes in and refusing to cultivate more land than was necessary for the support of himself and his family. Semi-starvation in towns became actual starvation; people were dying by the thousand from malnutrition and hunger typhus.

By the winter of 1920-21 the situation had become acute. The peasants' quarrel had always been with the landlords, and now that the Revolution had enabled them to get hold of the land for which they had always craved they only wished to be left in peace to produce as much as they could and pile up money on the old capitalist system. They had never thought much of Communism and now they hated it intensely. Still having arms in their hands from the Civil War, they began to form bands all over the country for the purpose of stamping out the Communists and the Jews.

Risings took place in many areas; the most serious being that which was led by Antonov in the Volga country, and early in 1921 it looked as though the Kremlin Government, which had withstood the world in arms, was now about to be destroyed by its own people.

Lenin hated the idea of having to send troops against his own land workers, but Trotsky was completely ruthless. He despatched Tukachevsky against Antonov's peasant army and numerous other generals against the other peasant bands. After the destruction of the unlucky Gaai's mounted troops in the Polish campaign, another Second Cavalry Army was formed and the command of it given to that handsome rogue, Kotovsky. Under Tukachevsky he chased the wretched Antonov through the province of Tambov and succeeded by a treacherous trick, although one requiring much courage, in massacring a great detachment of the malcontents. The insurrections were put down with an iron hand and the blood of her people again deluged the soil of Russia from the mass shooting of the peasantry which took place wherever they had risen.

The most serious crisis with which the Kremlin was faced, however, was a mutiny at Kronstadt among the sailors of the Baltic Fleet. They stood in a very different category to the peasants, since they were real dyed-in-the-wool Communists, and their mutiny was directed against the autocracy of the Kremlin, which, in their view, had completely sabotaged genuine Communist ideals.

The cry of the sailors was: 'Our Revolution. A swindle! Whatever happens it's always the same. Nothing alters. For the man in the street there's neither bread nor work.'

Kronstadt lies on the Gulf of Finland only a few miles from Petrograd. Zinoviev was Commissar of Petrograd at the time and the people detested him. Owing to the general discontent the Petrograd workers from the factories and the sailors from the fleet got together and began to demonstrate, in threatening masses, against the representative of the Kremlin Government. The old days were back again, the sole difference being that Zinoviev was now the hated tyrant instead of the Czar, Nicolas II.

Zinoviev was a poltroon and he panicked, terrified that the angry people would hang him. He had the Petrograd bridges guarded by detachments of *Chekists* and cadets from the Military College, but the workers crossed over by the ice on the river and he sat shaking in his room without taking any steps to stop them.

The men in the National Printing Works and the Naval Dockyards came out on strike, and the sailors of the *Aurora*, who had captured the Winter Palace for the soviets in the Bolshevik Revolution, now openly rose against the Kremlin. The anarchists of the Revolution, who believed that the world could really be run without anybody giving orders to anybody else, were in full revolt against the despotism which had muzzled the nation and they were backed by the starving population of the old capital.

The Kremlin was alarmed, and, ignoring Zinoviev, whom the rebels would certainly have torn to pieces, Lenin sent the inoffensive Kalinin, together with Kuzman, the Commissar of the Baltic Fleet, to reason with the sailors in the Fortress.

At Kronstadt 70,000 sailors were loose and boiling with excitement. They were old fighters, the very people from whom the original Revolution had sprung and utterly disillusioned by the Kremlin Government. They knew all about the peasant shootings and many of them were brothers of the murdered men. They meant to put a stop to this tyrannical and bloody despotism. On March 5th, Kalinin, and Kuzman arrived and a vast mass meeting was held during which an icy wind blew across the frozen Gulf.

Kuzman was the first to mount the improvised Tribune; a few planks covered with red bunting. He had been instructed to make no concessions and only told the angry crowd that the Communist Party would ensure the success of the Revolution.

He said that they had chosen an absurd moment to revolt as the nations in the west were about to recognise the People's Government and in a year or so there would be plenty of everything. In the meantime things must be kept going and they must have patience.

The sailors howled him down, yelling: 'It's you and your friends who have stolen all the food and clothing while the workers go hungry and cold. Throw him out, throw him out!'

Kalinin tried to speak but was unable to make his voice heard above the din. A sailor pushed him off the platform and, waving his cap, shouted: 'Look around you, Comrades, at the filth we've got ourselves into. All because of a handful of Communists, but they're not real Communists; they've only made fine nests for themselves in the midst of the Republic while wearing our label. We've got to get rid of these false Communists who incite the workers against the peasants, and the peasants against the workers. Let's clear out the scum and put an end to the murderers' shootings.' He received a terrific ovation, while Kalinin and Kuzman only wriggled out of the crowd and escaped in their car with difficulty.

The sailors and workers of Kronstadt now set up a Government of their own consisting of a Revolutionary Committee of Fifteen. It included nine sailors, four workers, a ship's doctor and a schoolmaster; the President was a sailor named Petrichenko, who acted with quite extraordinary energy.

In Moscow, Trotsky issued a proclamation calling upon the garrison, shops and population of Kronstadt to surrender under pain of the most drastic terrorism. Without the least foundation he stigmatised the rising as a fresh attempt against the Revolution by the Whites; but nobody believed this transparent fiction. The proclamation, which concluded with the words: 'This is the last and only warning,' was pasted up in the streets of Kronstadt and Tukachevsky was despatched with 60,000 picked troops to deal with the 70,000 disaffected sailors.

When Tukachevsky arrived, Vasiliv, President of the Kronstadt Soviet, had been seized and imprisoned; all the forts at Kronstadt were in the hands of the rebels with the one exception of Fort Red, and Petrograd was in a ferment.

Zinoviev proclaimed the city in a state of siege and issued an order that in case of street fighting all who resisted the Government must be shot down without mercy; the families of

Kronstadt sailors who lived in Petrograd were arrested and held as hostages.

The officers of the fleet urged the sailors to march on Petrograd on the grounds that if they failed to draw the Red soldiers there into their movement they were bound to be defeated; but the sailors wished to spare the unnecessary shedding of blood and nothing could be done with them. The very same sailors who, four years before, had thrust any Czarist or bourgeois who fell into their hands under the ice of the Neva with brutal laughter, and roasted their officers in the furnaces of their ships, now set their faces against violence of any kind. What they wanted was liberty and equality. They did not believe for one moment that Trotsky would dare to shed the blood of the sacred 'people'.

Tukachevsky had now concentrated his forces and his planes began to fly over the Gulf of Finland, dropping bombs on mutinous Kronstadt, aiming not at the forts, but at the long streets of poor dwellings where the families of the sailors lived. The rioters were utterly aghast and filled with the most bitter fury. If they had marched on Petrograd a few days earlier when Zinoviev's power was in ruins they might have re-written history, but the old capital was now in Tukachevsky's hands and he was ready to cross the Gulf of Finland with his army of 60,000.

He realised that the great spring thaw was almost on him; once the ice of the Neva melted it would be impossible to approach the fortress, and worse, the warships would be able to steam up to Petrograd and then, most probably, the city would get out of hand behind him. He therefore brought his batteries into action, without any attempts to parley, at dawn on March 7th. While they opened fire upon the rebel forts, Fort Red, which was still loyal to the Kremlin, turned its guns on the houses of Kronstadt town, and ruthlessly shelled the men, women and children of the civil population.

The infuriated sailors were now determined to resist to the last man and sent out a radio message: '*Let the whole world know that up to his waist in the blood of the workers, our brothers, the blood-lusting Trotsky has opened fire against the city of Kronstadt which had risen against the power of the Communists. We will conquer or die beneath the ruins of Kronstadt fighting for the sacred cause of the workers. Long live the Soviets!*'

Tukachevsky had minutely prepared his plan of attack. His troops were issued with white shrouds to make them less conspicuous against the background of the winter snow, and protected by the land batteries at Sestroretsk Point, Oranienbaum and Fort Red, he launched his men in echelon formation over the ice-covered bay against the forts.

The sailors met them with a murderous fire; a snow-storm darkened the sky; night fell and the Kremlin forces were still being urged forward, but they could not make any headway under the devastating hail of lead that the sailors brought to bear on them.

During the night Tukachevsky ordered a fresh attack. The screech of shells, the drumming of the artillery and the staccato clatter of machine-guns were fiendish. Great chips of ice, as dangerous as shell splinters, flew in all directions. Tukachevsky's crack troops, the Communist cadets, hurled themselves on the key point, Fort Seven, in vain. They were stopped by the sailors' barrage, hesitated, were overcome with panic and fled in all directions. With the coming of dawn the snowstorm passed and the early light showed thousands of corpses heaped over the ice, wrapped in white shrouds, stained with blood. The bay was a shambles of Tukachevsky's troops and, to complete the disaster, many of the Kremlin regiments mutinied, refusing to march again against the rebels.

In an attempt to restore discipline Tukachevsky and the *Cheka* battalions, who were with him, rounded up the disaffected units and shot *one man out of every five,* but even this butchery was insufficient to induce the men to renew the attack, so all their favourite leaders, the darlings of the army, were sent from Moscow. Voroshilov, Budenny, Kotovsky and Yegorov arrived, not with reinforcements but with a great number of dependable politicals, and went about among the men explaining to them how vital to the ultimate success of the Revolution it was that this revolt against the Central Government should be quelled.

The politicals seem to have done their work efficiently and the presence of Voroshilov and the other heroes of the fighting men, with their wonderful reputations for victorious leadership, doubtless had a very important influence in restoring the morale of the troops.

Tukachevsky made a new plan for a fresh attack to be launched upon the night of March 16th–17th. The bombardment opened directly dusk fell; the forts and ships replied, but a dense mist descended, making it difficult to range the guns accurately. The sailors stood by all night waiting for the assault while the troops on the opposite bank were taking up their positions. In the dirty white shrouds they looked like legion after legion of grey ghosts, visible one moment in the flash of the shore batteries and blacked out the next. Not a word was spoken, not a cigarette smoked, orders were transmitted in undertones; the only noise apart from that of the artillery duel was of water from the thawing ice splashing underfoot.

At midnight Tukachevsky's bombardment ceased and the firing from the forts died down. It was a calm Baltic night, not a shot sounded; the only sign of activity was that of the searchlights feeling about in the sky. At three o'clock in the morning the silent, grey-white columns went forward, paying out their telephone wires as they went; while on sledges behind them they drew machine-guns and light artillery.

An hour passed; suddenly the guns of the forts came into action again; a searchlight had picked up one section of the attackers and, trained straight upon them, blinded them with its glare. The darkness on each side vomited machine-gun fire; mighty shells from the naval guns rent open the ice, decimated whole companies of men and sent up great fountains of water.

Up to their knees in the slush of the melting ice the troops rushed forward to the attack. Cursing like the damned, dripping with sweat, the sailors, naked to the waist, rammed shell after shell home into the breeches of their guns. The troops gained ground and reached the ramparts; the sailors sallied out to meet them with revolvers and cutlasses. Desperate hand to hand struggles were waged round Forts Totleben and Krasnoirmetz, which were eventually taken. In Kronstadt fierce battles were in progress. The sailors refused to surrender, preferring to die in battle than be shot afterwards by the *Cheka*.

Tukachevsky stood upon the Petrograd bank of the gulf with the Red Army chiefs about him. The inhabitants of Kronstadt were now fleeing over the ice from the blood-soaked citadel in an endeavour to reach the Finnish shore. The sailors were still fighting like lions, trying to gain time for their families to escape falling into the pitiless hands of Trotsky.

By morning the last fort and ship had been cleared of their defenders and the Kremlin was victorious. The rebel comnittee sought refuge in Finland, and, as Trotsky had menaced, engeance was now taken upon their adherents. Tukachevky wiped out the sailors by the thousand.

It was Trotsky who had said in the old days before the Bolheviks seized power: 'The Kronstadt lads are animals, but when it comes to the last combat for the Revolution they will ight to the death.' The last combat had come, and fight to the eath they did. When Trotsky questioned his general afterwards about the fighting Tukachevsky said:

'In five years of war I never saw anything like it. It was not battle—it was sheer hell let loose on earth. For a whole ight the artillery fire made such a din that one could not hear neself speak and the concussions were so terrific that not a ane of glass remained in any of the windows in Oranienbaum. hey were madmen, those sailors. Every house had to be taken eparately. A wretched hut would keep a company at bay for alf an hour. And when you did get in you'd hardly credit it; othing but two or three sailors swimming in gore at the side f their machine-guns, dying and yet summoning their last unce of strength to grab at their revolvers and, with their last asp, muttering: "If I could only kill another of 'em." '

It was in the same month as the abortive rising at Kronstadt hat Lenin initiated a new policy. The peasant *jacqueries* and he sailors' revolution were not without cause. Every city, very township, every village in the vast Russian lands had een fighting in the last few years; post offices, railway stations nd other Government buildings were the natural strong oints which had been fortified by the defenders and, consequently, shelled or bombed to pieces by the attackers. Innumrable bridges had been blown up, hundreds of thousands of iles of telephone and telegraph wires torn down; trains could nly move slowly and irregularly from point to point; twoirds of Russia's rolling stock had either been captured or roken down. In the cities the plaster was peeling from the ouses and the streets everywhere showed great rents and oles. The factories were idle, thousands of people homeless, veryone haggard and poorly dressed in shoddy, home-made othes; sacking, window curtains, chair covers, any sort of aterial that they could cut up and stitch again into some ugh shape to keep the cold from their bodies. The struggle reconstruct Russia upon the lines of health, wealth and appiness for all was an impossible one unless some drastic

change of front was made by the Kremlin Government.
consequence Lenin initiated the New Economic Policy. T
N.E.P. was an abandonment of the original Communist do
trine that no one should be allowed to pile up profits for I
individual benefit; it permitted the resumption of priva
trading.

The capitalist countries rejoiced. They imagined that t
Kremlin had definitely abandoned its old programme an
finding Communism utterly unworkable, had decided to reve
to the capitalist system. This misconception of the N.E.P. ve
materially assisted Litvinov, Chicherin and the other dipl
mats in opening up trade relations again with the Unit
States and other countries, but, in actual fact, Lenin had n
abandoned his original principles at all. The N.E.P. was on
an emergency measure; firstly to encourage the peasant
grow more grain with the promise that he would be allowed
sell his surplus afterwards for *money,* and secondly, from t
view that it did not matter much about a few speculators ma
ing a little profit for themselves if the goods they manufa
tured or smuggled into the country were going to improve t
condition of the people and quieten their murmurs agair
the Government. It was never intended that the N.E.P. shou
be a permanency; it was to be a bridge used to palliate disco
tent while the Kremlin rebuilt the State organisation a
gradually established the internal trade of the country up
co-operative Communist lines, after which private trading w
again to be abolished.

With the resumption of private trading thousands of spec
lators poured in from all over the world. In the haunts whe
they gathered champagne began to flow again and silk stoc
ings to be seen upon the prettier women. The stuffs that th
could import were limited and irregular in delivery, so pri
were fantastic, and the Kremlin, who regarded these bou
geois as much more deadly enemies than even the old Mo
archists, itself forced up the prices to fantastic heights throu
its desire that the speculators should not be allowed to 
away with any large portion of their  rofit. Each priva
trader was taxed by the Government and promptly retaliat
by putting up the price of his goods; the Kremlin raised t
tax, the speculator put up his price again and so the vicio
circle went on.

A new class now began to establish itself. Those of the int

ligentsia who, by having gone to ground or living very very quietly, had escaped the fury of the Revolution, came to light again and proceeded to use their superior intelligence in marketing the goods of the speculators, helping them run their shops, and so on. They were not necessarily anti-Communist, but the N.E.P. was largely responsible for the rebirth in Russia of the class that the Communists had wished to destroy and that Trotsky, Dzerzhinski and the *Chekists* had done their level best to annihilate by three years of unceasing massacre.

The Soviet Foreign Office was working overtime to make pacts with many nations and they reached an understanding with Mustapha Kemal who had become Dictator of Turkey. Upon the overthrow of the old Turkish Government that spectacular figure, Enver Pasha, had sought refuge in Moscow. He continued as the Government's guest there, intriguing with them to lend him their support in a new attempt to set him up in Turkey where he had virtually ruled throughout the whole of the Great War, but the Russians knew that Kemal was far the better man and established direct contact with him.

Kemal, a great patriot and fine statesman, pursued a very sound and straightforward policy. He knew that the decay of the old Ottoman Empire had been caused by the constant drain on the Turkish population to police great tracts of territory which were nominally under the rule of Constantinople, but inhabited by alien and hostile peoples. Turkey had been stripped of these great provinces by the terms of the Armistice. Kemal surrendered them, only too glad in his wisdom to be shot of them, but when it came to allowing foreign diplomats to cut up Turkey herself and place large sections of the Turkish people beneath a foreign yoke he was adamant. With no more than the ragged remnants of an army which had been fighting almost continuously since the first Balkan war, nearly twelve years before, and the support of an impoverished people, he defied the 'glorious and victorious Allies' to come and fight him.

Lloyd George wished to do so, but his colleagues warned him that the people of Britain would certainly not stand for another war. The mischievous and ambitious Greek Premier Venizelos was, in this instance, used as the catspaw, and a large Greek army, supplied with abundant munitions by the Allies, was landed at Smyrna and sent against Kemal.

The Russians came to his support by sending their able General, Michael Frunze, to him in December, 1921, and, since he was completely without supplies or the means of securing them, turned over to him free of charge the vast quantities of Allied munitions and equipment which they had captured after running General Baron Wrangel out of the Crimea the previous winter.

Mustapha Kemal, who was a very great man indeed, showed magnificent generalship; by the following September he had captured Smyrna and driven the whole of the Greek Army back into the sea. Turkey and Russia buried their centuries-long enmity owing to the *rapprochement* between the two new Republican Governments.

The reabsorption of Russia into the Comity of Nations was sufficiently far advanced by April, 1922, for the Powers to call the Genoa Conference mainly with a view to looking into Russian affairs. Chicherin attended it and skilfully out-manœuvred the other statesmen, who had wished to present a solid front, by making a separate treaty with the German envoys dealing with the cancellation of Russo-German war debts and indemnities.

In the spring of 1922 Lenin fell ill. He suffered from severe headaches and, as one of the three bullets with which Dora Kaplan had shot him in 1918 still remained in the back of his neck near the spine, the doctors decided to remove it.

Lenin caused Stalin to be elected Secretary-General of the Russian Communist Party, an appointment which was not considered to be of any great significance at the time as numerous more prominent Bolsheviks held posts of apparently greater importance. The leader then underwent the operation for the removal of the bullet on April 23rd. A slight stroke followed causing temporary paralysis of the left hand and side. Lenin does not appear to have been in any danger, once the blood clot which caused the stroke was absorbed, but his devoted followers insisted on guarding his health with the most jealous care and through the summer months he was only allowed to watch the progress of his four-year-old child, the Revolution, from an invalid chair.

Enver Pasha, disgruntled at his lack of success in persuading the Kremlin to assist him against his old enemy, Mustapha Kemal, had gone off to 'hunt' in Bokhara on the borders of Afghanistan. He hated Britain and had some wild scheme of emulating Alexander the Great by a descent into India and collected a force of Basmachi and Afghans for the purpose.

The Bolsheviks had much too much on their hands to want a war, so in July, 1922, Enver turned his small army against them with the idea of making Bokhara an independent state. The Red general, Kakurin, defeated him and, dispersing the Basmachi through the wild mountain country, proceeded to hunt them down. One detachment of Bolsheviks entered a lonely valley to find a gathering of tribesmen seated in a circle on the ground holding a pow-wow. There was a sharp skirmish in which the Russians annihilated the enemy by means of a small quick-firing gun. When the victors examined the dead they were all found to be richly clad Basmachi Khans except one, who carried letters in German and a book of notes in Turkish under his oriental kaftan. It was Enver Pasha, who had been giving his last instructions to the rebel chiefs before retiring over the border into Afghanistan. So, in a small affray many hundreds of miles from the great centres of civilisation, died one of the most remarkable figures of the World War.

On October 30th, 1922, Mussolini marched on Rome, and exactly one month later declared in the Italian Parliament: 'I recognise the Soviets.' Italy was thus the first of the old Great Powers formally to acknowledge the Bolshevik Government, although MacDonald's minority Labour Government in Britain ran her close.

The other great powers, with the exception of the United States, followed suit; and the Kremlin was invited to send representatives to the Lausanne Conference.

By November Lenin was better and able to attend a meeting of the heads of the Party in the throne room of the Kremlin. His coming was unannounced and he slipped quietly into a chair by the door, but he was instantly recognised and given a tremendous ovation.

Vladivostok had just fallen to Blucher, and on November 14th the Chita Republic. in Central Siberia, proclaimed its adherence to the R.S.F.S.R. (Russian Socialist Federal Soviet Republic). It was just five years since the Bolshevik Revolution and now the whole of the territories of the old Russian Empire, excepting those European States which had seceded, acknowledged Soviet rule. The Kremlin Government was at last supreme and unchallenged from the Baltic to the Pacific coast.

# Epilogue

Between the wars Voroshilov became Minister of Defence and it was he who laid down the strategy that saved Russia from defeat in 1941.

Germany was the only enemy Russia had to fear. Having lost the 1914–1918 war against the West, it seemed that when she had recovered, her next bid for *lebensraum* would be to the East, with the object of acquiring the great corn lands of the Ukraine.

The training and equipment of the Soviet Army being greatly inferior to that of Germany, Voroshilov foresaw that an all-out offensive by Germany must penetrate many hundreds of miles into Russia before it could be checked. Nine-tenths of Russia's heavy industry being situated in European Russia, this would have led to the capture of Kiev, Karkov, Paskov, Odessa and other key cities, thus depriving the Soviet of the munitions essential to continue the war.

To counter this, during the 1930s Voroshilov ran down Russia's old munition plants and created huge new ones behind the Urals, with the added advantage that they were out of bomber range. (It is curious to record that, although the author had no knowledge of this at the time, his first novel, *The Forbidden Territory*, published in 1933, had as its theme this very operation.)

Voroshilov then conceived the strategy of the 'Chastity Belt', which was designed to push all potential German jumping-off areas further away from Russia's frontiers.

The first move was the annexation of the then independent, pro-German states of Esthonia, Latvia and Lithuania, and to deprive Roumania of a part of Bessarabia.

This strategy also explains two wars of aggression which, at the time, roused the indignation of the Western World.

(1) Shortly after Hitler invaded Poland in September 1939, Russia invaded and seized the eastern half of that country, thus securing a further 250 miles that a German army would have to fight its way over before it could enter Soviet territory.

(2) There then remained one highly vulnerable link in the 'Chastity Belt'—namely, pro-German Finland, the southern frontier of which lay fewer than 50 miles from Leningrad. Hence the Soviet attack on Finland in November 1939. The Finns defended their country with the utmost gallantry; but

Voroshilov, who took personal command of the campaign, succeeded in breaking the Mannerheim Line. On March 12th 1940 the Finns capitulated, and Finland's potentiality as a German base of attack was greatly reduced.

On June 22nd 1941 Hitler launched his offensive against Russia. Voroshilov's anticipations were realised. Within a few months the Germans over-ran the greater part of Russia's European territory. Victory or defeat hung upon two vital conditions:

(1) The enemy must not be allowed to cross the Volga. To prevent this, during the first phase of the war Voroshilov used only great masses of ill-trained conscripts. He held his finest regular divisions in reserve. The final result, when they were used, was the German débâcle at Tzaritsyin, later renamed Stalingrad.

(2) Leningrad must be held at all costs: (a) to prevent a German breakthrough south-east on Moscow; (b) its fall would have resulted in the cutting of the vital supply lines from Archangel and Murmansk by which the Allies were sending Russia the munitions without which she could not have continued to fight. Leaving his post as Minister of Defence, Voroshilov took personal command of Leningrad. Under the German General Von Lieb, with 29 divisions and the assistance of the Finnish Army, Leningrad was invested in September 1941. It proved to be one of the most terrible sieges in history. It lasted for a year and a half. During two ghastly winters horses, cats, dogs and rats were eaten; every stick of furniture was burned for fuel, innumerable mass assaults were made on the city, but Voroshilov would not hear of surrender. In the Spring of 1943 he launched his starving garrison in a counter-offensive and broke the German army of the North. It was the last and greatest triumph of his military career.

Voroshilov's name is still little known in the Western World, but his record in *two* world wars will give him a place in history as one of the greatest Generals of all time.

And his career did not finish with the ending of the war. In 1953, on Stalin's death, he became Chairman of the Praesidium of the Supreme Soviet. When Kruschev came to power, he was confirmed as President of the U.S.S.R.

DENNIS WHEATLEY

# Index

**If you would like a complete list of Arrow books please send a postcard to P.O. Box 29, Douglas, Isle of Man, Great Britain.**